THE INSTANT COMPOSERS POOL AND IMPROVISATION BEYOND JAZZ

The Instant Composers Pool and Improvisation Beyond Jazz contributes to the expansion and diversification of our understanding of the jazz tradition by describing the history and practice of one of the most important non-American jazz groups: The Instant Composers Pool, founded in Amsterdam in 1967.

The Instant Composers Pool describes the meaning of "instant composition" from both a historical and ethnographic perspective. Historically, it details instant composition's emergence from the encounter between various overlapping transnational avant-gardes, including free jazz, serialism, experimental music, electronic music, and Fluxus. The author shows how the improvising musicians not only engaged with the cultural politics of ethnicity and race involved in the negotiation of the boundaries of jazz as a cultural practice, but transformed the meaning of music in society—particularly the nature of improvisation and performance. Ethnographically, *The Instant Composers Pool* encourages readers to reconsider the conceptual tools we use to describe music performance, improvisation, and creativity. It takes the practice of "instant composition" as an opportunity to reflect on music performance as a social practice, which is crucial not only for jazz studies, but also for general music scholarship.

Floris Schuiling is Postdoctoral Researcher, Department of Media & Culture, Utrecht University.

Transnational Studies in Jazz

Series Editors: Tony Whyton, Birmingham City University, UK, and Nicholas Gebhardt, Birmingham City University, UK

Transnational Studies in Jazz presents cross-disciplinary and global perspectives on the development and history of jazz and explores its many social, political, and cultural meanings.

Jews and Jazz: Improvising Ethnicity
Charles Hersch

Jazz and Totalitarianism
Edited by Bruce Johnson

The Cultural Politics of Jazz Collectives: This Is Our Music
Edited by Nicholas Gebhardt and Tony Whyton

Jazz Sells: Music, Marketing, and Meaning
Mark Laver

THE INSTANT COMPOSERS POOL AND IMPROVISATION BEYOND JAZZ

Floris Schuiling

Routledge
Taylor & Francis Group

NEW YORK AND LONDON

First published 2019
by Routledge
711 Third Avenue, New York, NY 10017

and by Routledge
2 Park Square, Milton Park, Abingdon, Oxon, OX14 4RN

Routledge is an imprint of the Taylor & Francis Group, an informa business

Library of Congress Cataloging-in-Publication Data
Names: Schuiling, Floris, author.
Title: The Instant Composers Pool and improvisation beyond jazz /
    Floris Schuiling.
Description: New York ; London : Routledge, 2018. | Series:
    Transnational studies in jazz | Includes bibliographical
    references and index.
Identifiers: LCCN 2018021162 (print) | LCCN 2018028732
    (ebook) | ISBN 9781351254380 (ebook) | ISBN
    9780815368564 (hardback) | ISBN 9780815368571 (pbk.)
Subjects: LCSH: Instant Composers Pool. | Jazz—Netherlands—
    Amsterdam—History and criticism. | Avant-garde
    (Music)—Netherlands—Amsterdam—History—20th
    century. | Free jazz—History and criticism.
Classification: LCC ML3509.N48 (ebook) | LCC ML3509.N48
    A677 2018 (print) | DDC 781.65/609492352—dc23
LC record available at https://lccn.loc.gov/2018021162

ISBN: 978-0-815-36856-4 (hbk)
ISBN: 978-0-815-36857-1 (pbk)
ISBN: 978-1-351-25438-0 (ebk)

Typeset in Bembo
by Swales & Willis Ltd, Exeter, Devon, UK

MIX
Paper from
responsible sources
FSC
www.fsc.org   FSC™ C013985

Printed in the United Kingdom
by Henry Ling Limited

The best of all rulers is but a shadowy presence to his subjects.
. . .
Hesitant, he does not utter words lightly.
When his task is accomplished and his work done
The people all say, "it happened to us naturally."
—Lao Tzu, *Tao Te Ching*, 21

CONTENTS

FIGURES

Images

Musical Examples

SERIES FOREWORD

Since the 1990s the study of jazz has changed dramatically, as the field continues to open up to a variety of disciplinary perspectives and critical models. Today, as the music's meaning undergoes profound changes, there is a pressing need to situate jazz within an international research context and to develop theories and methods of investigation which open up new ways of understanding its cultural significance and its place within different historical and social settings.

The *Transnational Studies in Jazz* series presents the best research from this important and exciting area of scholarship, and features interdisciplinary and international perspectives on the relationships between jazz, society, politics, and culture. The series provides authors with a platform for rethinking the methodologies and concepts used to analyze jazz, and will seek to work across disciplinary boundaries, finding different ways of examining the practices, values and meanings of the music. The series explores the complex cultural and musical exchanges that have shaped the global development and reception of jazz. Contributors will focus on studies of the music which find different ways of telling the story of jazz with or without reference to the United States, and will investigate jazz as a medium for negotiating global identities.

Tony Whyton
Nicholas Gebhardt
Series Editors

ACKNOWLEDGEMENTS

This book would not have been possible without Susanna von Canon, the ICP's manager. When I came to see her for the first time after I started this research project, her response was (and I paraphrase slightly): "Great! We go on tour in three weeks. The bus leaves at 9—don't be late." I am enormously thankful for her openness, efficiency, and kindness. She has been more helpful than I could ever have imagined. The same goes for the ICP musicians: Han Bennink, Misha Mengelberg, Ernst Glerum, Mary Oliver, Tristan Honsinger, Wolter Wierbos, Michael Moore, Ab Baars, Thomas Heberer, Tobias Delius, and Guus Janssen. I thank them for welcoming me into their group, making time for interviews, sharing their scores, and for the great music they played during the years I spent with them. They have made my ethnographic work a real joy. I also thank Ernst Reijseger, Pieter Boersma, Peter van Bergen, Evan Parker, and George Lewis for our conversations about their experiences with the ICP. Gerard de Meij, who drove the ICP tour bus, deserves special mention for his good care, as do all the people who do such good work at the concert venues we attended. I am also happy to have gotten to know Amy and Andrea Mengelberg; it is sad that it had to be during such a difficult period.

For the use of their photographs, I am very grateful to Francesca Patella, Pieter Boersma, and Jaap van de Klomp, and I thank Barbara Wien for allowing me to reproduce the work of Tomas Schmit. The Dutch Jazz Archives have been an invaluable source of historical material; Ditmer Weertman and Marc Duivenvoorde have especially been very helpful during my research, but I wish to thank all the people who have kept this running during a time of budget cuts and relocations—keep up the great work. I would also like to thank Bert Vuijsje, Ajay Saggar, Bas Andriessen, Wim Berkers, and Jan Nieuwenhuis for their willingness to share their books, audio recordings, memories, and other forms of information. Jan and I discovered this kind of music together, and without him I would perhaps have never embarked on this project.

I have been extremely privileged for the various sources of financial help available for me to do this research. It would simply have been impossible if not for the Arts and Humanities Research Council, the University of Cambridge Home and EU Scholarship Scheme, and Corpus Christi College. The additional grants and awards from the Music & Letters Trust, the Society for Music Analysis, and the William Barclay Squire Fund for fieldwork expenses and conference attendance were also very helpful. After returning to the Netherlands, I was a recipient of a Veni grant from the Netherlands Organization for Scientific Research, which allowed me to finish writing this book.

The starting point of this research was a lecture by Sam Barrett in Utrecht, where Walter van de Leur remarked that little research was being done on jazz in the Netherlands. Already fascinated with Misha Mengelberg and the ICP Orchestra, I saw an opportunity. The ICP became the subject of my MA thesis, supervised by Barbara Titus, and then my PhD, supervised by Nicholas Cook. I am grateful to Sam, Walter, and Barbara for their help and support in the very early stages of this project, and particularly to Nick for his encouragement, and his uncanny ability to state clearly and succinctly what I was actually trying to say. In the course of my research I have had many inspiring conversations about my work with various other people, including Robert Adlington, Monique Ingalls, Tony Whyton, Nicholas Gebhardt, Kariann Goldschmitt, Georgina Born, Jonas Tinius, Eric Clarke, Loes Rusch, Emily Payne, Rachel Hodgson, Sean Williams, Michiel Kamp, Matt Pritchard, Ross Cole, Jenny Judge, Myles Eastwood, Michael Byrne, Sheila Guymer, John McKean, Andrew Goldman, and Ely Rosenblum.

Two particular research centres should also be mentioned for the way in which they were able to bring together exciting and innovative researchers. One is the Centre for Musical Performance as Creative Practice; the other the Rhythm Changes project. The conferences I attended as part of these two projects were particularly stimulating and have opened up important new directions for musical research.

Finally, and most importantly, I want to thank Ella, Gertjan, and especially Ceri-Anne for their relentless support, care, and patience.

INTRODUCTION

When he was young, Misha Mengelberg, pianist and leader of the ICP Orchestra, went to see Duke Ellington and his Orchestra in the Concertgebouw in Amsterdam. During the intermission, he went back into the concert hall and saw the Duke play piano by himself. As the second half of the concert was about to start, all the musicians of the band got back on stage and joined in one by one. Mengelberg later described this as a formative experience; he said that he was fascinated by what he called the flexibility and informality that he saw being displayed. He continued that this seemed to him to be much better than the kind of music where everything is determined in advance, because

> such music can never respond to what happens in its environment. Some music sounds bad in certain halls and better in others, sure. You can compose according to the space in which you know the music will be played. But the flexibility with which improvised music can respond to its environment goes far beyond that.
>
> *(Mengelberg 1992)*

Mengelberg and Han Bennink, the two founders of the ICP who were still part of the group during my fieldwork, have each compared improvisation to scenes from everyday life. Mengelberg has compared it to buying a train ticket: nobody thinks about what they are going to say in such an everyday conversation, but despite this lack of preparation these exchanges are usually successful (Andriessen 1996, 18). Bennink has compared it to crossing a busy street, where you have to pay constant attention and be able to respond as quickly as possible (Challenge Records 2012). The differences between these two comparisons indicate the stylistic differences between the two musicians. The differences between their descriptions and the usual accounts of improvisation are more striking. Neither seems to equate improvisation with a sense of personal expression; indeed, both of the scenes sketched would be rather awkward moments for personal expression. Neither also seems to value spontaneity: Mengelberg's example locates spontaneity in the most banal experiences, while in Bennink's case spontaneity is not so much a matter of joyous inspiration but a matter of responsiveness that could mean life or death. Neither scene, finally, depicts a situation of unbounded freedom, but of finding oneself in a situation that is already inhabited by social structures and material surroundings that one has to learn to deal with. This is not to say that expression, spontaneity, or even freedom do not have a place in the practice of the ICP. It does, however, suggest that improvisation has a very different significance for these Dutch improvisers.

In both definitions, and in the practice of the ICP Orchestra more generally, the improvisation is mainly defined in terms of responding to one's environment. From this perspective, it does not matter so much that the scene that Mengelberg describes, when watched without a child's naiveté, was probably prepared by Ellington, and may even have been a regular feature. This does not diminish the flexibility that Mengelberg perceived in this performance; indeed we might say that Ellington prepared just enough to make this flexibility possible, to construct part of the environment to which the musicians were responding. We might even say that Mengelberg, when describing his fascination for Ellington, is speaking as a composer rather than an improviser, as somebody who actually faces the choice whether to write a piece that determines everything in advance or that is able to more flexibly respond to its environment.

In its performances, the ICP uses an extensive repertoire of written material, most of it composed or arranged by Mengelberg. The orchestra is often praised for its ability to combine anarchic free improvisation with more traditional jazz drawing on the modernist bop of Herbie Nichols and Thelonious Monk as well as the big band repertoire of Duke Ellington and even older Dixieland-style jazz. Like Ellington's band, the ICP Orchestra is also frequently marked out for its combination of strong soloists (many of whom lead their own groups) and a highly polished group sound, a contrast that is made stronger because of the even wider range between entirely written-out compositions and entirely free improvisation in their concerts. Others comment on the influence of twentieth-century chamber music and other forms of western art music (Kurt Weill, Charles Ives) on their improvised and composed music, and yet others highlight the theatricality, humour, and absurdism that form an important aspect of their performances.

What personally drew me to the ICP, and what is perhaps most frequently emphasized by reviewers and audience members alike, is the way that the group can transition from a rambunctious collective improvisation to a brilliantly arranged big band tune in the blink of an eye, and then on to a soft piece of chamber music, without these transitions feeling forced or incoherent. Watching and listening more closely, you start to see that the musicians use cues and gestures, but you also wonder what is on their music stands apart from lead sheets and perhaps some written-out compositions. When hearing the group perform more often, you start to realize that the rambunctious improvisation contains pre-composed elements, that some of the background riffs in the big band tune are improvised on the spot, and that in fact the chamber music piece is completely improvised. ICP performances are exciting, because the agreements on the basis of which the musicians interact with each other are constantly up for discussion; even a moment of "free" improvisation is shown to have certain boundaries and conditions when it is interrupted by a musician who wishes to take the performance in a new direction. This establishes a strong emphasis on the actual practice of making music, and an ICP performance is about more than just the sound; this is also why their performances are often called theatrical. Sitting in the audience at so many ICP concerts over the last couple of years, I frequently heard audience members wonder aloud whether the music at that point was composed or improvised. This uncertainty creates a sense of magic, as it makes you wonder where this music is really coming from.

Usually it was both, and neither. As I discovered in the course of my fieldwork, the pieces that Mengelberg wrote for the group are not just vehicles for improvisation, but actually have a significant impact on the nature of improvisation as practised in ICP performance. They include lead sheets and fully composed pieces, but also game pieces, graphic scores, as well as other kinds of indeterminate and mobile forms. In addition, the ICP always includes some freely improvised sections in its concerts, and regularly features a conducted improvisation. Moreover, the musicians were often improvising precisely by playing notated material, not just in the sense that performers are always improvising to some degree because notation cannot specify everything, but actually radically reinterpreting written music in the course of an improvisation, or using one piece to interrupt another. In this approach, scores function not as "models" or "frameworks" but as sources of creativity for the musicians. This raises questions about the nature of composition, improvisation, and especially about the role of these pieces in the social and creative interactions that characterize their performances. Such questions interrogate our common assumptions about intentionality, agency, and creativity in performance.

This book is the first history of the Instant Composers Pool as well as the first in-depth study of the group's music. However, it does not aim to be a holistic description of the group's history or indeed of its music. Although I try to paint as rich and complete a picture as possible, my concern is specifically to understand the history and practice of "instant composition" as found in the ICP Orchestra. The first part describes the historical emergence of the concept in an encounter between various musical styles and historical developments, including jazz, experimental music, and the 1960s counterculture. The second part forms an ethnographic description of the performance practice of the ICP Orchestra, and formulates a theory of creativity in musical performance that can accommodate the interpenetration of composed and improvised material that characterizes their work.

"Beyond jazz" in this regard should emphatically not be understood as "outside of jazz". Rather, it signifies an in-between space where the ICP positioned itself in relation to jazz, experimental music, contemporary composition, and performance art, but not squarely within any of those categories. Inherent to this positioning was also a reconsideration of the meaning and significance of composition, improvisation, and the relation between notation and performance. This in-between position, then, also applies to their performance practice of "instant composition", in which improvisation is defined as itself a kind of composition, and perhaps more importantly, the use of notated repertoire is by no means opposed to its improvisatory character. In this regard, a lot of "jazz" is in fact "beyond jazz", Duke Ellington himself being a prime example. I hope therefore that both my historical approach and my arguments about creativity in performance will be relevant to the study of other figures and groups in the jazz tradition, beyond it, and outside it.

The Instant Composers Pool

The Instant Composers Pool was founded in Amsterdam in 1967 by Misha Mengelberg, Han Bennink, and Willem Breuker. Mengelberg and Bennink had been playing together since around 1960, when Mengelberg was studying composition and music theory at the Conservatory of The Hague, and Han Bennink was attending art school at the Kunstnijverheidsschool. Mengelberg comes from a classical music family; his great-uncle Willem Mengelberg was a world-famous conductor, his father Karel was a composer and conductor as well, and his mother Rahel Draber was a professional harpist. Bennink comes from a decidedly more working-class background, but his father was also a professional musician. Rein Bennink played drums, percussion, and reeds, spending most of his career playing swing and big band music for Dutch radio and television. Mengelberg and Bennink had a successful quartet with alto saxophonist Piet Noordijk and a range of different bass players, and were one of the primary groups to support visiting American musicians, most notably Eric Dolphy, which resulted in his *Last Date*, which was Dolphy's last released recording before he died shortly after. Breuker came from a working-class family without any professional musical activity. He developed a taste for jazz, free improvisation, and experimental music from a very early age, and was a rising star in the Dutch jazz scene, playing freely improvised music on saxophone and bass clarinet in various formations, but also writing his own experimental compositions. He joined Mengelberg and Bennink in 1966 and the ICP was founded the next year. The ICP became a cornerstone of improvised music in the Netherlands, as it was emerging in the late 1960s. Parallel developments were happening in the rest of Europe, where improvising musicians were asserting their individuality and independence, both from their African-American free jazz paragons and also from the musical cultures and infrastructures in Europe as they organized their own institutions, festivals, and record labels.

The ICP was founded at a time of strong political engagement in the Dutch musical avant-garde, where musicians were fighting for democratization in musical practice not just in improvised music but also, and perhaps even more so, in contemporary composed music. In fact, improvised, experimental, and composed music significantly overlap in Dutch post-war art music, and the ICP is a case in point, as we shall see throughout Part I. Mengelberg is a conservatory-trained composer, and was part of a group of activist composers (also including Louis Andriessen, Peter Schat, Reinbert de Leeuw, and Jan van Vlijmen) organizing various demonstrations and political concerts as well as taskforces and public debates to address not only the political content of music, but also the role of music in the broader society of the Netherlands. They mobilized many other musicians, including free improvisers like Breuker but also early music specialists like Frans Brüggen, in their attempts to reconsider the status quo in classical music performance. Mengelberg had been looking for alternative musical practices since the early 1960s, initially experimenting with performance art and briefly joining the Fluxus movement, where he got the idea of "instant composition" from Tomas Schmit's "instant poetry". Mengelberg's compositional output has primarily been written for the ICP. The ICP—and perhaps European improvised music more generally—should thus not only be understood as a part of jazz history, but certainly also as one of the ways in which contemporary composers found ways of operating outside of the scope of traditional concert practice.

The ICP was initially set up partly as a political initiative: a grassroots organization defending the rights of improvising musicians, a platform for people to find like-minded musicians, and an independent record label. As a "pool", the idea was that an ICP concert could feature any number of musicians associated with the group. After Breuker left the group in 1973, Mengelberg became the unofficial leader of the ICP: he organized regular rehearsals for musicians to learn various improvisation techniques, he wrote a diverse and substantial repertoire of compositions for the group to play, and created musical theatre pieces, played by the ICP musicians and a host of actors. Meanwhile, although there were still various groups playing under the ICP banner and recording on the label, in the late 1970s the group started to revolve more and more around a standardized line-up of musicians, first known as the ICP Tentet and later as the ICP Orchestra, which is how it still performed during my fieldwork in a line-up that has not drastically changed since the early 1990s (Figure 0.1).

The rhythm section of the group consists of Misha Mengelberg on piano, Han Bennink on drums, and Ernst Glerum on bass. Mengelberg has often acknowledged the influence of Thelonious Monk on his piano playing, and his influence has also been noted by others (Arndt 2002). However, his style is much more diverse, containing aspects of not only Monk, Ellington, and Herbie Nichols (another important influence), but also Cecil Taylor and Romantic piano repertoire; it emphasizes motivic development and contrapuntal harmonic textures, and really sounds like somebody developing their compositional thought as they

FIGURE 0.1 The ICP Orchestra line-up during my fieldwork. From left to right: Ernst Glerum (double bass), Tristan Honsinger (cello), Misha Mengelberg (piano), Michael Moore (alto saxophone, clarinet), Mary Oliver (violin, viola), Han Bennink (drums), Ab Baars (tenor saxophone, clarinet), Wolter Wierbos (trombone), Tobias Delius (tenor saxophone, clarinet), Thomas Heberer (trumpet)

Photograph by Francesca Patella

are playing—including all the hesitations and clumsy ideas. Bennink, especially compared to Mengelberg's aloofness, is a force of nature. A big man with a big stage presence, he has a remarkable energy, and is stylistically incomparable to anyone else. Players often criticized him for being too loud, and particularly his 1970s recordings contain some outright violence on the drums. In that period, he was more of a multi-instrumentalist than a drummer, playing saxophones, conches, trombone, trumpet, violin, and all sorts of percussion instruments. He has always been an excellent time drummer, however, and relates more to drummers from the 1950s and before than to other avant-gardists. Since then, moreover, he has returned to the standard drum kit (with the occasional extra prop) and during my fieldwork he frequently played concerts on only a snare drum. Glerum, out of the whole group, is perhaps the least "avant-gardistic". He has played in a number of contemporary music ensembles, and outside of the ICP mostly plays in straight-ahead jazz groups. In between Mengelberg's eccentricity and Bennink's abandon, he truly forms the musical anchor of the group. His tone is sophisticated yet straight to the point, and besides his walking bass technique he frequently makes use of his classically trained bowing techniques.

Glerum plays a double role, in that sense, as he is also part of the string section, together with Tristan Honsinger on cello and Mary Oliver on violin and viola. Like Glerum, Honsinger and Oliver have a classical education on their instrument. Honsinger attended the New England Conservatory and later attended Peabody, but moved to the Netherlands after hearing ICP records in the early 1970s. In Europe, he became involved not only in improvised music, but in improvised dance, mime, and theatre. His role in the ICP is not just that of a musician, but as he himself put it, to do "all the other stuff", frequently leading conducted improvisations, reciting texts, and singing. Oliver started out pursuing a career in contemporary music, premiering pieces by Iannis Xenakis, John Cage, and Brian Ferneyhough, before moving to improvised music. She did a PhD on improvisation in San Diego with George Lewis, and moved to the Netherlands in 1995, joining the ICP shortly after.

The brass section consists of Wolter Wierbos on trombone, Tobias Delius and Ab Baars on tenor saxophone and clarinet, Michael Moore on alto saxophone and clarinet, and Thomas Heberer on trumpet and cornet. Wierbos, like Bennink, combines virtuosic extended techniques, including multiphonics and split tones, with very traditional playing styles. He is particularly competent with the plunger mute, and often plays the melody line on more lyrical melodic pieces in the ICP repertoire. Delius is the most recent addition to the group, having joined in 2003. He greatly admires Sonny Rollins, and has something of his warm yet sharp tone. His playing is upbeat and has a percussive edge, but is mostly characterized by his snake-like melodies that twist irregularly through different registers with a broad range of dynamics within a single phrase. Baars is a master of extended techniques, both on the saxophone and on clarinet, for which he took lessons with John Carter. He has an extensive repertoire of cross-fingered notes and multiphonics, and a very abstract soloing style, using extreme timbres, but his playing also has a fragility that makes it emotionally very direct. Moore studied at the New England Conservatory in the 1970s, when Gunther Schuller, George Russell, Jaki Byard, and Joe Allard were teaching there. Shortly after graduating, he settled in Amsterdam in 1982. He is best known for his warm, lyrical tone, at times reminiscent of West Coast cool jazz musicians, and is in that sense perhaps the most "straight-ahead" player of the horns, although he is also capable of derailing the musical situation with an understated sense of humour and subversion. Heberer grew up in Germany, where he played with Manfred Schoof and Alexander von Schlippenbach, and joined the ICP in the early 1990s. He is particularly skilled at circular breathing, having recorded possibly the first continuously played solo LP, but his solos also frequently use a more classical tone, with big vibrato and laidback tempos in a style that seems to recall early jazz trumpet and cornet players.

Guus Janssen, finally, was not really a member of the ICP during my fieldwork, but frequently played with the group, sometimes sitting in for Mengelberg who was suffering from ill health. He became the standard pianist of the group when

Mengelberg stopped performing. He was trained as a concert pianist but chose to pursue a dual career as an improviser and a composer. His Septet in the 1970s featured many of today's ICP musicians, and like Mengelberg he has written much material aiming to combine compositional and improvisatory elements. His playing is influenced, apart from his classical education, by Lennie Tristano and boogie-woogie. He also plays harpsichord, organ, and a range of other keyboard instruments.

Beyond Jazz History

The history of jazz in Europe remains a somewhat marginalized part of jazz history, although this is fortunately changing both in jazz criticism and academic jazz studies. What is clear, however, is that concepts of a "European identity" in jazz obscure more than they clarify; they fail to account for the diversity of jazz in both Europe and in North America, and by distinguishing these traditions they also overlook the complex interrelations between musicians from these two continents. Moreover, such constructions of different national or continental identities in jazz disregard how the identity of jazz itself was frequently at stake in the intercultural exchanges that form part of this history.

As I said, "beyond jazz" is not the same as "outside of jazz", but rather signifies an in-between space, an interstitial moment from which to appreciate the contingencies of genre formation.[1] The ICP shows some strong similarities to the Art Ensemble of Chicago and other groups and musicians associated with the AACM active from the mid-1960s onwards, who can be said to be beyond jazz in quite a similar way, occupying a boundary position between jazz, experimental music, and performance art, and looking for ways to combine compositional and improvisatory practices (Lewis 2008; Steinbeck 2017). However, these musical similarities should not be over-emphasized, as the musicians of the ICP and those of the AACM were responding to very different environments, including lived realities of race, class, and culture. Whereas AACM musicians were struggling not to be pigeonholed as jazz musicians and to be taken seriously as composers and experimental musicians, the ICP was trying to get away from a restrictive environment of contemporary composition through free improvisation, while also realizing its own cultural distance from the jazz tradition.

The practice of the ICP cannot be fully understood without also taking into account their position vis-à-vis contemporary composition, experimental music, and performance art. Instant composition was the result of a complex negotiation of such cultural influences. In the first part of this book I trace its genealogy. I describe Mengelberg's early experiments with performance art, the relation of the ICP musicians and Dutch improvised music to American jazz, and the foundation and early years of the ICP in the context of the political activism in contemporary composed and improvised avant-garde music. Throughout these three chapters, there are constantly recurring negotiations of the idea of music as a social practice, of the meaning of improvisation, and of the relation between these two questions. The history of the ICP, and indeed the history of European improvised music more generally, shows how musicians have practically negotiated this entanglement of musical practice with the boundaries of genre, which in turn are bound up with cultural and national identities. For the ICP, this negotiation meant a reconsideration of the significance of improvisation as a social practice, the political efficacy of music performance, and indeed the meaning and value of improvisation itself. These were questions to which musicians of the ICP did not have an unambiguous answer.

As we shall see, the musicians of the ICP often ended up choosing music over direct political action, and indeed frequently dismissed descriptions of their music as a vehicle for political ideas. This is not to say that their music had nothing to do with politics. Of course, the very distinction between music and politics is a political one—something of which these musicians were all too aware. But it is to suggest that the very association of avant-garde improvisation with political subversion is something that needs to be reconsidered in the light of a more global view on different forms of improvisation. As the chapters in Part I will make clear, the ICP was an active part of the emerging counterculture, and this movement had important influences on their approach to music. However, this "counterculture" was by no means uniform, and neither was its influence on these musicians.

In this regard, the first part of this book does not simply form a "context" to the ICP's musical practice in the sense that it describes concentric circles around a single point which is the "text" of the ICP's performance practice. Such a metaphor cannot account for the variety of different contexts in which the ICP participated, and neither can it account for the dynamic, ambiguous, and variable connections between these contexts and the ICP musicians. The debates about groupings and inclusion that will recur in Part I—who was or wasn't "part of" Fluxus, or the jazz tradition, for instance—also suggest that contexts are not quite so easily delineated. In this sense, the very idea of "context" includes a degree of unwarranted generalization, something that Bruno Latour captures well in his description of context as "simply a way of stopping the description when you are too tired or too lazy to go on" (Latour 2005, 148). Of course, all writers and readers will at some point become too tired or too lazy, and some such generalizations are necessary for successful description. However, the three chapters of Part I will focus on the interstices and intersections between contexts to show how these categories are in constant formation, and how particular actions and events may resonate at different registers in society.

The practice of the ICP was developed in a reciprocal connection to these processes of formation. As an alternative to the metaphor of text and context, Georgina Born has proposed a topology of intersecting planes of social mediation (Born 2011). She suggests four such planes: musical practice with its creative interaction and division of labour; the imagined communities of audiences and subcultures; social identities like class, age, race, and gender; and finally the musical markets, institutions, and organizations. This approach takes as a given that the emergence of musical practices, identities, and institutions cannot be studied in isolation, but has to take into account "their complex interrelation and imbrication with contiguous musical systems existing in the same or proximate physical, geographical, historical or social space" (Born 2010a, 209). The advantage of this topology is that it makes clear the multiple levels at which musical behaviour and experience are socially mediated, thus avoiding the uniformity of the idea of "context", while identifying some of the specific dimensions in which such mediations may take place.

Born refers to these planes as making up the musical "assemblage", a term drawn from the philosophical work of Gilles Deleuze and Félix Guattari, who also use the term "planes" (Deleuze and Guattari 2013). Such assemblage theory is an increasingly common way to approach the concept of genre, not as uniform and stable musical category, but as an unstable, constantly redefined, and heterogeneous process of categorization, that moreover concerns not just musical qualities but also matters of identity and social behaviour (see for instance Brackett 2016). In 1991, Scott DeVeaux wrote an important critique of jazz historiography, questioning the validity of the overarching category of "jazz" when it implies "the idea that musics as diverse as those of King Oliver and the Art Ensemble of Chicago are in some fundamental sense *the same music*" (DeVeaux 1991, 530–531). Pointing out that jazz history is in fact filled with disputes about whether or not new, old, or revivalist styles could be called "jazz", DeVeaux argues for a way of writing history that does not pass over such debates in favour of all-encompassing categories, but attends to such moments of disagreement precisely to show the music's diversity and constantly shifting boundaries. Although DeVeaux did not use the term "assemblage", it is a useful concept to achieve such kinds of genre descriptions where the process of categorization does not presume an analytic totality but rather proceeds by negotiating difference. His argument inspired various jazz scholars to document how such genre boundaries have been used by musicians to claim positions of power, to cultivate outsider status, or to find new expression of racial or national identity (Gennari 2007; Ake 2002; Ake, Garrett, and Goldmark 2012).

Similar arguments in other genres have recently been made by Eric Drott, who describes genres as "acts of assemblage", and by Benjamin Piekut in his work on experimental music (Drott 2013, 10; Piekut 2011). Both draw explicitly on Latour's Actor-Network Theory (itself deeply influenced by Deleuze and Guattari), specifically his statement that "if you stop making and remaking groups, you stop having groups" (Latour 2005, 35). This view emphasizes the work involved in constructing, stabilizing, and maintaining such categories. As Piekut argues, genre is not "something that magically coalesced around shared [musical] qualities", but "a network, arranged, and fabricated through the hard work of composers, critics, scholars, performers, audiences, students, and a host of other elements including texts, scores, articles, curricula, patronage systems, and discourses of race, gender, class and nation" (Piekut 2011, 19). Piekut's work on experimentalism is particularly relevant to the history of the ICP, as experimental music has played a large part in the development of the group and its approach to performance. His argument further develops the work of George Lewis, who interrogated the idea of American experimentalism as a distinct genre, particularly the way in which it is implicitly distinguished from the African-American avant-garde (Lewis 1996). The music of various musicians and groups associated with the Chicago-based AACM, for instance, is clearly closely related to experimental music, but by virtue of its racial identity such practices were often designated as a form of "jazz". Lewis' argument centres on different definitions of "improvisa-tion", and how these conceptualize the role of history, identity, and agency in performance, questions that are intimately bound up with racial prejudice. Thus, Lewis shows how musical performance is, as Nicholas Cook would say, "not just a *metaphor* but a *metonym* of social interaction" (Cook 2012, 196); not just a sepa-rate sphere in which broader social issues are reflected, but a place where these issues are actively negotiated.

    Downbeat critic Kevin Whitehead, the author of the primary publication on Amsterdam's jazz and improvised music scene, in which the ICP plays a major role, calls this genre "New Dutch Swing" (Whitehead 1998), a term that has since stuck with some critics. On the cover of his book, he sums up the emer-gence of this genre as "jazz + classical music + absurdism = *New Dutch Swing*". Although he identifies important influences—indeed, in a different order they can be mapped on the three chapters of the first part of this book—such a for-mula implies a logical necessity that disregards the contingency and heterogeneity of this constant negotiation over boundaries. It is this contingent nature of the emergence of musical genres and practices that the first part of this book aims to portray. In these chapters, we will see repeated intersections between the various planes that Born identifies. In the first chapter, which describes Mengelberg's connection to Fluxus performance art and the ICP's ambivalent relation to the emergent counterculture which used similar performative means in their ludic protest, these intersections revolve around the question of the institution of "art" and whether artistic aims are at all compatible with the democratizing move-ments of the 1960s. Chapter 2 describes the relation of the ICP to American free jazz, and Dutch musicians' responses to claims of cultural ownership by some African-American musicians, while there was already a debate within the Dutch jazz community about the legitimacy of free improvisation vis-à-vis more tra-ditional jazz. This chapter directly addresses the previously mentioned debates about genre and processes of legitimization and authentication. The third chap-ter revisits the first's emphasis on politics, but through a focus on the political activism of contemporary composers, improvisers, and other musicians in the 1960s and 1970s. It specifically discusses the theme of organization, describing the foundation of the ICP in the context of activism for the reorganization of the musical infrastructure and the foundation of various other grassroots ensembles and organizations, as well as debates about the democratic organization of musical practice itself.

The three chapters may be seen as tracing "lines" along which the different planes of social mediation repeatedly intersect. For Deleuze and Guattari, part of the dynamics of assemblages is described by "lines of flight", which generate transformation and development, destabilizing and subverting the original status quo and thereby creating novel assemblages (Deleuze and Guattari 2013, 238–242). Such talk of "lines" may seem to go against their championing of chaotic and heterogeneous "rhizomatic" connections instead of "linear" roots (4–5). Indeed, it may seem antithetical to my description of Part I as a "genealogy" of instant composition, of which Michel Foucault argues the point is to subvert teleological historical narratives as it traces how practices, values, and concepts emerge not by any design or historical necessity but rather through chance, irony, discontinuity, and "haphazard conflicts" (Foucault 1977, 154). In describing the historical developments in Part I as "lines", I may seem to invoke precisely such a "linear" teleological narrative. Anthropologist Tim Ingold, elaborating on the work of Deleuze and Guattari, argues, however, that in such an understanding, lines are only a "sequence of dots", "succession of instants in which nothing moves or grows", while real lines are better thought of as a process, in a way that attends precisely to the erratic, unexpected variation through which they are formed (Ingold 2007, 3). In following these erratic lines in the emergence of instant composition, my aim is precisely to describe these processes of cultural and transnational musical encounter and exchange as what Steven Feld, describing jazz in Ghana, describes as "performances and imaginaries of connectedness, detoured and leaped-over pathways storied and travelled from X to Y by way of Z [. . .] These performances of connectedness are necessarily erratic, uneven, and ironic" (Feld 2012, 49).

Beyond Jazz Practice

In the second part of the book, I describe the results of ethnographic fieldwork conducted with the ICP Orchestra, exploring its approach to performance, composition, and improvisation in depth by presenting material drawn from interviews and observations. The ICP's practice draws particular attention to their music as a form of social practice, so my description of their music will focus primarily on this aspect. Although they have made several excellent recordings throughout their history, I will not go into much detail on any of them. Recordings are of very limited use in describing the creative interactions of musicians on stage—although I am certain that readers will notice new things about their recordings after reading this book.[2] Nor will I discuss the musical styles of the musicians or, in the case of Mengelberg's writing for the group, discuss his harmonic language or his talent for making arrangements. All of these things deserve further commentary and analysis, but they are not the primary concern of this book. My primary concern is to describe the role of the ICP repertoire in their musical practice, and for this reason I approach the pieces in their repertoire not as "works", but as notations, which is to say I see them as resources for making music in performance rather than representations of the music itself. More than a reconsideration of improvisation, then, this book is an attempt to formulate an account of music notation that makes it possible to describe its function within such an improvised practice.

If the first part of this book addresses the reciprocal relation between the sociality of musical practice and more large-scale social and cultural processes, the second part concerns the reciprocity between the sociality of musical practice and the theoretical assumptions and methodological approaches of music scholarship. By addressing this reciprocity, my aim is to extend the idea of in-betweenness and its subversion of given categorizations and distinctions to musical practice. The categorization of music into different genres also implies what Born calls "regional epistemologies" (Born 2010a, 209–210), conceptions of musical creativity and production, of improvisation and composition, and consequently on the role of human agency in music-making, on the relation of music to its social context, and indeed on ontological questions about what music is. As Philip Bohlman already argued in 1999, rather than binary distinctions between work-based and practice-based forms of music-making, between narrow understandings of the aesthetic and the social, an interdisciplinary and multicultural music scholarship calls for a pluralization of musical ontologies (Bohlman 1999). Recent work in cultural anthropology has similarly explored the idea that a "culture" is not just a matter of adopting or constructing a "worldview" but rather of constructing a world; not just developing different perspectives on the same reality, but actually constructing new realities (Holbraad and Pedersen 2017).

This ontological argument centres on the distinction between composition and improvisation. Classical music and jazz have frequently been distinguished along the lines of a difference between literate and oral musical cultures, and composition and improvisation have frequently been understood as similarly signifying such a difference. Just as literacy has often been taken to define the tradition of classical music, and the theories and methods of music scholarship were developed for the study of this notated tradition rather than the study of musical performance in general, improvisation has frequently been described in opposition to the use of notation. The practice of the ICP, however, in which notations are integral to their particular approach to improvisation, makes clear the need for a more nuanced vocabulary for speaking about performance and notation than the concepts of improvisation and composition allow. It is not simply the case that the ICP combines aspects of an oral and a literate musical culture; rather, in explicitly occupying an interstitial position, their practice makes clear the limited usefulness of concepts of orality and literacy to understand either classical music or jazz.

One of the central goals of this book is to show ways to consider the practice of improvisation that do not rely on this oppositional discourse. Discussions of improvisation in music scholarship have been entangled in a discourse of "otherness". Laudan Nooshin describes how early ethnomusicologists studying traditional Iranian music characterized it as "improvised" simply because it did not use notation, even though this tradition relied on the very precise memorization of a canonic repertory, and performances were appreciated on the basis of nuanced inflections of a standard melody rather than the invention of musical material in the course of performance (Nooshin 2003). She suggests that the praise of improvisation since the 1960s as a more authentic and socially desirable form of music-making than the work-centred discourse of classical music may be likened to the trope of the "noble savage", the "pure" primitive other who acts as a remedy to the decadence of western intellectualism.

Jazz has often been described as a music in which personal and collective interaction play a central role. Arguments in music scholarship for understanding music primarily as a form of social practice have frequently taken jazz as their example, and this goes back to the early twentieth century.[3] In other fields, sociologists and social psychologists writing about the collective negotiation of knowledge, practical skills, and aesthetics have frequently taken jazz as their primary example.[4] In management and organization studies, there is a large amount of literature that takes the collective creativity found in jazz as a model for shaping democratic and innovative work environments.[5] Sometimes these descriptions of jazz and improvisation border on the utopian, for instance in the work associated with the "Improvisation, Community, and Social Practice" research group in Canada, where jazz and improvisation are described as a model for an "ethics of cocreation" as it "accentuates matters of responsibility, interdependence, trust and social obligation" and promotes "dispersed authority" and "self-active democracy" (Fischlin, Heble, and Lipsitz 2013, 198).

It is easy to be sceptical of such ambitious claims—philosopher Gary Peters dismisses such discourses as "reduc[ing] improvisation to a glorified love-in dressed up as art" (Peters 2009, 3). However, not only does this celebration of jazz and improvisation imply an aesthetic acknowledgement of African-American musical practices that has long been denied, but I think moreover that such an ethical, social, and political approach to musical practices should not be discouraged—if anything we need more music scholarship to be sensitive to such issues. Jazz has in this regard been an important base for a more general turn to seeing music in terms of processes of social interaction. From this perspective, music is seen not primarily as an object, but as an activity—which includes composition, performance, listening, criticism, etcetera—a shift that Christopher Small has captured in his suggestion to change the noun "music" into the verb "musicking" (Small 1998).

Perhaps the most ardent advocate of this "performative turn" in recent times has been Nicholas Cook, most of whose work concerns classical music. He has criticized the way in which scholarship on this tradition has always focused exclusively on the composer as the creative genius and the musical text as a representation of all that is supposedly aesthetically relevant about music. Because of a focus on those aspects of music that could be written down, tonal and rhythmic qualities became the most essential musical parameters, and moreover "music" became identified with abstract and ideal "structures" of such tonal and rhythmic qualities, rather than the social, cultural, material, and emotional practice of making and experiencing sound. Thus he writes that "ways of thinking about performance that reflect the fundamentally creative role of the performer will have to come from somewhere other than the analytical tradition of Western 'art' music and jazz may well be one of those places" (Cook 2007, 338).

However, Cook simultaneously notes that much discourse on jazz represents it as uniquely or exclusively interactive and social, and he cautions that this has stood in the way of a more general view of music as creative interaction. He interrogates how it describes improvised performance as a form of social interaction "as opposed to" the performance of pre-composed music. He argues that a full understanding of the performance of written repertoire is dependent on interaction and mutual coordination as much as is the case with improvised music, not only because notation does not specify everything, but also because when something is specified, performers still have to turn it into *their* music and this requires close collaboration. Thus, he argues, distinctions between orality and literacy are inapplicable to the real experience of making music together (Cook 2007).

Nor can jazz properly be described as "oral". Kenneth Prouty, in his work on jazz education, notes the frequency with which the "orality" of jazz is emphasized, particularly in the context of how jazz musicians develop their musical abilities. He surveys the various textbooks, transcriptions, theories, and sound recordings that have mediated musical expression, pedagogy, and experience since at least the 1920s, and argues that:

> a rigid classification as either "oral" or "written" fails to explain what was really happening in the learning and performance of jazz. I might suggest the jazz composition occupies a musical space somewhere between the compositional traditions of Western art music and jazz improvisation. But I also believe that to classify this as a written tradition *vis-à-vis* improvisation is troublesome, as is the absolute classification of Western art music itself as a written tradition.
>
> *(Prouty 2006, 331)*

As we will see in Part II, the written repertoire of the ICP Orchestra is crucial to both the learning and performance of the group's musical style. Whereas Prouty is mainly concerned with how jazz is learned and taught, my main concern is how to conceptualize this interpenetration of the written material and the group's improvisations in performance. Considering how deeply embedded the idea is in music scholarship that improvisation is defined by the absence of music notation, I turn particularly to work in anthropology for different perspectives on improvisation and creativity. Specifically, to understand the interaction between the ICP musicians and their notations, I turn to theories of material culture: the study of the social and cultural relationships between people and things (see also Schuiling forthcoming a). In fact, this book may well be considered a description of the material culture of the ICP repertoire.

In describing the music of the ICP, then, I try to avoid a perspective that views music as existing purely in the moment or purely in the score, but as a multiply mediated practice emerging between musical people and musical objects: between bodies, skills, instruments, scores, and recordings that give existence to music in different ways. The idea of the musical assemblage discussed above is used not just to describe music's socio-historical formations, but increasingly also to describe the performance of music itself. The idea of the assemblage as a dynamic interaction between heterogeneous elements seems a fitting description for the interaction between musicians, instruments, studios, recording technologies, playback technologies, spaces, and listeners that makes up musical practice. Piekut writes that "whatever music might be, it clearly relies on many things that are not music, and therefore we should conceive of it as a set of relations among distinct materials and events that have been translated to work together" (Piekut 2014, 192). When applied to music notation, this perspective softens binary understandings of "text" versus "performance" and looks rather to the role of notation within this broader network of material and technological mediation that makes up the musical assemblage.[6] Notations, by mediating creative knowledge and coordinating social interaction, participate in the construction of musical contexts. In the ICP, musical notations have an active role in shaping both the forms of musical interaction between musicians and the musical structures that result from these. They function not as models or frameworks but rather as sources of musical creativity, of disagreement and musical subversion as much as compliance and collaboration. They can be seen as tools for shaping a musical performance, or as interfaces of virtual social, material, and musical relations (Schuiling forthcoming b).

Fieldwork and Ethnography

"Here: 'I think improvisation is much higher than composition, not because I cannot read and compose, but . . . I was born an instant composer.' I'd like you to start the piece with that."[7] Han Bennink was one of the few ICP musicians to make the effort to read and comment on a transcription of an earlier interview. This brief remark, apart from highlighting the values and cultural hierarchies associated with improvisation and composition, opens up a world of problems with fieldwork and ethnography. Of how, in the words of Susan MacDougall, such work is always simultaneously "sincere and instrumental" (MacDougall 2016). Bennink's primary frame of reference in giving interviews is probably journalism, and he may not know—indeed, no-one would expect him to know—what it means to be an (ethno-) musicological researcher. The focus in my research on the role of the ICP repertoire in their performances creates rather a special role for Bennink, who is the only person in the group not to read sheet music. Indeed, my description of the ICP in terms of Mengelberg's compositional, political, and music-philosophical ideas is in that sense slightly unbalanced as it diminishes the life-long role of Bennink in the development of the group.[8]

The sad irony of my fieldwork, given his central role in this book, was that Mengelberg was increasingly suffering from dementia in the course of my research. Although his health had already been decreasing for a number of years, having had a heart attack and a stroke since the 1990s in addition to other health problems, he had been diagnosed with dementia shortly before the start of my research. Dementia covers a broad spectrum of symptoms and can be very difficult to diagnose (Brummel-Smith 2008). It can have a number of different causes, and Mengelberg did not suffer from Alzheimer's disease. When I started my fieldwork, he had many clear moments and plainly understood who I was and what I was doing with the group. As his condition became worse, he increasingly suffered from aphasia, memory loss, and delusions, and he stopped performing altogether a few months after I completed my fieldwork. He died on 3 March 2017. Although we had some conversations and interviews, and some of his comments during my fieldwork have been taken up in this book, I decided in the early stages of my research not to plague him with in-depth interviews about his musical ideas and his past, because I had noticed that he occasionally found it exhausting to try to remember such things. The extent to which such interviews would really have been fruitful is a question in itself: he was well known for his tenacity and irony, which makes him notoriously difficult to interview. In one of our earliest conversations, I asked him general questions about politics, the protest movements of the 1960s, and philosophy. He denied any interest in politics, or any participation in the protest movements. He found the writings of Marx and Bakunin useless and boring when they were not totally incomprehensible. Nonetheless, when our conversation was over he commended me for asking the right sort of questions.

His situation does raise issues of consent and participation, and so it is important to discuss Mengelberg's role in the group during my research and particularly how the other musicians treated him. There is no denying that his role as the leader of the group had been played out. The other musicians, manager Susanna von Canon, and bus driver Gerard de Meij all took care of him very well, and I tried to help where I could, and everyone made sure that he did not overexert himself, got rest when he needed it, and took his medicine. Although some people in and close to the ICP occasionally raised doubts over whether his continued participation was a good idea, he performed with the group until a very late stage in his disease. Medical and music-therapeutic literature seems to indicate that this was probably a good decision overall. Music is generally acknowledged as an effective form of care for dementia patients, and music therapy in particular has been shown to be highly effective. Actively playing music rather than just listening to it is especially important, as it allows patients to communicate when normal forms of communication have become difficult, it allows them to participate with other people and so enhances social and emotional skills, it can help alleviate agitation and stress, and the employment of embodied skills can serve as a way to maintain a strong sense of self when loss of memory and aphasia make this more difficult.[9] What seems to me to be particularly important about his participation in the ICP is that it allowed Mengelberg not to be defined purely by his disease, but to continue to be appreciated as the person that he is (by musicians and audience alike) rather than as a person-with-dementia.

To be sure, performing music can be taxing, and the ICP performances could run very late. Mengelberg knew that he always had the choice whether he wanted to perform or go back to the hotel, and it was no problem if he decided to stop playing in the middle of the first set, or if conversely he suddenly decided to step up on stage. The improvisatory approach of the ICP performances also made his continued participation possible, and it is unthinkable that Mengelberg could have continued to perform in a similar way if he had been a concert pianist. At the same time, although musical skills outlast a large number of other bodily functions in dementia patients, there are indications that improvising music can be difficult for dementia patients for the same reasons that speaking can be (G. Aldridge 2000). He gave the impression of being happy to still participate in the group, to go along on tours and perform with them, and repeatedly expressed to me his pride and satisfaction in the way that the group functioned. The fact that he knew what was being expected of him in such situations, and that he could make the conscious decision to participate or not, indicated to me that there were no extraordinary issues of consent in his participation in my fieldwork. I found it important to include his voice in this book as much as possible, and will occasionally include comments that he made during my fieldwork. The considerations in including these statements—am I allowing people to speak with their own voice, was this statement made truthfully and in full awareness, are its inclusion and my critical perspective on it warranted by my concern for their best interests?—were the same as with any other musician in the ICP.

My arguments about orality and literacy also bear on the practice of ethnography and thus on the status of this book. Anthropologists, ethnomusicologists, and other ethnographers have long been aware of how the written text constructs and reifies "the field" which is in reality a social, embodied, practical, and diffracted process (Barz and Cooley 2008). However, this distinction between academia and the field should not necessarily be identified with an "official" and "vernacular", or "literate" and "oral" culture. Of course, academic positions are positions of power and one should be careful in using this to report on people who may not be in such a privileged position, but our ethnographic subjects are increasingly literate and media-savvy people. The multiplicity of mediation in today's culture affects not only our ethnographic subjects, diffracting the field even further, but also our own research process, which frequently includes not only audio and video recording, but also contact through email and social media. One's status as a writer also mediates the relation to other people in the field, but it is only one kind of mediation among others.

Similarly, this book does not aim to be an accurate or complete representation of the life, practices, and history of the ICP musicians, or even of my own experience in doing fieldwork. Rather, just like Mengelberg's scores, I see its purpose not in representational terms but in terms of the relations and connections it generates and constructs. The ethnographic part of this book in particular is explicitly theoretical, and as such it is an account of the things I have learned through my interactions with the ICP musicians, the questions they have raised for me, and the new ideas they have engendered. It is an example of "situated knowledge" (Haraway 1988), avoiding both the myth of objective representation and the self-awareness of reflexive ethnography, but acknowledging the relational nature of research and maintaining the open-ended, relational nature of this knowledge by opening it up to current musicological debates. I feel that the best way to do justice to the ICP's practice is not just to describe their practice as unique and to emphasize their difference from standard ideas about performance, composition, and improvisation, but to try to see what we may learn from them about improvisation, creativity, and the sociality of music in general.

Notes

1 Jason Toynbee, referring specifically to free improvisation, has argued that it has a tendency to describe itself as being beyond genre, while having a clearly identifiable sound, way of working, and cultural identity. He discusses this in the context of what he calls the "inevitability of genre" (Toynbee 1999, 107). My discussion of the ICP's music as "beyond jazz" is not intended to portray them as being beyond genre, but rather, as I explain further below, to take into account the negotiation of influences from various different genres in constructing their own musical practice. In other words, it takes into account the inevitability of genre while also addressing its contingency and multiplicity.

2 Paul Berliner and Ingrid Monson combined ethnographic observations with discussions of jazz recordings (Berliner 1994; Monson 1996), but the value of recordings has been debated, for instance by Robert Faulkner and Scott DeVeaux (Faulkner 2006; DeVeaux 2006).

3 In the early twentieth century, such arguments were made perhaps most prevalently (more than in the United States itself) in Weimar Germany; see for instance Pritchard (2011) (and Wipplinger 2017 for a more general discussion of the role of jazz in Weimar Germany). In post-war American music scholarship, the work of Charles Keil presented an important argument to this effect (Keil 1966). The influential work of Christopher Small on "musicking" also draws on his earlier work on jazz (Small 1987, 1998), and Nicholas Cook's arguments for a performative turn in

music scholarship have also been influenced by the work of Berliner and Monson (Berliner 1994; Monson 1996; Cook 2001).

4 See for instance Schütz (1951); Martin (2006); Faulkner and Becker (2009) in sociology and Sawyer (1992); Seddon and Biasutti (2009); and Bastien and Hostager (1992) in social psychology.

5 See for instance Orlikowski and Hofman (1997); Barrett (1998); Weick (1998); Zack (2000); Kamoche and Cunha (2001).

6 In the field of "book history" scholars started looking at books as windows into the cultural experience of the past, not by looking at their themes, metaphors, or narrative structure, but rather at their technological production, material form, dissemination, and consumption. In this approach, as D.F. McKenzie puts it, bibliographic aspects become sociological data as they provide insights into how books came to construct social relations in the first place (McKenzie 1999). The rise of digital editions and of literature that actively engages the possibilities of the digital era has also effected a convergence between literature scholarship and media theory and this has given rise to a broad reconsideration and differentiation of concepts like print, text, book, document, and notation. Katherine Hayles and Jessica Pressman summarize this approach by saying that it acknowledges that "recursive feedback loops between form and content are not only characteristic of special cases ... but are the necessary ground from which inquiry proceeds" (Hayles and Pressman 2013, x; see also Hayles 2002; Drucker 2013; Kirschenbaum 2008; Gitelman 1999).

7 Han Bennink, interview with the author, 4 January 2013.

8 It must be said that Bennink himself frequently refers to the ICP as 'Misha's group' and acknowledges his role as a leader.

9 For an overview of the positive effects of music on dementia patients, see Brummel-Smith (2008); Clair (2008); D. Aldridge (2000); Wall and Duffy (2010); Allison (2010).

PART I
Beyond Jazz History

1

PERFORMANCE ART AND LUDIC COUNTERCULTURES

Han Bennink and Misha Mengelberg played together for the first time on 4 September 1960 in jazz club Persepolis in Utrecht (Van den Berg 2009, 58). Both budding jazz musicians, they found each other through a shared interest in the music of Thelonious Monk. At this time, Bennink was in art school at the Kunstnijverheidsschool ("School of Applied Arts"), the current Gerrit Rietveld Academie. Mengelberg was a composition and music theory student at the conservatory of The Hague while simultaneously pursuing a career as a jazz pianist. In the world they inhabited, cool jazz was the fashion and Monk was seen as an offbeat and incompetent pianist. In contemporary art music, twelve-tone music was largely unknown and regarded with suspicion. Ten years later, the world had changed completely. Any sound could now be called music—indeed, any gesture, or even any idea, could be called music, poetry, or sculpture. The emergence of performance art had not only revolutionized the art scene, but through new international political movements like Situationism, "happenings" had become a hallmark of the emerging counterculture which aimed to transform public space into a ludic environment fit for the creative and nomadic existence of the human beings of the future. Bennink and Mengelberg, together with fellow ICP founder Willem Breuker, were right in the middle of these processes, and to some extent agents of what historians have called the "expressive revolution" (Righart 1998).

Categorizing the various "schools" in European improvised music, Mike Heffley writes:

> The Dutch were the louder anarchists, the humourists, the ironists, the rug-ged individualists and musical gamesters/tricksters radicalized around their own folk and music theatre traditions, nudged by the Fluxus movement to provide a grassroots populist (if also intellectually esoteric) alternative to both commercial pop-schlock and pompous classical *Kultur*.
>
> *(Heffley 2005, 66)*

The influence of the ICP on this description is palpable, and in this chapter we will see various important influences on this style of music-making. The influence of Fluxus, specifically, will be discussed at length, but its significance lies more in its "intellectual esoterism" than in its grassroots populism. Where Heffley connects Fluxus to a countercultural iconoclasm as a matter of course, we will see that the relation of Fluxus—and in fact of the ICP—to countercultural politics was by no means straightforward.

Mengelberg's time in Fluxus is often mentioned in relation to the ICP, but is hardly ever discussed in detail. Most journalistic articles and concert programmes refer to it only to say that it was a form of absurdist performance art. Kevin Whitehead, in his book about improvised music in Amsterdam, argues that Fluxus was not so important for Mengelberg at all: "Mengelberg's Fluxus connection is often cited, but his involvement was short-lived" (Whitehead 1998, 35). He cites Mengelberg in an unpublished interview with John Corbett: "Fluxus was nothing. Fluxus was a bunch of idiots who all did their things and saw at a certain point that some other people were working in similar amorphous directions" (Whitehead 1998, 35). This indeed seems rather dismissive, but it can also be understood as an admonition that Fluxus was a very heterogeneous movement with no clearly outlined programme, which is not to say that some of the ideas in Fluxus did not have an important influence on his musical thought. Jürgen Arndt cites Mengelberg as saying something similar but more positive: "Fluxus did not have a program; it stands for nothing. Fluxus only means current. I felt there was a very intense connection to Dadaism, and in my opinion, Dada was the most brilliant art movement of this century" (Arndt 2012, 355). Indeed, he even becomes uncharacteristically personal in his description of that period:

> This was the first time for me where I had the impression with everything I tried musically—sense and non-sense—that there were other people in the world doing these things and talking about them. There, I felt more or less at home.
>
> *(Arndt 2012, 357)*

The influence of performance art was also playing a role in the upcoming counterculture. The 1960s countercultures in the Netherlands, like many of the other protest movements emerging globally in this period, are notable for their close engagement with contemporaneous forms of performance art, and indeed in the "aestheticization" of their protests. However, although there was clearly a relation of the Dutch counterculture to performance art, the connection with Fluxus specifically is rather tenuous. Mengelberg describes his fascination with Fluxus mostly in artistic and musical terms; his sense of the movement providing a place for him is based on a shared aesthetic rather than political outlook. The question of Fluxus having aesthetic or political aims was an important point of discussion within the group, and as we shall see, this was in fact a more general point of contention in the encounters between artists and activists. The description of both artistic and political avant-gardes in terms of "happenings" challenging authorities and traditions too easily overlooks the heterogeneity of the various performance art movements and their relation to the counterculture—which in fact was itself not a uniform movement. In this chapter I take a close look at this diverse environment, not as a space neatly separated into schools (Fluxus, Darmstadt, happenings) and subcultures (beat, Provo, hippies), but rather as a heterogeneous landscape of overlapping networks and alliances.

The political efficacy of avant-gardes was famously questioned by the work of Peter Bürger, which is a prime reference in art historical literature on avant-garde art movements (Bürger 1984). Although Bürger acknowledges that very little avant-garde art is actually political in content, he makes its political practice, namely the attack on art "as an institution" through the reintegration of art with everyday life, into one of its definitive characteristics. When writing of the avant-garde, Bürger is mainly thinking of Dada and the post-war movements that continued its legacy, of which Fluxus was one. One of his core arguments is that the former ultimately failed to fulfil its ideals of abolishing art as an institution, and consequently that the latter was a lost cause from the start, because it institutionalizes an already failed historical avant-garde. Although Bürger's work remains the starting point for most research on the avant-garde, few art historians would still accept his argument without qualification (Foster 1996; Sell 2008; Mann 1991; Harding 2013). Rather than seeing *the* avant-garde in terms of its attack on *the* institution of art, recent work proposes to be more sensitive to the different contexts, aims, and premises of specific artists. Fluxus participants had very different attitudes towards the institution of art, and disagreed about whether its criticism should even be a core concern of the movement; such differences are not easily classified under one definition of an "avant-garde".

As we shall see throughout Part I, questions of whether their artistic practice was conducive to, contiguous with, separated from, or even opposed to political action were continuously debated by the ICP musicians and the wider contemporary music scene. This chapter will describe perhaps the most radical challenge in these debates, namely whether the very category of "music" or "art" would not have to be abolished. The ICP musicians—and indeed many other contemporary musicians in the Netherlands—did not go along with the more radical movements in this period, but chose to keep making music, even "art", although they would continue to be politically engaged. Somewhat paradoxically, then, the main influence of Fluxus on the ICP is an aesthetic one, and it is a particularly important one for the very concept of instant composition which was based on Tomas Schmit's Fluxus work on "instant poetry". This chapter thus provides a set-up for the more in-depth political arguments of contemporary musicians discussed in Chapter 3, but also lays the foundation for some of the theoretical discussions of Part II.

Mengelberg and Performance Art: Early Encounters

Mengelberg was part of a group of composers who all studied with Kees van Baaren, which included Louis Andriessen, Peter Schat, Reinbert de Leeuw, and Jan van Vlijmen.[1] As will be discussed in Chapter 3, Mengelberg and his fellow students would organize various demonstrations and political concerts from the mid-1960s onwards. In his book on avant-garde music in 1960s Amsterdam, which deals mostly with composed music but reserves a chapter for the ICP, Robert Adlington describes the situation of this generation of composers as follows:

> As students in the late 1950s, they were the first composers to gain a school-ing in serialism, a schooling that they sought to deepen through further lessons with prominent figures of the postwar avant-garde, and involve-ment in influential trade meetings such as the Darmstadt Ferienkurse. Yet even before this training was complete, these composers were exposed to drastically different models of creative practice, in which absurdity and hap-penstance took priority over intricacy and precision. Simultaneously, the global tensions of the cold war were reaching their height, and in Amsterdam local expressions of dissent were gaining new focus. From this conjuncture inevitably arose difficult questions about the purpose of progressive artistic pursuits. Did the future of music lie in serialism—in 1962 still a novelty in the Netherlands—or in indeterminacy? How might either of these relate to the creative public manifestations emerging on the streets of Amsterdam? What was the point of composition in the face of the atom bomb?
>
> *(Adlington 2013, 23–24)*

The description captures well the various radical changes that were to happen in the course of the decade. In his book, Adlington presents an essentially Bürgerian argument: the political aspirations of the avant-gardists largely failed because of a blindness to the political (bourgeois) nature of modern music and the institutions in which it is embedded. Of the "Van Baarenites", Mengelberg most consistently pursued the forms of "absurdity and happen-stance" to which Adlington refers. While his fellow students remained mostly within the confines of contemporary art music—either as composers, conduc-tors, or in other capacities—Mengelberg consciously moved outside it. If the others wondered whether the future of music would be in serialism or inde-terminacy, Mengelberg moved in circles where people more fundamentally questioned whether there should be a future for music at all.

In 1958, his first year as a conservatory student, Mengelberg visited Darmstadt. Originally going to see people like Karlheinz Stockhausen and Boulez, he was put off by their "pomposity" (Schouten 1973, 58), and was much more fascinated by the lectures of John Cage, who happened to give his famous lectures/performances that year:

He was smoking six cigarettes at a time but also manipulating them, burning them or laying three on an ashtray and burning the fourth. I remember the manipulating more than the lecture. His talking was also interfered by David Tudor playing. I remember thinking that the lecture, manipulating and playing should appear as one . . . I hated musical theatre in the classical sense, but there were new possibilities.

(Whitehead 1998, 24)

The work of John Cage and especially the forms of performance art that followed it had a decisive influence on Mengelberg's approach to music, perhaps even more than jazz. That is to say, while jazz and classical composition seem to have co-existed in his musical practice just fine, it was this upcoming avant-garde that began to transform his approach to both, thus informing his response to the "difficult questions about the purpose of progressive artistic pursuits" to which Adlington refers.

Cage's lecture directed Mengelberg's attention to new modes of performance that would have a long-lasting impact on his musical aesthetic. Mengelberg's first experiments in such new forms of performance art were done in the context of the "Mood Engineering Society" (MES), a movement initiated by Dutch visual artist Willem de Ridder. Although very short-lived, and by all accounts a failure, the MES brought together a diverse and talented group of artists and musicians, and formed an explosion of new approaches to music and performance at a time when twelve-tone composition was still a very controversial method in composed music in the Netherlands. Originally a painter, De Ridder started showcasing human-size (and larger) wads of blank canvas as "paper constellations" from 1960 onwards for people to interact and play with. These crumpled-up canvases turned the end (or failure) of artistic expression into possibilities for new forms of playfulness. Later initiatives similarly revolved around playful interaction as a new direction for traditional art forms, such as his "Society for Party Organization", which organized parties as a form of "auto-theatre" in which there was no distinction between performer and spectator (De Ridder 2008). Such ideas were also the basis for the MES, for which De Ridder primarily gathered composers and musicians. He initially approached electronic music pioneer Dick Raaijmakers, who had assisted Edgard Varèse with his *Poème Électronique* in 1958 and was now working at the Studio of Electronic Music connected to Utrecht University. Through Raaijmakers, he probably got to know other contemporary musicians. These included Andriessen, Mengelberg, and Schat.[2]

In an open letter in 1962 Schat and De Ridder propagated "auto-theatre" and interaction as opposed to the traditional, unidirectional mode of stage performance. They note that "contemporary music is simply contemporary life", noting that when art and life are separated, masterpieces and "art" emerge, which clearly is to be avoided (Beeren 1979, 35). In the programme book of the first MES concert, they criticized the fact that all the new theatres and concert halls that were being built in the post-war reconstruction perpetuated the "goggle-box theatre" of the Renaissance with its "feudal arrangement of seats and balconies" instead of providing a more flexible set-up in which "the space could be adapted to the work of art rather than the other way around" (De Ridder 1962). This concert programme itself fulfilled such an auto-theatrical function: it was large and unwieldy, and a small "paper constellation" had been attached to the front page of each programme. Experimental typography meant that audience members had to move the programme around, thus participating in the creation of movement and sound before the concert itself had even started. The concert opened with a piece by Mengelberg, *Exercise for Flute*, with a graphic score containing scratches and ink stains (Beeren 1979, 39). Other pieces included a piece for acoustic piano and tape by Raaijmakers, a piano and piccolo improvisation by Rob du Bois, a graphic piece for piano and flute by Andriessen, tape pieces by Jan Boerman and Jaap Spek, and Schat's *Sextet*, which gave both musical and choreographic instructions to its six performers. De Ridder's contributions were an experimental choreography to a tape piece, and a piece called *Monochrome*, in which De Ridder stood silently on stage until the audience started to murmur, which triggered De Ridder to reproduce any sounds coming from the audience (De Ridder 2008).[3]

Although these pieces may have struck the audience—and probably the performers themselves—as belonging to a general "avant-gardistic" aesthetic of weirdness and absurdism, none of the pieces except for De Ridder's actually fulfil the idea of "auto-theatre" in any way. The performances clearly maintained a traditional division of labour between performers and audience. Only two MES concerts followed, with roughly the same programme as the first, before the group fell apart. The first person to distance himself from the group was Peter Schat. Schat's case is an interesting one, as it illustrates the disagreements and uncertainties underneath these early radical gestures. He had visited Darmstadt together with Mengelberg in 1958 and was an active participant of the Situationist International. From 1960, Schat had been a student of Pierre Boulez, and so was caught between two very different worlds: the high modernist aesthetic of Boulez, which wanted to advance music as an art, and the radical avant-garde of the MES and Situationism that aimed to subvert the very concept of art and build towards a playful society. In 1962, even before the third concert, he quit the MES and decided to focus on his composition work.[4] Many other people involved in the MES withdrew their support, something De Ridder later blamed on a concern for their compositional careers over their commitment to the ideals of the MES: where Schat wanted to make "great masterpieces", De Ridder wanted to put an end to official music culture altogether (De Ridder and Levy 1983, 8). This disagreement over the question of whether the idea of modern art was compatible with the ideals of the avant-garde—significantly, whether composers were able to reconsider their own role as composer within the desired transformations of art and society—was not just a matter between Schat and De Ridder, or even internal to the MES, but was representative of a tension in many contemporary avant-gardes; we will see the same tension arise in Fluxus, and in the forms of political activism described in Chapter 3.

Mengelberg's response to these issues was rather different from Schat's, and belies De Ridder's suggestion that their aims and methods were quite so clear-cut. In an interview in 1973 he recalled:

> They played a flute piece of mine, about which I said: that has nothing to do with it. I reject any responsibility for this production [. . .] I said: let's wait until we can give some meaning to that name with real "mood-engineering" and then make pieces that do that. But nobody had the patience for that.
>
> *(Schouten 1973, 58)*

Such recollections and hindsight may not be entirely truthful, and as we will see in Chapter 3 such participation without taking responsibility is an unfortunately typical stance of Mengelberg. However, he does acknowledge that his contribution did not fulfil the stated aims of the movement; it suggests that the disagreement in the MES was there from the start. Moreover, if we take him at his word, the comment does show that, perhaps even more than a political awareness, the MES triggered a thought process in Mengelberg about how musical performance might be changed so that the social relations in performance might be reimagined. In other words, even if he did not fully agree with some of its more radical aims, it did precisely initiate a reconsideration of his own role as a composer within his musical practice.

Fluxus

Around the same time as the MES activities, Fluxus was emerging as a movement in New York. The name "Fluxus" at this point was only used as the title of a newspaper published by George Maciunas and not to refer to themselves as a group, but a network of composers and visual artists was already taking shape: composers such as Maciunas, George Brecht, Allan Kaprow, and Dick Higgins were studying there with John Cage, and meanwhile Yoko Ono, Toshi Ichiyanagi, Henry Flynt, and La Monte Young were also active in the same city. Ono and Maciunas organized concerts for experimental performances, where these and other artists presented their work (O. Smith 1993). The first concerts where the name "Fluxus" was actually used were organized in Germany. Maciunas went to Germany in 1961, where he met many other artists exploring performance art partly inspired by John Cage, such as Nam June Paik, Wolf Vostell, Ben Patterson, and Emmett Williams. Together with these artists, he started to organize concerts in Wuppertal and Düsseldorf and then in September 1962, in Wiesbaden, he held the first official "Fluxus Festival" over the course of four weeks. Thus he "founded" the Fluxus movement, which would include a newspaper, a mail-order firm, sub-divisions, a headquarters, and copyright protection, and appointed himself the chairman of this "collective resembling a multinational corporation" (Dumett 2008, 316).

To give an idea of these concerts: at the Wuppertal concert, Benjamin Patterson performed his *Variations for Double Bass* in which a double bass is first tuned to toy instruments, then played with a clothes pin, paperclip, comb, feather duster, and other items, and finally a letter is posted through the instrument's f-hole. In Düsseldorf, Nam June Paik performed his *One for Violin Solo*, where he slowly lifts a violin over his head over a duration of 5 minutes before smashing it to pieces. Pieces such as these are early instances of what have come to be considered "typical" Fluxus performances, which have been an important influence on performance art and conceptual art and perhaps therefore have mostly been described in art historical literature rather than histories of music. However, performers, who were mostly composers, consistently called these performances *music*. This term was applied whether there were musical instruments involved or not—so it applied equally to Philip Corner's *Piano Activities*, in which a grand piano was methodically demolished with hammers, bricks, and saws, as it did to Paik's performance of La Monte Young's *Composition 1960 #10* (which reads "draw a straight line and follow it") by dipping his head in a bucket of paint and dragging it over a sheet of paper. Moreover, the Wiesbaden festival involved the latter two pieces but also more "ordinary" musical performances of pieces by composers loosely associated with Darmstadt including Stockhausen, Györgi Ligeti, Fredric Rzewski, Konrad Boehmer, and Toru Takemitsu (Drott 2004, 213).

Like the MES, then, Fluxus initially had room for "serious" art music. Whereas in the MES the composers who wanted to continue making "music" withdrew from the movement, in Fluxus these modernist compositions were gradually expunged by Maciunas himself (Drott 2004, 215). As Fluxus fanned out over Western Europe in 1963, such pieces disappeared from its programmes. Although Maciunas increasingly tried to establish a common programme for Fluxus, few other participants felt bound by his ideas (D. Higgins 1998). Despite such disagreements, a few shared characteristics can be identified in what are now generally seen as typical Fluxus performances: they were fundamentally non-expressive, frequently refusing any interpretation, they were usually simple and minimalist, playful, experimental and often absurd, and usually very specific in that they consisted of a particular action, situation, or idea. These Fluxus performances reconfigured art as a game, in which anyone could invent new rules to play by. Even this general description is specific to the earliest phase of Fluxus in the early 1960s, after which the movement mostly focused on mail-order "Fluxboxes" which would contain various pieces and instructions by Fluxus artists.

MES-leader Willem de Ridder had been to the concert in Wuppertal where he had met Paik and Maciunas (De Ridder 2008). De Ridder would become the main organizer of Fluxus events in the Netherlands, of which there were six in total, plus two exhibitions (one by Paik and one by Ben Vautier) and a television programme (Beeren 1979). Mengelberg, who unlike his other fellow MES-members was apparently still interested in pursuing this kind of performance art, joined him:

> I understood it was a kind of follow-up to Dada. Dada never had made an impact on music, but I found it the only art movement of the twentieth century that mattered, and I still do. Dada is—well, not exactly sacred, but something that I have almost always found more important than jazz. I joined Fluxus straight away in 1963 because I belonged there naturally.
>
> *(Van den Berg 2009, 91)*

Another important participant in the Dutch Fluxus movement was Wim T. Schippers, with whom Mengelberg and the ICP would collaborate until the early 1980s. Schippers would become a major Dutch conceptual artist, playwright, voice actor, and television presenter and producer. At this time, Schippers was also a student at the Kunstnijverheidsschool, a few years above Bennink. In 1961 he formed the "A-dynamic group" together with Ger van Elk and Bob Wesdorp, advocating art without intentions or directions; a fundamentally uninteresting and impersonal form of art (Beeren 1979, 36–38). An emblematic piece was the "fact" of Schippers emptying a bottle of lemonade in the North Sea in 1961 (Beeren 1979, 66).

De Ridder, Schippers, and Mengelberg were the primary Dutch contributors to the Fluxus concerts held in the Netherlands (Figure 1.1).[5] In De Ridder's *Card Piece* a small note is passed around, saying "please pass this to your neighbour as quickly as possible" (Beeren 1979, 94). In his *Laughing 1962* a number of performers would come on stage wearing laughing masks and stand there for a while doing nothing. Schippers' *Economical Concert* was to consist of a "small to medium" firework explosion, but its performance was forbidden by the fire brigade. His *Not Smoking. Not Eating. Smoking. Eating.* featured five performers doing exactly that. Mengelberg, in his *Game* ("Spel"), looked at a watch lying on a piano. In *Journal II* he handed out candy to audience members, before sitting down in the audience to blow bubbles accompanied by a transistor radio, with a thread connecting him to his wife Amy, who sat on stage knitting (Figure 1.2). His most frequently performed piece was *In Memoriam Hans van Sweeden*, a monotonous and repetitive piano piece in memory of a friend and fellow composition student who had committed suicide in 1963 (Van Gasteren 1983). Such "musical" performance had by this point become quite unusual in Fluxus events. Mengelberg played music more often in such performances: another *Journal* featured him playing a piece by Mozart an octave too low and claiming it was by Beethoven. Schippers recalls that he and other Fluxus participants sometimes worried that his pieces were too close to actual music, and indeed in comparison some of them may have been quite traditional (Dekker 2008).

FIGURE 1.1 Poster for a Fluxus concert in Amsterdam. The poster promises "the newest music and anti-music—the instrumental theatre. Concert for breathing in and out, music for piano and savoury snacks, trio for violin, viola, cello and polishing wax, composition for alarm clocks, singer, cough drops and many other interesting works from USA—Japan—Europe from 1958 to the present."

Maciunas returned to the US in late 1964, after which Fluxus more or less disappeared from the Netherlands with him. De Ridder would still be involved: he had been made the official representative of Fluxus in Northern Europe and was in charge of the mail-order firm that distributed the Fluxboxes in this region. Schippers agreed to sell pounds of salt through Fluxus, but that was his only contribution; Mengelberg was not involved (Hendricks 1995, 461–462). Schippers and Mengelberg would no longer

FIGURE 1.2   Misha Mengelberg performs his *Journal II* at a Fluxus concert in Scheveningen, 13 November 1964

Photograph by Egbert Munks

have any official affiliation with Fluxus. However, Mengelberg continued to make and perform new "journals", such as his *Journal 1–10–66 for Cello, Piano, and Christmas Tree* in which a Christmas tree is decorated while the cello and piano play a duet (Van den Berg 2015, 25). Maciunas wrote a letter to De Ridder in 1964 with a list of people who might be involved in the mail-order firm, with Schippers' involvement being marked out as essential and Mengelberg's only marked with a question mark (Friedman 1998, 114). In a 1975 letter to curator Harry Ruhé, Maciunas marked out some artists as "real Flux-people", some as "allies", which included De Ridder, but also some as having "nothing to do with Fluxus—ever". This last category included Schippers; Mengelberg is not even mentioned (Ruhé 1979, n.p.).

With such strict boundaries being drawn, it is worth taking a closer look at Maciunas' aims for the movement. Maciunas would certainly have agreed with Bürger that his primary aim was to abolish the institution of art. In a letter to Tomas Schmit from January 1964, at that point still the representative of Fluxus in Northern Europe, he wrote: "The goals of Fluxus are *social* (not aesthetic)" (J. Becker and Vostell 1966, 199). Already since 1962 he had been advocating "propaganda actions" and "terrorism" directed against museums and concert halls and aiming to "reduce the attendance of the masses to these decadent institutions" (H. Higgins 2002, 77). This anti-artistic aim is recognizable in each of his Fluxus manifestos. The first sets up what he then still called "Neo-Dada" in opposition to the artificiality, abstraction, and "illusionism" of traditional art. Neo-Dada instead produces "concretist" works, showing concrete reality rather than any representation of it, and the manifesto states that

the furthest step towards concretism is of course a kind of art-nihilism [. . .] The "anti-art" forms are directed primarily against art as a profession, against

the artificial separation of a performer from audience, or creator and spectator, or life and art.

(Jenkins 1993, 157)

In his 1963 "Fluxus Manifesto" this anti-artistic aspect gets greater emphasis,
as he states as his aim to "Purge the world of bourgeois sickness, 'intellectual',
professional & commercialized culture, PURGE the world of dead art, imita-
tion, artificial art, abstract art, illusionistic art, mathematical art,—PURGE
THE WORLD OF 'EUROPANISM'!" (O. Smith 1993, 24). In his final
1965 manifesto he calls the aim of Fluxus "art-amusement", to create simple,
amusing, and insignificant pieces that only serve to underscore the fact that
anyone can produce such things, and thus to subvert the idea of the artist as
gifted creator (Maciunas 1965).

Such calls were met with growing resistance from other Fluxus artists.
Jackson Mac Low wrote in a letter to Maciunas:

> I'm not opposed to serious culture—quite the contrary. I'm all for it & I
> hope & consider that my own work is a genuine contribution to it [. . .]
> I'm against the overbalance of museum culture . . . as against present-
> minded and presently "useful" cultural activities and would certainly like
> to see the balance tipped the other way, but I would not want to elimi-
> nate museums (I like museums).
>
> *(H. Higgins 2002, 77)*

Similar ideas were expressed in letters by Dick Higgins, Nam June Paik, and
Tomas Schmit. The most famous example of this emerging rift in Fluxus was
the demonstration against Stockhausen's *Originale* in April 1964, organized
by Maciunas together with Henry Flynt. Stockhausen had dismissed jazz as
a "regressive" form of music and the protesters thus accused him of racism
and "cultural imperialism", and viewed the notion of art itself as upholding
white supremacy (Jenkins 1993, 169; H. Higgins 2002, 71–75; Piekut 2009).
However, Stockhausen had himself participated in some of the early Fluxus
events, and indeed some Fluxus participants were involved in the performance
of *Originale* taking place in the concert hall, including Paik, Higgins, Mac Low,
Brecht, and others (H. Higgins 2002, 72).

Among the Dutch Fluxus artists, there seem to have been similar disagreements
about the purpose of Fluxus. Once again, De Ridder consistently felt art needed
to be abolished completely. Both Schippers and Mengelberg, meanwhile, seem
to have had the same ambivalence about Maciunas' anti-art sentiments as those
expressed by Mac Low; although they were critical of museums and the art world,
they were not for the complete abolition of art, and though both continued to
make "serious" artistic work, this work does challenge traditional notions of art.
Mengelberg and Schippers' theatre work (and Schippers' subsequent work for
television) certainly seems to fulfil Maciunas' aims for "art-amusement", being

farcical and entertaining, but also explicitly cultivating an amateuristic style. Their productions often featured amateur performers, such as Cees Schouwenaar, who became a regular actor in Schippers' theatre and television work. He had originally been a market vendor before they asked him to perform with them, and his lack of experience or talent apparently made him an attractive performer for them, as Mengelberg explained: "When Cees Schouwenaar [sang], everything about it was outrageously bad and clumsy. And that's good, that made it work" (Dekker 2008). Schippers' television programmes also made ironic use of clichéd sitcom dialogues and stock décors. However, already in 1962 the a-dynamic manifesto had rejected Dada's anti-artistic sentiments, since this implied an expression of intention, thus being at odds with the group's a-dynamic aims (Beeren 1979, 38). Moreover, Schippers has, besides all of his television and theatre work, always produced sculptures and installations that have been exhibited in museums.

Mengelberg, who had kept composing and playing jazz during his time in Fluxus and with the foundation of the ICP would devote his career to music rather than performance art, more clearly rejected the idea of abolishing art. In a 1976 interview he says that the "abolishment of the completely rigid musical infrastructure" should be a long-term (rather than short-term) goal, and that institutions should not be meddled with. "Let those orchestras fool around for a bit. As long as there's an audience, they can play Brahms symphonies until the year 2500 if you ask me" (Van den Berg 2015, 57). As will be discussed in Chapter 3, Mengelberg did participate in demonstrations and action against the Concertgebouw and other aspects of classical music infrastructure in the second half of the 1960s, but these actions were not geared towards the abolition of serious art, but precisely to make more room in the serious artistic and musical infrastructures for experimental contemporary forms of music. Similarly, the goal of the ICP and part of the rhetoric behind the term "instant composition" was to validate improvised music as a serious art form.

That is not to say that none of Maciunas' aims can be recognized in Mengelberg's work for the ICP. The role of the repertoire written by Mengelberg for the ICP, described in detail in Part II, corresponds very well to Maciunas' (and De Ridder's) call for artworks that do not express the genius of a gifted creator but rather form an opportunity for playful interaction. Second, the use of melodic, ironically sing-song material in the ICP repertoire from its foundation onwards, in the context of the highly modernist sounds of free improvisation, certainly fulfils Maciunas' idea of "amusement" to subvert the pretentions of modern art. However, such ideas of de-professionalization should also not be exaggerated; although Mengelberg has always been rather self-deprecating about his own qualities as a pianist (indeed, he can be said to cultivate an image of being a poor pianist), he has always had a very high standard for his fellow musicians, and for instance did not participate in the celebration of amateur musicianship as some other improvisers did in the 1970s. Some of these issues will be explored in more depth in the next two chapters. At the same time, a counterculture was emerging in Amsterdam that drew on elements of performance art to change all of society, not just art, into a space for human playfulness. This forced Mengelberg and the other ICP founders to reconsider their avant-gardistic activities not just in artistic, but also in societal terms.

Cultural historian Andreas Huyssen writes that when it came to politics, Fluxus was in fact much less radical than is often thought. Although Fluxus is regularly connected to the ludic forms of protest and demonstration in the 1960s, such links appear difficult to validate historically. In fact, Huyssen argues, Maciunas and Flynt's failure to politicize Fluxus "points to the overall closeness of Fluxus to the non-political and allegedly non-ideological 1950s" (Huyssen 1993, 144). In other words, it may better be seen as an outgrowth of a tradition of aesthetic modernism and experimentation rather than as an iconoclastic postmodernism breaking with this tradition. In the 1950s there had already been a strong political relationship between the USA and West Germany, and part of this relation was to stimulate progressive and experimental art as emblematic of the liberties of the "free world". Darmstadt was a case in point, and Cage's presence there only perpetuated this Cold War strategy, despite Mengelberg's (and nearly everyone else's) perception of his presence there as a maverick or an outcast.[6] Amy Beal, in her study of this Cold War connection between the USA and West Germany, writes that "there might have been no Fluxus movement without the American occupation of Germany (and Japan) and the contexts of the Cold War that brought American and non-American artists together" (Beal 2006, 121). Huyssen also notes the significance of the term "Neo-Dada", as Dada was rediscovered as a historical art movement in the 1950s and was the subject of various retrospective exhibitions (Huyssen 1993, 144). Fluxus' reliance on Dada as a model for subverting the institutions of High Art was thus dependent on the workings of these very institutions to have preserved the art of Dada in the first place. Mengelberg's association of Fluxus with Dada underscores this significant retrospective aspect of Fluxus.

James Kennedy's history of the Dutch 1960s argues that perhaps the most important agents of cultural change in the Netherlands were not the figures of the counterculture, but the authorities against whom they were fighting (Kennedy 1995). Rather than repressing these radical politics, they facilitated and sometimes even encouraged them; partly because they agreed with some of their progressive ideas, and partly because they wished to maintain the peace and calm in the public sphere. A similar argument may be made about the emergence of avant-garde forms of music and art (see also Chapter 3 on this point). If Bürger argued that the post-war avant-garde's radical aspirations were subverted by its dependence on the institutions they were attacking, we have seen above that these aspirations were not universally shared. Of course there was a general anti-artistic strain to Fluxus, especially in the way its performative mode subverted the possibilities of commodification and museumization. Wolf Vostell declared that Marcel Duchamp had made "the mistake of declaring the urinal to be a sculpture but not to consider that using the urinal was an equally artistic activity" (Brill 2010, 134). Thus emphasizing process over product, the concept of flow—in every possible sense of the word—was intended to undermine any reified concept of the artwork.

However, museums quite easily found a way around this. Wim Beeren, one of the foremost curators of contemporary art in the Netherlands at the time, suggested that

> the museum can intermediate between the solitary decisions of independent artists and the interested visitor [. . .] Our value as a museum could consist in the fact that we maintain contact between "everyday life" and creativity, at a moment that these seem to be so far apart. This despite *homo ludens*.
>
> *(Leeuw-Marcar and Anselmo 1969, 14)*

The statement is striking not only because it suggests museums to some extent could go on to function as they always had, but moreover that despite the efforts of Fluxus and other avant-garde movements to merge art and everyday life, and despite the public currency of concepts of "ludic man" in contemporaneous protest movements (about which more in the next section), most museum visitors felt alienated by these forms of art. Thus, far from abolishing art institutions, the Fluxus artists and other post-war avant-gardists were reliant on them, and set out to negotiate new relationships with them.

In a catalogue of a retrospective exhibition of avant-garde art in the 1960s, Mengelberg and the ICP are only mentioned once after the last Fluxus events in late 1964. This was at an event for the seventy-fifth anniversary of the Stedelijk Museum in 1970, the country's foremost centre for contemporary art. The anniversary week was coordinated by Beeren, and had the explicit aim of presenting art that normally takes place outside of the context of museums. For one evening, he had invited Willem Breuker to curate a night of music performances, and Breuker had programmed himself with an ICP group, a mandolin orchestra, two fanfares on the street outside the museum playing different compositions at the same time, and a solo performance by Mengelberg. Such examples indicate that far from being opposed to each other, there existed a dynamic relationship between contemporary artists and musicians and the institutions that presented their work. Beeren thought the new art forms could play an important role in transforming society, and that museums could help in trying to achieve this aim (Schumacher 2010). Artists were happy to collaborate with them.

Ludic Protest

In an interview in the 1990s, Mengelberg reflected:

I did not agree with the 60s idea about elites. Because apart from elites that want to keep people out, there are also those who do not aim to exclude. They are just small because they are concerned with something that is not appealing to everyone. In that sense everyone who is highly skilled in a certain profession makes up an elite.

(Andriessen 1996, 23)

Such a perspective, with the benefit of hindsight, suggests a rather more realistic idea of the effectiveness of avant-garde art to transform society than the one espoused by Maciunas. It leaves room for the possibility that audiences may actually be alienated by attempts to integrate art and everyday life, and it acknowledges that elites and institutions are to some extent unavoidable, which is significant in the context of the emerging counterculture. Various activists and artists in the 1960s professed the classless society was near, or even could be achieved in the here and now, and imagined a society centred around the personal expression and creativity of "ludic man". In these protest movements, absurdism, playfulness, and provocation were used as a means to question the status quo, and performance art was an important source of inspiration. The two primary historians of the 1960s in the Netherlands, James Kennedy and Hans Righart, agree that the 1960s were "less politically charged" than in many other countries, comparable to some extent with the United Kingdom (Kennedy 1995, 217; Righart 1998). Kennedy writes that it "was a country *without any obvious social, political or economic crises*" (Kennedy 1995, 217–218). Righart has characterized the social upheaval and protest movements as a cultural rather than a political development, calling them an "expressive revolution" (Righart 1998, 87).

Emblematic of this expressive revolution was the Provo movement, an Amsterdam-based anarchist movement centred around Roel van Duijn, active from 1965 to 1967. Provo "happenings" were intended to "provoke" unlawful and violent action from the police, thus exposing the "true nature" of authority. Some of their actions were as simple as handing out raisins to policemen, while some were more provocative and eventful, featuring ritualistic performances with body-painting, public nudity, collective music-making, and so on. Their most notorious demonstration was during the wedding of princess Beatrix to Claus von Amsberg in March 1966, a former member of the Hitlerjugend and the Wehrmacht, where Provo spread smoke bombs, causing chaos and obstructing the news coverage of the event (Van Duijn 1985, 113–130; Pas 2003, 161–182). More than with such explicitly political demonstrations, however, the Provo movement was concerned with transforming the urban space of Amsterdam as a public space conducive to the creativity and playfulness of its people, rather than a commercial or merely functional space. This aim of establishing utopia in the here and now was also expressed in their "white plans", intended to re-appropriate and democratize various aspects of public space. These included a "white bicycle plan", distributing bicycles around the city as a form of public and free transportation, "white police plans" campaigning for unarmed police forces whose main duty was to perform social work, "white women plans" campaigning for women's emancipation and birth control, "white housing plans" for social housing, advocating a regulated form of squatting, and various other plans proposing feminist, ecological, and socialist measures.

There were two primary artistic influences on Provo's thinking about urban spaces: one was painter and former COBRA-member Constant Nieuwenhuijs. In the late 1950s he turned away from COBRA's expressionism and was briefly involved with the Situationist International, a group of artists and political theorists led by Guy Debord. Debord envisioned a post-capitalist society in which labour would be replaced by "ludic recreation" and "total participation", and where everyone would be an artist (Debord 2011, 349–350). Constant (always referred to by his first name) similarly imagined a future in which, because of technological advancement, labour would become unnecessary and this would mean a new era of "homo ludens". For this future, Constant created his vision of New Babylon, an architectural environment for playful, nomadic subjects, consisting of labyrinthine and futuristic structures spanning over whole continents, and ultimately enveloping the whole globe (Brinkman et al. 2016). Provo took over this concept of New Babylon and saw its own actions as realizing this utopian idea in real life; Constant, in turn, praised Provo for turning the Spui square into one of the spaces that would form the basis of New Babylon (Beeren 1979, 172). On this square was the second main artistic influence on Provo, namely the ritualistic demonstrations of Robert Jasper Grootveld, mainly intended as a protest against the tobacco industry (and advocating the use of cannabis). These protests featured an enigmatic combination of biblical texts, pseudo-shamanic primitivist rituals, and aspects of the Dutch Saint Nicolas tradition from which Grootveld created his own personal mythology.

Grootveld had been involved in happenings since the early 1960s, with a wider group of artists that included poets Simon Vinkenoog and Johnny van Doorn, film maker Louis van Gasteren, visual artist and author Jan Cremer, and various others. Although Fluxus events are retrospectively often referred to as "happenings" and in other countries (for instance, Germany and the United States) were closely affiliated, none of these people participated in Fluxus events, and moreover their happenings represented rather a different aesthetic than the "intellectually esoteric" style of Fluxus (to quote Heffley).[7] Vinkenoog, who was the oldest and had a wide international network, had organized the *Open het Graf* ("Open the Grave") event in 1962, together with Living Theatre actor Melvin Clay and film maker Frank Stern. The theme of the evening was necrophilia, and the space was decorated with, among other things, rotting meat and cow's intestines. The opening act was Jean Jacques Lebel, who came on stage with a cardboard television around his head, carrying a cardboard penis and vagina, with the word "nigger" written on his face, shouting "Jacky Kennedy!" and "Khrushchev!" Another performance involved Johnny van Doorn, who, tied to a chair by hands and feet, was thrown on stage, and struggled to get loose while kicking and screaming; when he had freed himself he threw the cow's intestines into the audience before passing out. Various performers were under the influence of psychedelic drugs, which were handed out in the course of the event (Beeren 1979, 55–58). Perhaps the most notorious event of this group was the unveiling in 1965 of the "third eye" of Bart Huges, a medicine student who had drilled a hole in his forehead believing this would achieve a permanent high (Beeren 1979, 96).

In a television programme made by De Ridder and Schippers in 1963 presenting an overview of contemporary art with special attention given to Fluxus, no such performances are mentioned, and the two are more eager to associate themselves with Pop Art, Zero, and Yves Klein (By 1963). The a-dynamic manifesto of Schippers and Van Elk did praise Constant's New Babylon project, but did so precisely for its impossibility of ever being realized (Beeren 1979, 37). As we saw above, the utopian Situationist politics of Provo would certainly not have been shared by all Fluxus artists (Provo came quite close to some of Maciunas' aims for the movement). Fluxus was also less concerned with occupying public space. The first event in Amsterdam had involved some public performances, but this had ended in a skirmish when some audience members began to set De Ridder's "paper constellations" on fire (D. Higgins 1964, 71). A later concert in Scheveningen included a public element in addition to a regular concert hall event, but this was more of a conceptual experiment: the performances were there for passers-by to enjoy if they noticed them (there is no indication whether these performances included the smashing of instruments or whether they featured more inconspicuous actions like smoking or not eating). Moreover, the same concert also featured a third concert in a closed space without any audience present, balancing out the simultaneous public performance (Beeren 1979, 88).

Despite these aesthetic and ideological differences, there are some interesting connections between Vinkenoog's circle, Provo, and the ICP musicians. Both *Open het Graf* and the unveiling of Huges' "third eye" involved jazz—at the former, one of the performances included recorded music by Charles Mingus, while the latter involved a live jazz group (Beeren 1979, 58, 96). Vinkenoog had a longer history of including jazz in his performances; since the 1950s, as he was making his name as a "beat poet", he had organized "jazz and poetry" evenings. In fact, even two years after *Open het Graf* he organized such an evening with American visitor Ted Joans reading poetry to music made by the Piet Kuiters Modern Jazz Group. The event was recorded by Louis van Gasteren, a regular participant in Vinkenoog and Grootveld's happenings, and it would be one of his first short films (Van Gasteren 1964). In her dissertation on the cultural history of post-war jazz and improvised music, Loes Rusch describes the event as an example of the sophisticated, intellectual, and modern image of jazz in the Netherlands—something she offsets against the free improvisation of the ICP that would cause a schism in the Dutch jazz scene (about which more in the next chapter) (Rusch 2016, 31–32). Although her reading of this film seems accurate, this makes the event all the more striking considering the involvement of Vinkenoog and Van Gasteren, and shows the permeability of what we would in hindsight perhaps cast as radically different schools and aesthetics.

In other words, although the aesthetic differences between Fluxus and happenings (or even between these forms of performance art and "modern jazz and poetry") are significant, these movements did take place in the same geographical and social space—indeed, as late as 1971, Mengelberg performed with Johnny van Doorn in something as seemingly anachronistic as a "jazz and poetry" evening (Author Unknown 1972). The closest that Vinkenoog, Provo, and the ICP founders came to collaborating was through their activities in the Sigma Centre, which opened in 1966 and combined artistic practice and community work in a fusion of Provo and Situationist ideals, helping visitors to develop their artistic creativity for when they would no longer need to work (Adlington 2013, 144–145; Pas 2011). As a space that allowed recreational drug use, it would be an important centre for the emerging hippie movement. There were also experimental theatre, poetry, and music evenings (including popular, improvised, and composed music) and "teach-ins". Mengelberg and his former fellow conservatory students organized composition workshops, and other workshops on various artistic disciplines were programmed at the Centre—including one on improvisation by the aforementioned Piet Kuiters (who had since moved from modern jazz to free improvisation). Kuiters had been collaborating with Danish saxophonist John Tchicai, who had earlier been part of the New York scene, recording with Archie Shepp, John Coltrane, and Albert Ayler. After playing with Mengelberg at the Sigma Centre, Tchicai would be one of the first international musicians to become part of the ICP.

Breuker was also involved in the Sigma Centre, and was in many ways much closer to the chaotic aesthetic of happenings and Provo. Although his performances never featured any intestines, he did describe his concerts in the mid-1960s in similar terms:

> Nobody knew exactly what was going on. I put in all the ideas I had in mind, to combine kinds of music, do stupid things with music. I'd take some music of Beethoven or Mozart, and remove page two, save page three, rip out page four, make a new combination. Turn the paper upside down, whatever. People were very interested in these evenings. They were a kind of Happening. People could go out and come in again, sit or drink or smoke, whatever they liked. Everybody had a very good night.
>
> *(Whitehead 1998, 59)*

Like various other improvising groups and musicians around 1970, Breuker also took to the streets quite regularly, unlike Mengelberg. One of his projects for Sigma was his *Lunchconcert for Three Barrel Organs*, performed publicly on the Dam Square in August 1967 (Beeren 1979, 124) (Figure 1.3). Describing his intentions to a journalist, he said: "You must go and meet the public, your fellow man [. . .] You must take to the street" (Adlington 2013, 108). Barrel organs are to this day a frequent appearance on Dutch streets, and they usually play popular and folk music material. Breuker, however, had composed a series of atonal pieces for the instruments, which rather threw the listeners who happened to hear the performances, some of whom responded angrily. With its provocative and public nature and its subversion of expectations of familiar elements, this seems to align with Provo's aims—indeed, with his beard and glasses Breuker looked very similar to Provo frontman Roel van Duijn and one might forgive bystanders for thinking this was another Provo happening.

However, the musicians' activities in the Sigma Centre also brought to the foreground fundamental differences between their aims and Provo's. For one thing, for professional musicians, these forms of creative expression were not preparation for a society without paid labour—this *was* their job, and they expected compensation for their efforts. The free participation of audiences, meanwhile, particularly of rowdy Provos, was experienced by musicians as a disruption of their music rather than a collaboration. Provos, conversely, although they had initially supported the Sigma Centre, found that the musicians' activities were too much concerned with their own individual creativity and artistic development rather than the cultivation of collective creativity and the inclusion of the general public (Adlington 2013, 148–156). The *Lunchconcert*, for which Breuker had to

FIGURE 1.3   Willem Breuker performs his *Lunchconcert for Three Barrel Organs* on the Dam Square in Amsterdam, August 1967

Photograph by Pieter Boersma

learn the meticulous method of writing for barrel organs, is a case in point. If such a provocative piece seems to align with Provo's aims, it was in fact exemplary of the kind of Sigma activities that caused Provo to retract its support from the Centre not long after it opened.

Breuker had engaged more closely with Provo a year earlier, with his composition *Litany for the 14th of June, 1966*. It was performed at the finale of the annual jazz competition in Loosdrecht, and caused such a controversy that he became a national celebrity overnight. The piece referred to riots in Amsterdam on the 13th, after a demonstration of construction workers tied to the Dutch Communist Party had been interfered with by the police. In the tumult that followed, in which various activists had joined the side of the construction workers, one of the construction workers died of a heart attack, leading many to believe he was a victim of police brutality. Provo had only been indirectly involved in the demonstrations (some of the youths that joined in the riots had ties with Provo), but to them this represented yet another instance of excessive violence by the police, of which they had already had enough experience that year. When the right-wing, anticommunist newspaper *De Telegraaf* published the coroner's report the next day, Provo and the construction workers stormed their offices, suspecting a cover-up (Kennedy 1995, 294–295). These two days of riots peaked what had already been a violent year, and were perceived as a radicalization of Provo despite their tangential involvement and public dismissal of the actions (Pas 2003, 202–206).

Breuker's *Litany* (which can be heard on Breuker 1966) was a 10-minute piece for eighteen musicians, containing alternating sections of fully composed material, graphic scores, and free improvisation. Singer Sofie van Leer recited excerpts of reports taken from *De Telegraaf* as well as other newspapers (Adlington 2013, 97–98). The work would have had a big impact even without its controversial topic, and indicates the consciously provocative nature of Breuker's music at this point. He sympathized with Provo's actions, even though he was not directly involved in them, as he explained in 1978:

> I was not really a Provo, but all the things that happened then were also happening to me, also when they weren't around yet. I still feel sympathetic to Provo, that's just how things go, but I don't translate my political opinions into music.
>
> *(Buzelin and Buzelin 1994, 17)*

This disavowal of political intentions is not just a matter of hindsight; in an interview published in the same month as the *Litany* performance, he had stated that jazz was not a form of "protest music" to him (Vuijsje and Witkamp 1966, 228). In 1967 he said: "Last year I wrote *Litany for the 14th of June* without political intentions. Those riots just made an enormous impression on me.

We don't make political music, but you can imagine we are not right-wing" (Visser 1967). Breuker had been at the riots himself, yet he denied that the piece was "a program piece of a street incident. Rather perhaps a sketch of the atmosphere" (Adlington 2013, 107). Considering the disagreements at the Sigma Centre some years later, Breuker's dismissal of political intent with his *Litany* performance is significant—as is the fact that this watershed in Dutch-improvised music was in fact a largely pre-composed piece, an individual's artistic expression rather than a collective effort.

As a provocation, the piece was certainly effective in getting media attention:

> It was described as the end of music, as the beginning of total anarchy. That's what people wrote about us. So I got a lot of gigs, because every-body was curious to hear what the end of music sounded like.
>
> *(Van den Bos 2015)*

Like Breuker, Mengelberg also saw the value of provocation and increasingly employed it in his music performances. Already in 1963, in a performance with Johnny Griffin he took a solo in a very fast rendition of Thelonious Monk's "Rhythm-a-Ning" only to start playing a very slow and plaintive "I'm Getting Sentimental Over You" (Van den Berg 2009). He sometimes lit a firecracker by way of a piano solo, perhaps inspired by Schippers' *Economical Concert*. In 1966 he was awarded the Wessel Ilcken prize, the most prestigious Dutch jazz prize (still awarded annually, but now as the Boy Edgar Prize). In the concert following the award ceremony, Mengelberg handed out toy instruments and fireworks to the audience, and played table tennis and chess with bass player Ruud Jacobs (Van den Berg 2009, 93).

The composition they played was *Vietcong*, perhaps the only Mengelberg piece with a politically charged title. Musically, the piece is insignificant; it con-sists of a repeated pentatonic motif giving way to free improvisation. Still, the title was intentionally provocative, and this was more important than any message the music might convey. When the jazz quartet of Mengelberg and Bennink, featur-ing alto saxophonist Piet Noordijk and bass player Rob Langereis, was invited to play at the Newport Jazz Festival in 1966, Mengelberg wanted to perform the piece and explicitly announce its title—in fact it was the only piece of which he always announced the title in his performances (Van den Berg 2015, 22). Although this may have made for a bigger impact of the group on this international stage (they played as an opening act before the start of the official programme), Noordijk ultimately convinced him not to do it (Van den Berg 2009, 88). The piece once more shows the importance that Mengelberg and Breuker accorded to provocation as a way to get attention, which was perhaps more important than any serious political message.

Indeed, the awareness of the efficacy of such provocation to get atten-tion was certainly something the ICP musicians shared with (and for which they perhaps were inspired by) Provo. In Niek Pas' history of Provo, its sophisticated use of media to sustain a public image in a period where the media landscape was diversifying and democratizing is the central narrative thread (Pas 2003). Provo and its allies (including Grootveld) used techniques drawn from commercial advertising to create a public image of themselves that was much larger than they actually were (Pas contends that Provo really only consisted of ten people). Moreover, they could use this public image to playfully subvert and mystify their actual aims and intentions so as to elude precise definition and identification. As noted in the Introduction, Mengelberg has always held up an elusive image, never giving unequivocal answers in any interview. In the early years of the ICP, moreover, their advertisements and press releases imitated commercial slogans in much the same way that Provo and other countercultural movements and publications did. In fact, the very name "Instant Composers Pool", with its conscious reference to "instant coffee" (Whitehead 1998, 40) and other instant foods that were quite a new phenomenon in the 1960s, can be considered a kind of Pop Art commentary on mass-produced goods. An advert from 1970 opens with a list of commercial slogans:

- *Ready while you wait*
- *The music is flying off the shelves*
- *Current today, old-fashioned tomorrow*
- *Pretentious yet subcultural*
- *Sounding products reach the consumer without middle-men*

(Mengelberg 1970)

Such ironic statements were copied in various concert announcements and reviews, and the general public will certainly have associated the ICP with a left-wing urban youth culture because of them. The "far-out" titles of pieces and especially theatre productions (including "A Pound of Lost Time", "Consequences of Chicken", "A Thousand Curtains", "Wallpaper", and "Reveries of a Shitty Dog"—the latter a reference to a Rousseau novel) also undoubtedly added to such associations. Despite such physical proximity and general stylistic similarities, however, the histories of Fluxus and the Sigma Centre show that the ultimately aesthetic concern of these musicians was at odds with the political aims of the 1960s counterculture. In Chapter 3 we will see such aesthetic and political aims clash again, this time in the political activities of musicians and composers themselves.

Fluxus, Performance, Media

Apart from Provo, the fascination with provocation and antagonism described above also goes back to Mengelberg's encounter with John Cage in 1958. In an interview in 1981, while acknowledging that this was probably a misinterpretation of Cage's aesthetics, he says:

You suddenly saw all those tinkerers [in Darmstadt] implode. What I learned in that period was that the only real kicks to be had in that area emerge from schadenfreude, anger, and pestering. That is the most beautiful thing there is.

(Van den Berg 2015, 67)

This comment cultivates provocation as an aesthetic more than a political ideal. As I suggested at the start of this chapter, the main influence of Fluxus and performance art on Mengelberg was an aesthetic one, although it was what might be called a "relational" aesthetic in the sense that it does not concern abstract structural qualities but rather the social practice of making music (see Chapter 6). The ICP was certainly part of a broader countercultural movement celebrating new forms of artistic and cultural expression, and as we shall see in Chapter 3, taking action to restructure society in more democratic and egalitarian ways. Still, they consciously chose to pursue their highly specialized form of music rather than a form of music-making that was more conducive to the ideas of collective creativity that were being advocated by groups in their close proximity. To conclude this chapter, then, I will describe the ideas about performance and improvisation that Mengelberg derived from Cage and Fluxus, as these directly influenced the concept of instant composition.

The main influence of Fluxus on the ICP is sometimes thought to be found in the ICP's music theatre. Both Breuker and Mengelberg made theatre productions throughout the 1970s and 1980s. These productions were usually absurdistic, partly improvised pieces, in which music played an important theatrical role. Breuker's theatrical works were often farcical productions with slapstick comedy, while Mengelberg's, produced together with Schippers, were generally more ironic and intellectual. In 1969 the ICP staged its first theatre production, Breuker's *The Life of Wolfgang Amadeus Mozart*, taking its title and plot from a little comic book that was part of a coffee brand's promotional series on "Famous Men", and in which Mengelberg played Mozart (Buzelin and Buzelin 1994, 36–37). If such a piece corresponds to some Fluxus aims in its absurdity and amusement, and its irreverent attitude to music history, it was explicitly a form of "theatre", with a plot and actors fulfilling particular roles, which was quite far removed from the Fluxus aesthetic, or from the MES' concept of "auto-theatre".

This was also the case with the productions of Mengelberg and Schippers, although these did experiment more with forms of improvisation and collage, the order of scenes and musical numbers sometimes being decided backstage in the course of performance. This led to a way of working in which "the performance was sometimes more enjoyable in the dressing room than for the audience."[8] We get a glimpse of this from Peter Cusack, who described *Een Behoorlijk Kabaal (A Considerable Noise)* in 1976:

There was Derek Bailey, the Brötzmann trio, various ICP groups, Louis Andriessen [. . .] one actor and two actresses doing various sketches (all lines read from scraps of paper in the hand), etc. etc. etc., all in no apparent order or plot but during which other things might also happen. Stage dragons would appear, cabbages or newspapers would drop from above, smoke would start wafting from the chimney of an often-collapsing cottage façade, people would walk into other peoples' acts, two acts might occur simultaneously, or there might be nothing much happening at all.

(Whitehead 1998, 106)

However, even if these theatre pieces fit the general spirit of the expressive revolution of the 1960s, being quite clearly a form of music theatre, they do not show the specific influence of Fluxus.

The more particular influence of Fluxus on the ICP is of a more conceptual nature, and deals directly with their reconsideration of improvisation and composition. Mengelberg's encounter with Cage, and particularly with his experimentation with aleatoric and indeterminate forms of composition, really made him "reconsider the responsibility that you have for what you write down on the page" (Van den Berg 2015, 20). After Mengelberg had gone to Darmstadt, he composed various pieces that were influenced by Cage's style. I already mentioned his *Exercise for Flute*; another piece was his *Musica per 17 strumenti* from 1959, which although just over 10 minutes long prescribes not much more than one note to each musician, and thus consists mostly of long stretches of silence. It was awarded the prestigious Gaudeamus music prize by a jury consisting of Györgi Ligeti, Ernst Krenek, and Karlheinz Stockhausen in 1961 (Van den Berg 2009, 89). Although it consisted largely of stretches of silence, it did not engage with Cage's theories of music and silence, but rather expresses Mengelberg's reception of these ideas as a kind of musical pestering of performers and audience. In a conversation with Andriessen, Mengelberg said that Andriessen had been right when he once said that the piece dealt essentially with the question of musical narrative: "It's like a magic show. You sit there waiting: will a rabbit jump out of the top hat, or not? Or will it be a white handkerchief? Or perhaps the rabbit eats the handkerchief?" (Van den Berg 2015, 32).

In fact, Mengelberg disagreed with Cage's philosophy of music and silence, particularly in the way it proposed the construction of "sound objects", sounds in which no tonal tendency or even intention of the composer or performer could be detected. Mengelberg has always referred to Cage's ideal to "just let sounds be themselves", not to form a musical narrative through functional harmonic or other means, as "banning literature from music", something with which he fundamentally disagreed. This idea was an important influence on Fluxus, which broadened Cage's definition of music as possibly being any kind of sound to any kind of action, movement, or even the presence or absence of something. George Brecht said about him:

Cage was the great liberator for me . . . but at the same time he remained a musician, a composer . . . I wanted to make music that wouldn't only

be for the ears. Music isn't just what you hear or what you listen to, but everything that happens . . . *events are an extension of music.*
(Kotz 2001, 72)

La Monte Young's "draw a straight line and follow it" is an early example of an action or event being considered music, and such pieces would become increasingly influential in Fluxus. Brecht's own scores are a good example: his string trio instructs the performers to polish their instruments, his *Vehicle Event* simply says "start, stop", and his *Piano Piece 1962* says "a vase of flowers on(to) a piano".

Mengelberg rejected this strategy of calling anything "music", or rather disagreed that there could be such a thing as letting sounds (or movements, or events, or ideas) be "themselves". In a conversation with Cage in the 1980s, he illustrated this by recounting the "shortest story" he knew: "BANG! Meow . . ." (ad van t veer n.d.). In a 1981 conversation with Andriessen and writer J. Bernlef, he gave a more detailed and explicit explanation that any sequence of events is going to be put into a logical narrative by a listener anyway, because that is how human hearing is conditioned. Moreover, the presentation of "sound objects" that have no meaning or intention is *itself* a frame giving meaning to these sounds:

> The whole idea of listening to sound objects is literature in itself [. . .] You hear a dog barking in the street while stirring your cup of tea. As a composer I would hear that as polyphony. But I can only make that clear to you by using Cage's trick of isolating those things or by putting some silence before and after it. That takes about six seconds. And then you think: gee whiz, I wonder what he means by that. That's a trick.
> *(Van den Berg 2015, 74)*

Already in 1965, Mengelberg distances himself from Fluxus in this respect: "It isolates things that are much more interesting in everyday life" (Baaij 1965). In everyday life, he once explained to Derek Bailey, such isolations precisely never happen:

> One of the things that inspires me in making any gesture, musically and theoretically, is its relation with daily life, in which there is no such thing as an exclusion [. . .] Of course I don't mean daily life transformed into music, but in certain respects there are parallels between music and daily life. For example in the respect that very vulgar things are happening near to very aesthetic things: people go pissing one moment and have deep philosophical thoughts the next. Or maybe both at the same time.
> *(Bailey 1993, 131)*

Mengelberg's questioning of Cage's idea of sound objects is significant considering Fluxus' aim to merge art and everyday life, as it suggests that this isolation, the frame which makes a Fluxus event into a performance, defeats this very purpose. Mengelberg thus rejects the idea of a pure performative presence central to much performance art by emphasizing the socially mediated nature of all expression.

Hence this understanding of music also bears on that of improvisation. In his comment to Bailey, Mengelberg continues:

> Improvisation starts for me at the moment it is needed and it's always in a context in which there are fixed points to refer to. So, the term "free" is meaningless. The sort of improvisation I am interested in is the sort that everyone does in their lives. They improvise in taking six or seven steps to the door, scratching their heads with one or two fingers. Group improvisation takes place according to common points of education, aims and subjects and is interesting as far as the material reaches. When there is nothing more to develop it should stop.
>
> *(Bailey 1993, 131–132)*

There is an identifiable strand of Fluxus that in fact thematized the idea of the mediation of all expression. For one, Fluxus performances were by no means sites of free expression in which everything was possible, but usually revolved around specific, identifiable, and delineated actions, usually with a predetermined end. Moreover, these events were usually "scripted" in that they were almost all based on a textual instruction or "event score", which admittedly often left much room for interpretation. Such event scores have an obvious connection to Cage's graphic scores, indeterminate works, and particularly his *4'33"*. However, rather than seeing such a score as a representation of sound objects, one could also perceive its *mediating* function in constructing the frame in which such sound objects come into existence in the first place (which Mengelberg describes as a "trick").

These ideas are central to the emergence of the concept of "instant composition". A crucial aspect of Mengelberg's perspective on improvisation is that it is never purely spontaneous, but always relies on individual memory and experience:

> I think [improvisation and composition] are hardly different. The processes of considering musical activities are very similar. Only the procedure is different: in improvised music you have a lot of baggage to unpack and employ on the spot, while as a composer you have to be much more elaborate about it. Then you sit at a desk and use your baggage to fill a sheet with musical notation, with suggestions of how something should be played by a group of musicians that you do not necessarily belong to yourself.
>
> *(Andriessen 1996, 22)*

The term "instant composition" itself derives from a series of "instant poems" made by Tomas Schmit in 1963. His "instant poems" are glass jars filled with scraps of paper, letter, or even just ash and ink, that read "shake well before reading!" on the lid (Wien, Lukatsch, and Vollmer, n.d.) (Figure 1.4). Mengelberg first met Schmit when the latter performed his *Cycle* in one of the Fluxus concerts in Amsterdam, in which Schmit poured water from one bottle to the next, going around in a circle "until all water is spilt or evaporated" (Stiles 1993, 64). Schmit was also on Maciunas' list of artists having "nothing to do with Fluxus—ever". He would become a good friend of Mengelberg and Bennink, and some of his works from the early 1960s speak directly to the various understandings of improvisation under discussion. His "instant poetry" features a degree of humour, indeterminacy, and found objects, but crucially they meditate on the possibilities of expression given in texts from the past, but also in the materials that are used to create such expressions (letters, ink, paper).

If Fluxus can be said to have been participatory, it is the "do-it-yourself" quality of its scores that justifies such a characterization, and this DIY aesthetic is clearly present in the work of Schmit. Art historian Anna Dezeuze compares this DIY component with Claude Lévi-Strauss' concept of "bricolage", a way

FIGURE 1.4   Tomas Schmit, *Poem V: Shake Well Before Reading*

© 2018 Tomas Schmit Archiv, Berlin. The Gilbert and Lila Silverman Fluxus Collection Gift

of working that makes do with whatever is at hand to achieve present needs (as opposed to the careful planning ahead that Lévi-Strauss calls "engineering") (Dezeuze 2010; Lévi-Strauss 1966). This corresponds to Mengelberg's idea of improvisation starting when it is called for, and always happening within a particular context. Event scores in this sense create a particular context; they give a performer material to develop, after which the event is over, even if this takes as long as it takes for a bottle of water to evaporate. Schmit's *Typewriter Poem* from the same year explores this theme further (Figure 1.5). The score shows a typewriter keyboard with numbers on some of the keys to indicate their order, resulting (possibly) in the sentence "if your typewriter is different from mine, this may be difficult to read" (Jenkins 1993, 159). The piece clearly reflects on the creative space between score and result, and on the forms of technological and linguistic mediation that inhabit that space. In 1967 Breuker wrote *Piano Distance* for Mengelberg, a piano piece that follows the same principle as Schmit's *Typewriter Poem*, indicating a sequence of notes to be struck using a schematic representation of the piano keyboard (Whitehead 1998, 60).[9] The cover of an ICP record designed by Schmit once again highlights this theme: it shows "new ways of drawing a circle" with a pair of compasses, all of which presume the ability of the drawer to make

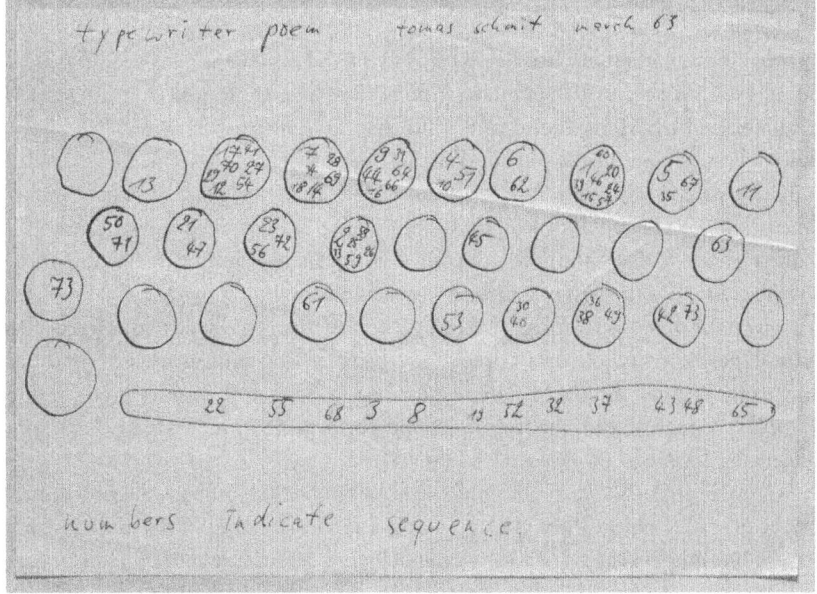

FIGURE 1.5   Tomas Schmit, *Typewriter Poem*

© 2018 Tomas Schmit Archiv, Berlin. The Gilbert and Lila Silverman Fluxus Collection Gift perfect circles by hand, thus defeating the point of using a pair of compasses (Bennink and Mengelberg 1971).

Such pieces reflect on the way in which the functional qualities of objects inform human action, and much of their wit consists of questioning or destabilizing this relation. Art historian Kristine Stiles, who describes Fluxus performances as "the music of *action* animating *things*", writes:

> Fluxus performances require both performers and viewers to consider the function of thought in the ways in which the body interacts with things: they draw attention to the behavioural processes that relate thinking and doing, and compel both performers and viewers to confront and then, perhaps, revise conditions of being.
>
> *(Stiles 1993, 65)*

Various Mengelberg pieces exemplify this interrogation of the functionality of objects. His early *Music for Two Pianists*, possibly developed in the context of the MES, featured a performer playing the keyboard, and a second performer (in this case Louis Andriessen) sitting underneath the piano making percussive sounds by knocking in various places and occasionally shouting something. It was described by Mengelberg as follows: "*Music for Two Pianists* is a piece in which I've attempted to humanize the piano. I don't know what on earth that might mean, but I've been concerned with it and I just don't know another word for it" (Dekker 2008). The theme of "humanizing" inanimate objects also returns in his earliest theatre piece *Hé, Hé, Hé, Waar is de Marechaussee?* ("Hey, Hey, Hey, Where Is the Military Police?"). It is a short dialogue between a man (played by Mengelberg) and a life-size doll who is his wife, and whose lines are projected onto a screen. Another piece that intervenes in the everyday functionality of objects is his 1973 composition *Met Welbeleefde Groet van de Kameel* ("With Kind Regards From the Camel"), a large-scale composition, lasting about half an hour, written for a group of ICP musicians (Figure 1.6). In the middle of the piece, a chair is sawn in pieces with a mechanical saw, and reconstructed in the form of a camel. When the camel is ready, the musicians play pages of crotchets in a completely uninteresting unison melody without any sense of tonal direction. This section lasts as long as the entire piece before it, and is specifically intended to bore the performing musicians, who can stop when they want to (Whitehead 1998, 106).

In this regard, the piece not only exemplifies a fascination with the functionality of everyday objects, but also represents a reconsideration of the functionality of written music, making it part of Mengelberg's "relational aesthetic" of pestering of musicians and audiences. Around this time, Breuker would leave the ICP to start his own musicians' collective, and shortly after Mengelberg would start assembling a standard line-up of musicians that would form the basis of the current ICP Orchestra. Although Mengelberg had been writing music for the ICP since

FIGURE 1.6   The ICP performs *Met Welbeleefde Groet van de Kameel*

Photograph by Pieter Boersma

its foundation, the development of this standard line-up meant that he would really start to concentrate on the question of how to write music in such a way that allowed musicians not just to perform the music "as written", but to negotiate the functionality of these scores and find new ways to interpret them so that the written material would be fully integrated into an improvised musical practice. It is this repertoire and associated performance practice that will be the main subject of Part II. We saw above, however, that Mengelberg's interest in the mediation of human behaviour by technologies and the material environment led him to reject the idea of "free" improvisation. This signifies a confrontation between the aims and concerns of the ICP and those of the American avant-garde jazz musicians that had influenced them in the early 1960s, for whom the notion of free improvisation was symbolic of their struggle against racism and systemic oppression in the United States. This question of improvisation and cultural identity will be the main topic of the next chapter.

Notes

1 To say that these composers were "fellow students" is a little misleading, as they did not attend conservatory together—Schat graduated the year Mengelberg started his degree, during which period Van Baaren left Utrecht Conservatory for The Hague—but they were all students of Van Baaren, who supposedly regularly addressed

political issues in his teaching, and was a close family friend of Mengelberg's parents. Apart from this common mentor, the Notenkrakers were quite a heterogeneous group, and we will see various forms of disagreement in their political outlooks and practices in this chapter.

2 Furthes MES participants included electronic music producers Ton Bruynèl and Jan Boerman, both close collaborators of Raaijmakers, Jaap Spek, who was a sound engineer assisting Karlheinz Stockhausen with his electronic music experiments, flautist Govert Jurriaanse, pianist and composer Rob du Bois, visual artists Hans Claessen and Lancelot Samson, and actor Will Spoor (Beeren 1979, 35, 38–42).

3 This piece has a striking resemblance to Emmett Williams' early Fluxus piece *Duet for Performer and Audience* from 1961; it is unclear whether De Ridder would have seen this piece performed when he went to the early Fluxus events in Germany.

4 These disorientating years in Peter Schat's early career, navigating between Boulez and the Situationist International, are described by Adlington (2013, 21–57).

5 Others were former MES-members Jaap Spek and Lancelot Samson, visual artist Bob Lens, and photographer Anna Beeke.

6 Martin Iddon provides a very detailed account of "the Cage shock" in Darmstadt; see Iddon (2013, 196–228).

7 The identification or distinction of Fluxus and happenings seems to have been another issue about which there was no clear consensus within Fluxus. Tomas Schmit, for instance, said that "every time I hear Fluxus and Happenings spoken of in one breath I shudder as if I saw a carp fuck a duck. It is possible to draw a dividing line between Happening and Fluxus. The two have very little in common and very much that keeps them apart. Happenings are expressionistic and symbolic, whilst Fluxus essentially portrays the opposite. It says farewell to the mania of perfection. It's concrete, simple, and offers two pleasant hours without great expense" (Berghaus and Schmit 1994, 87).

8 Han Bennink, Guus Janssen, and Ab Baars, conversation with the author, 14 October 2016.

9 Whitehead does not refer to it as Piano Distance; Pieter Boersma told me that this was the title (conversation with the author, 26 March 2018), and it can be heard on the ICP OOO album and seen being rehearsed on the photographs included in the ICP 2012 Box Set (Various Artists 2012).

2

GENRE BOUNDARIES

The ICP and Jazz

The founders of the ICP were part of a broader movement of European musicians in the 1960s who, mainly influenced by free jazz, started to assert their independence from American models. This is sometimes referred to in German scholarship and criticism as the "Emanzipation" of European improvised music (Ernst-Berendt 1977; Jost 1979). In Germany, the first years of this declaration of musical independence were referred to as the *Kaputtspiel-Zeit*, the period in which musicians played loud and fast music until it was "kaputt". German bassist Peter Kowald stated that:

> The main point was to shatter the old values, that is to say: to let all harmony and melody fall away . . . The *Kaputtspiel-Zeit* first and foremost made everything that is musically possible of equal value. Today it is clear for the first time that most Americans of our generation, as far as musical influence goes, can go hang.
>
> *(Jost 1979, 174)*

In one of the earliest books on the topic, German musicologist Ekkehard Jost describes the emergence of European improvisation as follows:

> Only with the Sturm-und-Drang period of Free Jazz in the USA, did the all-encompassing hegemony of American Jazz in Europe begin to be undermined. In the liberation from the structural principles of traditional jazz, from chord changes and the rhythmic regulation of the beat, younger European musicians simultaneously began to detach themselves from the almost obligatory influence of their former American models. The concept of *free music*, from which the term *jazz* was conspicuously erased, was intended to enable

people to develop freely, without regard for traditional norms or outdated ideas about sound. What followed was a tremendous psycho-musical tour de force, which not only shattered the familiar system of jazz improvisation, but consequently also questioned the identity of jazz itself.

(Jost 1987, 12)

Jost's language is rebellious, and his metaphors—hegemony, liberation—suggest an imperialistic oppression of European jazz musicians by their American counterparts.

Since then, various other critics and scholars have described improvised music in Europe as an autonomous development, with its own cultural and musical identity that can compete with American jazz (Nicholson 2005; Heffley 2005; Cerchiari, Cugny, and Kerschbaumer 2012). On the one hand, such descriptions are important interventions in historical narratives of jazz that present it as a uniform genre. A genre, moreover, that is strictly confined to North America: to this day, jazz histories generally ignore the global circulation of jazz since the very beginnings of the genre, save half a page on Django Reinhardt, some descriptions of the influence of Caribbean rhythms on New Orleans jazz, and perhaps a comment on the African and European tours of American jazz musicians. In this regard, it remains essential to affirm and describe musical developments outside the USA as significant contributions to jazz history in their own right. On the other hand, the construction of alternate or even oppositional identities, of a "European" improvised music independent from the jazz tradition, is problematic for various reasons. It ignores the background that almost all European improvisers had in jazz; they grew up with the genre, it may even have been the music their parents listened to, and it continued to be a source of influence long after the "Emanzipation". In fact we will see below that some of the first steps towards a sense of autonomy in Dutch jazz were taken in close interaction with American models. Moreover, by constructing a uniform European identity it ignores the broad stylistic diversity of European jazz and improvised music. More fundamentally, however, such constructions of a European identity in jazz do not attend to the global circulations in which this European activity was embedded, which included African, Asian, and significantly African-American musicians as part of a global movement of free improvisers negotiating their position vis-à-vis the jazz tradition. Finally, it suggests that European jazz musicians were only really starting to be autonomous from the mid-1960s onwards. Although this period shows a growing self-awareness, from a historical point of view European jazz musicians had always already been giving new meanings to jazz by recreating the music in their own ways: even if they mainly tried to "imitate" American examples, such practices tell us much of what they considered "true jazz" and how they positioned themselves in relation to it. Consequently, the argument for an independent musical genre seems to achieve too much; it risks presenting European free jazz as an exotic variant, not an integral part of jazz history.

Thus it risks a threefold erasure: of the African-American roots of the music, of the global circulations and collaborations cutting across nations and continents, and of the highly developed forms of jazz already existent in Europe. Rather than the oedipal logic of patricide suggested by the "Emanzipation" and the "Kaputtspiel-Zeit", we need a more rhizomatic account of artistic influence that can successfully negotiate the complex interrelations and ironies at work in such transcultural developments.

Significantly, as I shall argue in this chapter, musicians were themselves more than aware of such complexities—which does not mean that they had any unambiguous answers to them (far from it). The belligerent attitude represented by Kowald and Jost was not shared by ICP musicians.[1] The ICP seems to always have consciously occupied a position on the boundaries of jazz. Rather than a vehement distanciation from jazz in European improvised music, the ICP seems to have been much more ambiguous about this matter. Compare this excerpt from a small advert in jazz magazine *Jazzwereld* in 1970 promoting the ICP and inviting musicians to join:

> In our opinion, the most timely, universal and differentiated improvisation discipline at the moment is jazz. Now we would not claim that we make jazz, for that is a matter that has not only musical but also sociological and geographical aspects.
>
> Regarding our endeavours, we owe much to folks like: C. Parker, T. Monk, D. Ellington, C. Hawkins, C. Taylor, F. Waller, H. Nichols a.o.
>
> With regard to jazz, Black Power has loosened the chains of meter and tonality. PRAISE BLACK POWER.
>
> *(Mengelberg 1970)*

This is the same advert that opens with the quasi-commercial slogans mentioned in the previous chapter, so there is clearly some ironic mystification to it. Still, as a commentary on the ICP's relation to jazz, it is revealing. Mengelberg's language contains none of the belligerence of Jost, but on the contrary readily admits influence from a range of musicians spanning the history of jazz. The refusal to use the word jazz to describe the practice of the ICP stems from an awareness of musical and social differences rather than a wish to overturn a perceived oppressor. The last phrase is particularly ironic. Mengelberg's praise for Black Power, for reasons that are "purely musical", implies a complete ignorance of the wider social situation of black Americans and their political concerns. This faux-naivety seems to suggest that these musical developments cannot be detached from their particular social environment. The list of musical influences has a similar ironic purpose. The formal use of initials and last names detaches them from a historical context, as though they all just happen to be black jazz musicians. This advert alone shows much of the complexity and irony involved in intercultural encounters as well as the awareness that musicians can have of them.

Before Improvised Music

Jazz became a popular music in the Netherlands after World War I, when syncopated music began to replace the light classical and operetta repertoire in the larger cities (Wouters 1999). In the course of the 1920s, Dutch jazz groups started to emerge, including Theo Uden Masman's The Ramblers, who made the first Dutch jazz record in 1929 and would continue to play until the 1960s. Jazz was an urban, modern, progressive music, and its popularity was met with strong condemnation from the generally conservative establishment. Newspapers reported on "the dance problem" and its incitement of wild and pornographic behaviour. Official investigations were conducted, government reports were written, and the liquor licensing laws were altered in an attempt to regulate public dancing (Van de Leur 2012).

Partly in response to this public debate, jazz enthusiasts founded *De Jazzwereld* (not to be confused with the post-war *Jazzwereld* to be discussed below), perhaps the earliest jazz-devoted periodical in the world. They informed their readers of upcoming concerts, gave them practical advice on how to play instruments, and of course defended their music against the public condemnation. As has been shown in the case of American jazz periodicals, the Dutch jazz critics defended their music against moral and political criticisms through a distinction between what was "real jazz" and what was not. In the Netherlands, this was done specifically through conjuring up the image of the "noble savage". Real jazz, it was argued, unlike its commercial derivatives, was an expression of the African sensibility, "in civilization far below us", but for that matter all the more pure and innocent—a simple expression of a simple race (Van de Leur 2012).

Without the explicit racism, the general framework established by the pre-war critics still informed post-war jazz criticism to a large degree. A significant event was a 1956 concert by Lionel Hampton's big band in the Concertgebouw, Amsterdam's main classical concert hall.[2] Hampton's exuberant performance style caused the audience to become ecstatic, and the police cut the concert short for fear of riots. The event caused national outrage, with headlines condemning the "demagogue" Hampton across all Dutch newspapers. The response in *Rhythme*, the country's main jazz magazine of the 1950s, was telling. Siding with the public morale, it wrote:

> the concept of jazz, which did not have a very good name anyway, has been further devalued. After all, the general public perceives the Hampton gambol as "jazz" and all those who wish to educate that crowd about jazz music can now start all over again.
>
> (Rhythme *Editors 1956)*

For the intellectual jazz critics, jazz was sophisticated—albeit with an edge of primitivism. Hampton had been a topic of controversy in the pages of *Rhythme* before; in 1953 the magazine cited various responses to a Hampton concert, including Michiel de Ruyter, who would become one of the most important Dutch post-war jazz critics, who wrote that it was

> an orgy. This is not to say: "primitive", as the so-called "primitive jungle-rhythms" of the negroes are complicated, beautiful, and functional. It was only pounding, without swing, without meaning [. . .] I saw a negro in the crowd, dead still and unmoved. Probably because he appreciates good rhythm, not the sound of a pile-driver.
>
> (Rhythme *Editors 1953*)

Over the course of the 1950s, jazz transformed from dance music for teenagers into a more niche repertoire for connoisseurs. Whereas in 1949 the cover of *Rhythme* stated it was the monthly magazine for "modern music", including "dance, entertainment, and jazz music", by 1961 its slogan had changed to "the Netherlands' only jazz periodical". Throughout the 1950s, the emphasis had been on jazz, but it was still discussed as one popular music among others. With rock and roll increasing in popularity, jazz was presented as a more sophisticated genre for those who understood music. The May 1957 issue, for instance, recounts an anecdote about Elvis Presley who, when asked about his vocal range, "blatantly admitted" that he knew little about music and that it was not necessary in his genre (*Rhythme* Editors 1957). This was clearly taken as "proof" of the inferior quality of his music. In October 1960, the magazine announced that it would become exclusively devoted to jazz (Kop and Voogd 1960). With this decision, it definitively marked jazz as an autonomous genre, distinct from popular musics, and with its own historical trajectory; one of the new features of the magazine would be a recurring segment on the history of jazz.

This new way of valorising jazz meant that the music was no longer just seen as an expression of a primitive black sensibility, but as a musical art form with its own autonomous development and evolution, to which one could contribute in the present. This was in a way an important step to make something like the European "Emanzipation" possible. With the presentation of jazz as an intellectual and artistic pursuit, the groundwork was laid for many of the claims of artistic authenticity later used by free improvisers. Even though the "vanguard" was still made up of African-Americans, their musical quality was not dependent on the expression of a racial identity from a mythical past, but on their artistic achievements. And in fact it was around this time that we see an emerging recognition of Dutch jazz musicians. Michiel de Ruyter had produced three LPs between 1955 and 1957 as a series of *Jazz Behind the Dikes*, intended to showcase Dutch talent in "modern jazz" (Rusch 2016, 27–28; Various Artists 1955a, 1955b, 1957). The music generally adheres to the West Coast cool style of playing, with its soft tones, counterpoint, and rich instrumentation—particularly noticeable in Herman Schoonderwalt's septet as recorded on the second LP. Bennink, who was still a teenager at the time, recalls that the sophisticated style of the Modern Jazz Quartet meant that it was generally regarded as the quintessential jazz group:

> In school we would make lists: do you pick Percy Heath or Paul Chambers on bass? That was difficult enough. And on drums, Mel Lewis or Shelly Manne? Buddy Rich or Gene Krupa? We would draw up tables, and compare the best combinations. Percy Heath and Kenny Clarke, that was the *ultimate rhythm section* for [us]. That is how I learned to play, following Ruud Jacobs' advice. He got me off of Max Roach and onto Kenny Clarke.
>
> *(Van den Berg 2009, 39)*

In the early 1960s, however, critics generally felt that the most contemporary expression of the historical development of jazz was free jazz. *Jazzwereld*, appearing from July 1965 to May 1973, had the explicit goal to inform its readers of the "new thing". Clearly, tastes were rapidly developing compared to the popularity of cool jazz a few years earlier. In their 1966 readers' poll, in the international rankings, John Coltrane, Ornette Coleman, Archie Shepp, Miles Davis, and Albert Ayler topped the "best musician overall" chart, and Ornette Coleman's *At the Golden Circle* records and John Coltrane's *Meditations* and *Ascension* vied for "record of the year" (*Jazzwereld* Editors 1967, 21–23).

With this new jazz style, moreover, there developed a sense that Dutch jazz musicians could contribute something to it. In 1963 the first Wesssel Ilcken Jazz Prize was awarded, indicating a growing sense of the artistic qualities of Dutch jazz musicians. Bert Vuijsje wrote in that same year that:

> Until recently, most Europeans chose to imitate. In the Netherlands, too, we have seen how various musicians started out as boppers, played West-Coast in the early 1950s, and changed to hard-bop in 1956. Concerts by Dutch jazz musicians were consequently tedious, even pointless occasions, considering the many concerts by great American musicians. However, the Holland Jazz Concert that recently took place at the Amsterdam Concertgebouw, showed that in the last few years some exciting developments have taken place [. . .] Especially those musicians engaging in avant-gardistic experiments have attracted attention.
>
> *(Koopmans 1977a, 156–157)*

Vuijsje was almost certainly thinking of Mengelberg and Bennink as belonging to that latter category. Mengelberg's name starts to pop up in *Rhythme* from 1958 onwards, and he seems to have been perceived as a bit of an oddball from the start. Although his first mention notes only that he played "strikingly good solos" (*Rhythme* 1958), in 1960 a reviewer states that his "sombre and humourless Monk-jazz reached only a handful of people" (Niemans 1960, 28) and he is later mentioned as "only enjoying limited recognition, and only among certain audiences at that" (Kop 1960, 9). His playing, deeply influenced by that of Thelonious Monk, did not sit well with the general popularity of cool jazz. It did strike a connection with Bennink, however, who knew how to play Monk's repertoire (Van den Berg 2009, 58–59). The two started playing together more and more often, and in 1962 formed a quartet with alto saxophone player Piet Noordijk and bass player Rob Langereis (the quartet would change bass players frequently; apart from Langereis, Arend Nijenhuis and Jacques Schols were regular members of the group). The quartet became the most popular jazz quartet in the Netherlands. Noordijk, Mengelberg, and Bennink were Wessel Ilcken Prize-winners (Noordijk had won it in 1965), and in the 1966 readers' poll in *Jazzwereld* Noordijk was named best alto player, Bennink best drummer, Mengelberg best pianist and best musician overall, the group as best combo, and one of their records as record of the year (*Jazzwereld* Editors 1967, 18–20).

Although the emergence of free improvisation is usually described as a radical break, both from bop-based forms and from American examples, avant-garde elements were in fact integral to the practice of a number of progressive Dutch musicians. For the quartet, free playing was seemingly part of the various experiments and directions that defined "modern jazz"—which also included modal playing and the post-bop styles that Miles Davis was pursuing with his second quintet. In the recordings of the Mengelberg Quartet we can hear a mixture of bluesy, lyrical styles with more adventurous material. Mengelberg's solos contain clusters and parallel ninths and sevenths, but generally stay within a tonal framework. The 1966 record *The Misja Mengelberg Quartet* (Misha Mengelberg Quartet 1966; Mengelberg changed the spelling of his name to Misha somewhere in the late 1960s) contains two pieces juxtaposing composed material with spans of free improvisation ("Auntie Watch Your Step" and "Journey"), but also features rhythm changes ("Driekusman Total Loss"), a bluesy swing tune ("To John Hodjazz"), a ballad ("Peer's Counting Song"), and a two-chord modal tune ("Samba Zombie"). In 1967, the year the ICP would be founded, Bennink still played drums on a Dixieland album of the Stork Town Dixie Kids (Van den Berg 2009, 128). The Mengelberg Quartet was not the only band with such eclectic tastes. Boy Edgar's Big Band was particularly well known for its combination of Hilversum studio musicians and musicians with more avant-garde tastes; a recording from 1966 features compositions by Theo Loevendie (today probably best known as a composer, but then part of the emerging free jazz scene) and an early piece by Willem Breuker (Whitehead 1998, 29–30).

Not only was free improvisation cultivated as an integral part of a forward-looking "modern" jazz scene, but the growing self-awareness of Dutch musicians was similarly not developed in opposition to American jazz musicians, but precisely through close interaction with them. Bennink's father worked as a drummer in one of the studio bands (De Zaaiers) in Hilversum, where most of the Dutch radio and television studios are located (Flothuis 1968). Partly through this connection, Han got to play with many of the major Dutch jazz musicians, including the brothers Ruud and Pim Jacobs (bass and piano respectively), who together with singer Rita Reys would become the stars of the Hilversum scene. Pim presented the television show *Dzjes Zien*—phonetic for "jazz scene" but also a pun as "zien" means "to see"—and Bennink was often invited to play on the show, which led to early gigs with Wes Montgomery, Clark Terry, and Johnny Griffin, among others (Van den Berg 2009, 53). The Mengelberg Quartet were also a popular group for visiting Americans to play with: in 1964 they played and recorded with Gary Peacock and with Eric Dolphy (making his *Last Date* record, which would be his last recording before his death a few weeks later; Dolphy 1964), and in 1965 they played with Ted Curson (Misha Mengelberg Quartet 2011). In 1966, the quartet was invited to play at the Newport Jazz Festival, which, although people were aware they had been programmed in a quiet spot, was taken as a sign that this quartet—and, *pars pro toto*, perhaps Dutch jazz more generally—was worthy of international recognition (Figure 2.1).

FIGURE 2.1   The Misha Mengelberg Quartet performs at Newport in 1966. From left to right: Misha Mengelberg, Piet Noordijk, Rob Langereis, Han Bennink

Photograph by Jaap van de Klomp

Playing with these American musicians had a strong effect on their self-awareness. Dolphy stayed for a little over a month, during which he played several jazz clubs with Mengelberg, Schols, and Bennink as his rhythm section, did a concert with Boy Edgar's Big Band (mostly consisting of Hilversum players at this point, including Noordijk), and performed on Dutch national radio (which would be released as the *Last Date* album). The Dutch musicians were impressed with his professionality and musicianship, and more than a little starstruck. Bennink recalls that during rehearsals Dolphy would sometimes call a halt with a wave of his arm:

> I hated that wave of his arm. I just hoped it wasn't me that had made the mistake. Dolphy was so professional, such an exemplary musician, and such a good instrumentalist that he showed off his skill. For me, that was part of his style. He was a musical centipede. I could hear that he could do everything.
>
> *(Hylkema 1993)*

Bass player Jacques Schols had similar insecurities about playing with him:

> It was an afternoon, and we were trying each other out. Then you start getting used to the others. You become less cautious. At first, I prayed that every note was OK and he didn't turn round. It showed, of course, a lack of self-confidence.
>
> *(Hylkema 1993)*

However, playing with Dolphy, rehearsing and touring with him for a month, seeing a professional jazz musician at work, and learning to play his difficult pieces, was a transformative experience. Days after Dolphy had died, from a diabetic attack that was not treated because the doctors saw a black man and figured it was a drug overdose, Bennink received a letter from him inviting him on tour through Europe. "He also mentioned Bobby Hutcherson. I was amazed. I thought there must be better drummers around than me. But for some reason he had really enjoyed playing together." For the more traditional Hilversum players in Boy's Big Band, seeing Dolphy in action was transformative too, as he took away a lot of the prejudice surrounding free jazz. Alto saxophonist Tinus Bruin recalls:

> I even had one of his records. I didn't like it much [. . .] I came from a different generation: People like Carter and Hodges, Ben Webster and Hawkins. But this . . . ! I didn't know what to do with it [. . .] I didn't think it was very pretty. Quite the opposite, I can say.
>
> *(Hylkema 1993)*

The Hilversum musicians were sceptical about the technical abilities of a free jazz musician:

We said to each other: well, let's hear it. We were sitting around with the guys, talking about his playing. He came in with a great arrangement. And then he started to play: I thought . . . this is no joke. The stuff he played was fantastic.

(Hylkema 1993)

Increasingly, various Dutch musicians were venturing into avant-garde terrain themselves. Generally recognized as the first Dutch free jazz musician is drummer Pierre Courbois, who played on Gunter Hampel's *Heartplants* (cited by Joachim Ernst-Berendt as the first European free jazz record; see Ernst-Berendt 1977, 222–223) in 1965, and had led the Original Dutch Free Jazz Group for a couple of years. Willem Breuker started to play regularly with Courbois, because of whose connections in Germany he appeared on a number of the earliest European free jazz records—including those of Hampel but also of Peter Brötzmann and the Globe Unity Orchestra, together with Bennink (Schlippenbach and Globe Unity Orchestra 2001). Breuker was starting to make a name for himself, playing in clubs and competitions. In April 1966 Bennink asked him to perform at the opening of an exhibition of his visual art, together with Ted Curson. Mengelberg and Bennink were impressed with Breuker and asked him to join the quartet with Noordijk and Langereis. However, when Breuker joined the quartet, the balance was upset. Tensions had already been rising; as mentioned in the previous chapter, Mengelberg was starting to integrate his Fluxus activities into his jazz performances. Bennink enjoyed such subversive acts, but Noordijk and bass player Rob Langereis did not. Noordijk:

If I can't get behind it, I'm just making a fool of myself. So I don't do it. And then you got the jokes, lighting fireworks on stage or throwing bombs. That was about Vietnam. Misha stood there with bombs! I could not support that. I thought: Jesus Christ, why do we have to throw bombs? I am an anti-militarist!

(Vuijsje 1983, 84–85)

With the addition of Breuker to the quartet, who in July 1966 had his performance of *Litany*, the disagreement about free improvisation divided the group as it started to divide the Dutch jazz scene more generally. The quintet disbanded, and after about a year of playing as a trio and quartets with bassists Victor Kaihatu and Maarten Altena, Breuker suggested they should form the ICP (Figure 2.2) (Whitehead 1998, 38; Van den Berg 2009, 128–129).

With the founding of the ICP, there crystallized a growing distinction between what was called the "avant-garde" and the more traditional "mainstream" jazz players. Loes Rusch has analysed in detail how there emerged a *richtingenstrijd*, a "battle of directions" between these movements, where the improvising musicians' "deliberate, but by no means consistent" rejection of the

FIGURE 2.2   The four members of the ICP in 1967. From left to right: Willem Breuker, Misha Mengelberg, Maarten Altena, Han Bennink

Photograph by Pieter Boersma

jazz label in favour of "improvised music" connoted a more authentic approach to music (Rusch 2016, 48). Breuker said in 1975:

> What does "jazz" really mean? It is different from what we do. When I started performing in clubs where famous Dutch musicians used to play, I told myself: "It is ridiculous to copy the Americans! What does that have to do with Amsterdam or the Netherlands?"
>
> *(Buzelin and Buzelin 1994, 152)*

As Rusch argues, part of this construction of genre boundaries was the association of improvised music with high art and creative autonomy, whereas the label "jazz" evoked "undesirable images of commercialism and uncreative, slavish studio work" (Rusch 2016, 47). In 1971, for instance, Breuker complained that improvised music was still seen as a form of entertainment music, just like jazz had been:

> Conversely, serious [classical] music is more highly regarded and better paid. My opinion is that we belong to neither category, because both those kinds of music are fundamentally reproductive. The existing classifications are not applicable to our practice, which is purely creative.
>
> *(Jazzwereld 1971)*

Free Jazz and Free Improvisation

Clearly, apart from a reconsideration of their music as creative practice, such comments reflect a clash of identity politics. Although I have thus far emphasized the close interaction between Dutch and American musicians in the emergence of improvised music, before long Dutch musicians (and European musicians more generally) would emphasize their own musical identity, distinct from American examples. Free jazz itself was for a growing number of African-American musicians an expression of radical black politics. With the growing racial tensions in the USA, letting go of harmonic and rhythmic frameworks was symbolic of the self-determination and self-definition that black Americans were trying to achieve, and improvised collective expression indicated the possibility of expressions of black collectiveness elsewhere.[3] For some black American musicians, the rejection of the term "jazz" was equally a sign of emancipation from societal limitations. As Archie Shepp put it: "If we continue to call our music jazz, we must continue to be called niggers. There, at least, we know where we stand" (Wilmer 1987, 23). Notwithstanding such commonalities, of course, the identity politics of European and American improvising musicians clashed.

Dutch musicians and critics were not opposed to the political views expressed by black Americans—quite the contrary. Eric Drott, writing about free jazz in France, suggests that part of the reason that French musicians avoided the term "jazz" was precisely that they were sensitive to the politics of cultural appropriation, with playing music that was perhaps not properly "theirs" to play (Drott 2011, 135). Mengelberg's advertisement mentioned earlier and Breuker's idea that jazz had nothing to do with Holland or Amsterdam suggest similar considerations may have played a role in the Netherlands—aside from the implicit claims to artistic authenticity vis-à-vis more traditionally minded Dutch jazz musicians. Indeed, Dutch jazz criticism was initially very sympathetic to the political views of American musicians. In the US, musicians and their supporters (such as Frank Kofsky) attacked mainstream jazz critics, particularly those writing for *Downbeat*, for discussing their music in purely aesthetic terms and not paying attention to its political context, thus diminishing its significance (Baraka 1999; Monson 2007, 238–282). In *Jazzwereld*, however, there was elaborate attention to the social situation and political views of American musicians. In this sense, Dutch jazz criticism was generally similar to that in France, whose reception of the politics of free improvisation has been discussed by various authors—in fact, Dutch jazz critics actively followed French publications, and their writings show influences not only of Amiri Baraka, Frank Kofsky, and A.B. Spellman, but also of Phillippe Carles and Jean-Lous Comolli as well as other French critics.[4]

The principal writers for *Jazzwereld* were a group of young journalists, in their early twenties, who all worked as music critics for a variety of left-leaning Dutch newspapers. This included Bert Vuijsje, Peter Smids, Simon Korteweg, Martin Schouten, Pé Hawinkels, and Rudy Koopmans (Rusch 2016, 118). *Jazzwereld* was a platform for them to inform audiences about jazz, but also to discuss its aesthetic and political merits with those already initiated (and with each other). This inclusion of political and societal considerations was an explicit concern for them. Moreover, in a country with a rather small jazz scene, they had very close ties to Dutch musicians—Koopmans in fact sponsored the first ICP record, without which the ICP might never have existed, and was the foundation's first chairman; Mengelberg is listed as one of the editors of the early issues of *Jazzwereld*. As such, the magazine formed an important forum for a younger generation to explicitly express their music-political ideals, and this makes it a very important historical document. Although many of the polemics seem somewhat exaggerated in hindsight, and the amount of theoretical and philosophical terminology occasionally borders on the pretentious, *Jazzwereld* offers a valuable insight into this significant period of Dutch jazz history.

Particularly influential were the writings of Koopmans. He was a professional sociologist and always made sure to include sociological considerations in his discussions of jazz. A book by Koopmans from 1977, entitled *Jazz: Improvisation and Organisation of a Growing Minority* (Koopmans 1977a), included a chapter from Kofsky's *Black Nationalism and the Revolution in Music* as well as a chapter on Ornette Coleman taken from A.B. Spellman's *Four Lives in the Bebop Business*. The following quotation gives a taste of Koopmans' writing style as well as his aims in jazz criticism:

> For an understanding of jazz *music* we cannot do without an understanding of the jazz *world*, and this world is not isolated. The visual arts, literature, film, theatre and music can be seen to belong to the realm of ideas—to say it in a stately manner [. . .] As everyone with a little bit of sense knows by now, the ruling ideas are those of the ruling class(es). This means nothing other than that the political economic power relations are also reproduced on the social and cultural level. In this publication I will therefore constantly draw attention to the jazz *world*.
>
> *(Koopmans 1977a, 8)*

Koopmans drew on existing ideas of American jazz critics to interpret the status of jazz in terms of a broader class struggle. This allowed him to stress the similarities between the situation of African-American and Dutch musicians:

> In the Netherlands, too, this is the music of a minority. We can see this in the earnings, the working conditions, the place of improvised music in cultural policy and the policies of mass media, the way it is treated by record companies, and the way in which improvised music is (not) integrated into educational systems, including music, and in many other phenomena.
>
> *(Koopmans 1977a, 9)*

Initially, Dutch musicians responded sympathetically to the politics of free jazz musicians; they recognized a similar political outlook, although they acknowledged that they were obviously dealing with a very different political context. This raised the question for them of what the political significance of their own music could be. An early example of such considerations is evident in a *Jazzwereld* "discussion", organized in 1966, between radio presenters, critics, and musicians, including Breuker, Mengelberg, and American trumpeter Ted Curson who was on tour in the Netherlands at the time. It concerned the aesthetic merits of free jazz and—inevitably—the question of whether this music could still be called jazz. After Mengelberg had questioned the meaning of "freedom" and declared his disinterest in what the music should be called, Curson intervened:

> Can I say something? I think there is some sort of misunderstanding. These musicians do not call their music jazz; in fact they object to even being associated with jazz. What they want is something more personal. If you hear Ornette, that's Ornette Coleman's music. If you hear Albert Ayler, that's Albert Ayler's music. For these musicians "jazz" means slavery, prejudice, sex, because that's where the name "jazz" really comes from. It's all very emotional.
>
> *(Vuijsje and Witkamp 1966, 225–226)*

Up to this point the discussion of free jazz had been rather abstract: are we, on the basis of musical characteristics, able to identify elements of jazz in free jazz, or do we, on the basis of philosophical considerations, reject the whole idea of genre in the first place? But Curson's involvement turns this theoretical question into a personal one. Mengelberg is reluctant: "But is it really important how we call it? I would describe what I play as . . . well, jazz. For me it is not contaminated" (1966, 226). Theo Loevendie responded more sympathetically: "I think we had best stop talking about the name 'jazz'. Apparently the word is emotionally loaded, and in the emotional climate of this new development the term is rejected" (Ibid.).

Later in the discussion, Bert Vuijsje (writer for *Jazzwereld*) introduced a statement from Archie Shepp:

> We see jazz as one of the most meaningful social, esthetic contributions to America [. . .] It is anti-war; it is opposed to Viet Nam; it is for Cuba; it is for the liberation of all people [. . .] Jazz is a music itself born out of oppression, born out of the enslavement of my people.
>
> *(1966, 227)*

Mengelberg responded to this statement (after noting that Shepp himself still used the word "jazz") cautiously but affirmatively:

I believe that all music in a certain period more or less has political implications [. . .] I believe that the creative powers in jazz are generally more
to the left than to the right. It's difficult to speak apodictically about that.
Of course it's the poverty suffered by the most honourable jazz musicians
because they don't want to compromise their music. But there are also
other factors: the new music demands a discipline that probably, when
translated into other matters than music, more or less corresponds with an
insight that in any case casts a critical eye on the whole status quo of the
political situation.

(Ibid.)

Loevendie adds that in his eyes, jazz is "protest music"—something Breuker
disagrees with, which is particularly significant as this discussion took place
around the time of his performance of *Litany*. When asked by Mengelberg
about his views on this question, Ted Curson says:

I am actually against it. Because jazz is one of the last pure things we have
on this world [. . .] I love Archie Shepp . . . I've known him for years, but
if you really want to be engaged, you have to go to demonstrations, stand
next to Malcolm X, support Martin Luther King.

(1966, 228)

Loevendie again tries to establish a consensus: "Could we all agree on the idea
that social circumstances influence the music you make, but that mixing up
musical and political considerations too much, like Archie Shepp does, defeats
the purpose of the music?" (1966, 229).

Clearly, this encounter sparked a reconsideration of their own musical politics. The foundation of the ICP the following year was the start of a broader
movement aiming to improve the social situation for Dutch improvising
musicians—these developments will be discussed in the next chapter. Like their
American counterparts, Dutch musicians would fight for self-determination and
cultural self-definition, and in that sense they could relate to them. However,
as the black power movement was growing after the assassinations of Malcolm
X and Martin Luther King Jr., Pan-Africanist aesthetics were also increasingly
heard in the work of free jazz musicians. Influenced by John Coltrane, their
music expressed a sense of spirituality, or they combined free jazz with the
grooves of soul and funk, which of course were other important contemporary
musical expressions of black pride. To Dutch musicians, the idea that "the creator has a master plan" meant very little, and it is understandable that on them,
as perhaps on other white European musicians around 1970, the significance of
such expressions was lost completely. In fact, in an interview with Bennink in
the 1970s, he writes off such ideas as forms of commercialism—not just the use
of soul and funk grooves, but also the expressions of spirituality, which he may

have associated with the emerging hippie movement. He discussed Pharoah Sanders' *Jewels of Thought*, Albert Ayler's *New Grass*, Sonny Sharrock's *Black Woman*, and Sunny Murray's *Homage to Africa*, among others, and said:

> Don't think they can't play music! Of course they can. I played at a festival in Berlin one and a half years ago with Sanders and Sharrock. That was fantastic! They know how to play, but they don't. They stopped doing it [. . .] They're pandering to the tastes of the audience. They aim to please. Or rather, they want to reach them. Love! [. . .] And don't think it's just the free guys. No, Art Blakey also jumped the bandwagon. Suddenly he's walking around with big hair and floral prints. And Cannonball. And Clark Terry. With bells around their necks, like mountain goats.
>
> *(Koopmans and Vuijsje 1970, 18)*

Bennink saw such developments as a stagnation or even a "regression" in the development of jazz:

> I read that you can go on a "jazz trip" from the Netherlands to America. Well, that seems completely unnecessary, at least for me. Those trips are going the wrong way! They should organise trips for the Americans to come here!
>
> *(Ibid.)*

He added: "Believe me, it's really true. The best music is being played in the Netherlands these days" (Ibid.).

At the same time, of course, black American musicians were increasingly vocal about the political intentions behind their music, and critical of European musicians. AACM member Joseph Jarman, expressing views comparable to those of the Nation of Islam at the time, said in an interview in the next issue of *Jazzwereld*:

> On the other hand you have these people in Europe who gain popularity as avant-gardists, like [Han Bennink and John Surman]. I have nothing against them, we can get along and they believe in what they are doing. But it has been done before. By black people [. . .] You know, all culture is actually black. The music these kids are playing is black, the clothing, dancing, everything. But they don't even know [. . .] The only thing white culture ever made was technology, that's what they're good at. But it is not enough. They need black people to learn how to live [. . .] Our culture has always been held back, while they stole and imitated everything.
>
> *(Wolters 1970, 8–9)*

Despite their origins in very similar aesthetic and political outlooks, the concerns of these two avant-gardes were increasingly drifting apart. Bennink, looking back on the interview more recently, explained with a little embarrassment: "It was mostly because the music coming from Europe wasn't regarded as real music in America. They were kicking us down, and we needed something to kick back" (Van den Berg 2009, 167).

This had to do not just with identity politics, or the competition for a small European market, but also with mutual misunderstandings of highly fraught politics. In the preceding years, there had been some attempts at collaborations by the American and European avant-gardes. In 1969 there was a *Free Jazz Treffen* in Baden-Baden, where an improvisation featuring musicians from both continents (mostly Germans and members of the AACM) was later released as *Gittin' to Know Y'all* (Various Artists 1970). Although details of the event are unclear, accounts highlight the tensions that emerged in the interaction. George Lewis calls it "an uneasy attempt at musical hybridity", and emphasizes how from both perspectives the other group must have appeared as rather alien—something he sees exemplified in the ironic "y'all" of the record's title (Lewis 2004). In the aforementioned interview, Bennink mentions another concert in Frankfurt in 1970, which for him was the first time meeting the Art Ensemble of Chicago, and his (rather patchy) account was corroborated to me by Evan Parker, who had been present at the event as well. At this festival, Lester Bowie of the Art Ensemble made another attempt at a musical collaboration. The Europeans (perhaps also because they were asked by the festival organizers rather than Bowie personally) reacted indignantly, having the impression that they should be happy to be so "privileged" to play with American jazz musicians for a fee that they considered to be too low, and most of them declined.[5]

At the concert itself, Bowie prefaced the music with a speech, calling for a unification of Germany. Although this was received with applause by the audience, the musicians were affronted, as many of them were sympathetic to the Soviet Union. At the time, steps were being taken in the West towards unification— German chancellor Willy Brandt was actually in East Germany during the festival for this purpose—but it was on the premise of an anti-communist political stance that the musicians did not support at all. For musicians from the United States, at that point governed by Richard Nixon, to advocate German unification was seen by the Europeans to support such anti-communist politics—or at the very least, it showed a lack of understanding of the political situation in Europe (just like Bennink's comments in the interview showed a lack of understanding of that in the USA). During the performance of Bowie's big band, Paul Rutherford (a "card-carrying communist", as Parker put it) started to interrupt their concert with his trombone.

Such clashes between the two avant-gardes should not be taken as indicative of the general relationship between them, as musical collaborations were negotiated ultimately on an interpersonal, individual basis. In fact, Malachi Favors responded to Rutherford's interruptions by inviting him on stage to play along, which he did. Breuker, Mengelberg, and Bennink have each collaborated numerous times with American improvisers, and in fact developed some strong friendships with some of them. Still, such instances provide some context to the initially difficult relations between the European and American improvising avant-garde, as they were embedded in such different political contexts that it was difficult for them to find common ground. Bennink was critical of the Afrocentrism of late-1960s free jazz, and more generally, the Marxist framework in which Koopmans and other Dutch jazz critics interpreted free jazz made it difficult for them to appreciate this development. In 1972 Koopmans published a polemical essay on the late music of John Coltrane, specifically criticizing its religious and spiritual connotations. Koopmans ridiculed what he called the "Great Jesus Sentiment", accused Coltrane of mysticism and occultism, and criticized his fans for treating him as a prophet rather than a musician (Koopmans 1972a).

It was not that such connotations distracted from the music; Koopmans explicitly rejected an aesthetic appreciation from a purely musical point of view, arguing that it deprived much free jazz of its essential qualities. Rather, the religious and spiritual content was ideologically suspect for a Marxist sociologist. He cites the French critic Jean Echenoz of *Jazz Hot* who had argued that such mysticism was a response to white supremacy and an attempt to rebuild elements of an African-American sensibility; it should not be understood as a move away from politics, but as simultaneously a spiritual and political gesture. Koopmans was not having it:

> It sounds plausible, but isn't. When one is in an underdog position, in a position of defensiveness, one isn't free to choose one's battlefield and weapons. One can dream, as Coltrane and his followers do, but they confuse dreams and analysis. They confuse astrology with economics, chiromancy with sociology.
>
> *(Koopmans 1972a, 14)*

The general opinion of the *Jazzwereld* writers was that after John Coltrane's death, free jazz as a whole had gone downhill—its pan-Africanist aesthetics and mysticism did not appeal to them at all, and neither did fusion or the ongoing bop-based styles; both were deemed horribly commercial. In the final issue of *Jazzwereld*, Vuijsje reflected that part of the blame for its decreasing popularity lay with the

> disastrous development of avant-garde jazz since the death of John Coltrane. A magazine that, without any silly pep-talk, wishes to be an honest reflection of the situation in jazz, will at a time of such musical malaise unavoidably become rather sombre in tone.
>
> *(Vuijsje 1973)*

All these considerations show that the rejection of the jazz label in favour of "improvised music" was not simply a matter of declaring their musical autonomy, but was in fact a much more complex process featuring all kinds of musical, political, and cultural considerations. Moreover, it was by no means uniform. Bennink, in 1970, clearly still strategically opts for the jazz label (if they want jazz trips, they should come here). In an interview with Mengelberg and Bennink from 1971, Bennink is more ambiguous about their relation to jazz, and his comments recall Ted Curson's emphasis on the "personal" styles of Ornette Coleman and Albert Ayler:

Vuijsje: In the beginning you were part of the jazz scene, playing with Johnny Griffin and stuff like that. That gradually disappeared. How do you see the relation of your duo to the jazz scene?

Bennink: I think we make such a personal music together that it really does not refer to anything. It does have a jazz background. That's all there is to it [. . .] We've got such a personal sound, it relates to nothing. Only if you listen well, you can still hear: yes, those birds used to play jazz.

(Vuijsje and Schouten 1971, 19)

In the early years of the ICP, their music barely referred to jazz. If Mengelberg had said in the "Discussion" article in 1966 that jazz for him was not "contaminated", the advert from 1970 discussed at the start of this chapter also suggests a more ambiguous relation to jazz.

The relation of jazz to left-wing politics, especially to class struggle and racism, was also an ongoing issue of uncertainty. Mengelberg clearly was still trying (and failing) to come up with a point of view that could accommodate both the black power politics of free jazz and the Marxist politics of European improvisers. In 1979 he wrote a piece on improvisation for the *Neue Zeitschrift für Musik*:

Jazz contains an implicit protest against racism. In 1961 Stokely Carmichael went to Cuba, to experience that racism is only a transformed aspect of the class struggle. In this period . . . *(damn it—as if such socio-popular simplifications explain anything—better listen to "Monk's Music" with Trane, Hawkins, Blakey and so forth—further on in the text, this is just an essay—it does not necessarily need to succeed).*

(Mengelberg 1979b, 259)

In the late 1970s, Bennink and Mengelberg had formed the ICP Tentet, which was soon to become the ICP Orchestra. This was an important shift for the ICP, moving from an interest group for improvisers to an ensemble with a more or less standard line-up. This development meant, among other things, a return to a jazz repertoire, as Mengelberg wrote arrangements of pieces by Herbie Nichols, Thelonious Monk, and Duke Ellington—the first references to these pieces appear in concert reviews from 1980 (Lagerwerff 1980), and they were recorded in the ensuing decade (ICP Orchestra 1986, 1987, 1992a).

Interestingly, this return to jazz coincides with (or even predates somewhat) the "jazz renaissance" of the 1980s in American jazz, where a young genera- tion of musicians (centred around trumpeter Wynton Marsalis and bolstered by the writings of critic Stanley Crouch) dismissed most of the avant-garde and fusion music since 1960 and advocated a return to blues and bebop-based forms. In avant-garde circles, too, the "loft jazz" scene in New York combined con- ventional melodic and rhythmic elements in a generally avant-garde framework (Heller 2017). In Dutch jazz criticism of the 1980s, straight-ahead jazz (Dutch, American, or otherwise), loft jazz, fusion, and European improvisation are more or less described equally as part of a diverse musical landscape. Marsalis is described as a brilliant (though somewhat stylistically limited) trumpet player, and although his critical commentary on free jazz is mentioned, this did not lead to any of the critical debates they would have had ten years earlier. A review by Koopmans of the *Herbie Hancock Quartet* with Marsalis, Ron Carter, and Tony Williams seems characteristic: although he criticizes the record for its emphasis on technical dis- play over content, he is mostly pleased about the fact that Hancock has returned to acoustic jazz rather than fusion (Koopmans 1983).

In an interview with Mengelberg in 1989, he is asked whether one needs to know "the jazz tradition, the classics" in order to play free. Although he initially rejects this idea as unnecessarily "academic" and restrictive, and argues that one can improvise in many different ways and that people without such a background (mentioning ICP's trombonist Wolter Wierbos) can bring new things to the music, he does not reject this approach *per se*. "I teach music theory at the Amsterdam Conservatory, and I attest that they pay a lot of attention to bebop there. I believe that that's a very good way to learn; it just shouldn't be the only approach" (Suurmond 1989, 6). In this sense the approach of the ICP around this time is quite consistent with the approach of American avant-gardists, seeing jazz as one optional style among many. It was at this same time that Mengelberg and Bennink increasingly started to play and record again with American musicians, including some active in the loft scene, such as George Lewis, Anthony Braxton, Keshavan Maslak, Steve Lacy, Roswell Rudd, and Kent Carter.[6]

Still, Mengelberg would continue to place himself on the border of the jazz tradition. In the 1990s, he maintained that jazz no longer existed and that it had died around 1960. In an interview in 1993 he responds to the question of what black musicians like Eric Dolphy have meant for him:

> Of course it is not only Eric Dolphy. It is Duke Ellington, Thelonious Monk, Herbie Nichols, Anthony Braxton, George Lewis, to only name a few. Jazz music; once upon a time. I think it actually exists no longer.

Since thirty years or so. It is long ago that there was jazz. Jazz is the music of black people in evil America, an urban music, very exciting. Those were the days, when there was jazz.

(Mengelberg 1994, 180)

In Whitehead's book, talking about the death of jazz, he says:

Well I try to do something to the corpses that makes them live, maybe for another five minutes. I'm interested more in life than—no, scratch that from the record [. . .] Did I ever bother you with my ideas about cannibalism?

(Whitehead 1998, 162)

Unlike the neoclassicists who were "rescuing" or breathing new life into jazz, then, the ICP was cannibalizing jazz, using the parts of an "obsolete" style to create new approaches to improvisation.

Improvisation Beyond Jazz

From that perspective, Mengelberg's list of black American musicians who influenced him calls for further comment. As we saw earlier, plenty of black musicians opposed being labelled as "jazz" musicians, and his inclusion of Anthony Braxton and George Lewis, both of whom made their music after Mengelberg's presumed "death" of jazz, is noteworthy. His listing of influences, although once again acknowledging his debt to American examples, does seem to confine them to a separate genre of "jazz" rather than to accept them into a multicultural genre of improvised music. George Lewis has in fact argued that there is a history of presenting narrow and implicitly racialized constructions of jazz to exclude it from "universal" categories of music, which in practice turn out to be mostly made up of white composers. Lewis has often highlighted the importance of compositional work for AACM musicians, and consequently has been quite critical of the implicitly racialist historiography of "experimental music" in which the work of such African-American musicians has never really been included. Indeed, a composer such as Anthony Braxton is still often associated with jazz, while John Cage is never described as an improvising musician, even though many of his performances in the 1970s with David Tudor and Gordon Mumma were increasingly resembling free improvisations (Piekut 2017). In the construction of a European identity of improvised music, he sees a similar potential for erasing black history. In a 1996 interview with Bas Andriessen (no relation to Louis), answering a question about the existence of a "Dutch school" in improvised music, Mengelberg seems to make such a distinction explicit: "I think that improvised music that does not directly refer to jazz is international" (Andriessen 1996, 24). Such comments seem to dismiss the status of jazz as one of the twentieth century's most important musical avant-gardes.

However, Mengelberg's ideas on the identity of jazz, as we have already seen, were complex and contradictory, and another reading of his comment is possible. We might also read his praise for these musicians precisely as an acknowledgement of their role in twentieth-century music, while respecting the African-American cultural origins of jazz. The ICP's recording of the Nichols repertoire is remarkably straight, especially in comparison to the anarchic and raucous material on all their previous recordings. Leaving aside the freely improvised introductions, the group plays the pieces mostly in the standard head-solos-head form. The reason for this way of working may partly have been Mengelberg's wish to valorise the work of Nichols, who remains rather unknown to this day. The only existing recordings of Nichols are in a piano trio format, and Mengelberg wanted to arrange them for a larger group as a homage to the pianist:

> My only critique of Nichols is that he never found the right musicians [. . .] With such a trio, you don't even realize half of the music's potential [. . .] So I think that Nichols would have been very satisfied with the ICP, and he could borrow [the orchestra] straight away.
>
> *(Dekker 2008)*

In the case of Monk, Mengelberg always admired him as a composer as well as a jazz pianist, and even brought transcriptions of Monk's music to his classes with Kees van Baaren to analyse and discuss them (Dekker 2008). In the first issue of *Jazzwereld*, an article by Mengelberg is printed in which he discusses the motivic relations in Monk's "Criss Cross" and compares the different recorded versions of this piece, which sets a very different tone than the primitivist jazz criticism of only a few years earlier (Mengelberg 1965). When interviewed about his Monk arrangements in the late 1980s, he said:

> Monk has always had a great significance for me as a composer, and that is still true today. Without having necessarily to imitate him, I think the way he makes musical gestures is still exemplary. And I have tried to extend the line from Monk to what we are doing at the moment.
>
> *(Van den Berg 1987, 73–74)*

In the same interview he also praised Anthony Braxton, both for his compositional work and for his irreverent attitude to fixed ideas about the jazz tradition:

> I think Anthony Braxton is one of the few people with an own voice, somebody who is doing his own thing. Those enormous telephone books, all those written out pieces without a note of improvisation, that has to exist as well. I think I still find that record with Dave Brubeck his best move. A great choice. A-plus, I would say. The real boppers always

hated Brubeck enormously, but I never cared whether someone stuck to the Parker bebop bible or not.

(Van den Berg 1987, 79)

Indeed, American and European improvisers, despite the clashes described above, are best seen as part of an international, multicultural genre of improvised music. Braxton and especially Lewis can be heard on recordings with various ICP musicians. Indeed, in its combination of composed and improvised elements, the ICP is closer to the Chicago scene than to many other European improvisers. To put this in a larger context, it is necessary to understand the position of the ICP not only vis-à-vis American jazz, but within improvised music more generally. The emergence of improvised music was an international affair from the very beginning. The early ICP recordings feature plenty of Dutch musicians, most importantly Willem van Manen, Rob du Bois, Peter Bennink (Han's brother), Bert Koppelaar, Gilius van Bergeijk, Michel Waisvisz, and Maarten Altena. But there are also many international musicians on these recordings, including Peter Brötzmann, Derek Bailey, Paul Rutherford, Evan Parker, Anthony Braxton, Steve Lacy, Steve McCall, and John Tchicai. ICP musicians and other Dutch improvisers such as Leo Cuypers and Pierre Courbois also played on the recordings of Gunter Hampel, Brötzmann, and Globe Unity Orchestra, as well as British recordings on the Incus label with Bailey and Parker. Parker comments:

> To provide context, remember how few people were interested in playing this way then. It really was reassuring to know you weren't alone, you weren't crazy. Or if you were crazy there were other people who were just as crazy as you.
>
> *(Whitehead 1998, 50)*

From the 1980s onward, such international collaborations only increase, with American musicians such as Lewis, Larry Fishkind, Steve Lacy, and Roswell Rudd, as well as South Africans such as Dudu Pukwana and Sean Bergin, playing frequently with ICP musicians.

Despite such international collaborations, some musicians and critics have described various "schools" of improvised music. I already mentioned Heffley's characterization of Dutch improvised music in the previous chapter, noting how his description was indebted to the music of the ICP. This is also true, to different degrees, of other such descriptions. Parker, though noting the oversimplification inherent in such generalizations, describes Dutch improvised music as

> more about remarkable personalities—sort of Meetings with the Remarkable Men [. . .] Dutch music is always about the strong idea, associated with the remarkable individual. And about clarity [. . .] The

Dutch are not much interested in what Misha calls mood music which is music where the musician becomes lost in the process, transported into what I understand is for Misha a grotesque, trancelike state, where all rational decision-making gets lost, and the idea becomes less important than the experience.

(Whitehead 1998, 46)

Bas Andriessen's interview with Mengelberg was part of a series of interviews with various Dutch improvisers, all of whom were asked the question of whether there was something characteristically Dutch about the music they made—most of them, unlike Mengelberg, affirmed this. Bennink responded:

somebody like Breuker is very Dutch. And so are Misha and I, especially because of Misha. I'm not sure what this is. The English have this pointillist way of improvising: Derek, Evan, Paul Rutherford, Hugh Davies all had this. It was forbidden to play blue notes. We were a lot rougher in that regard, our music was more about shock value. The German thing is more or less personified by Brötzmann. Die-hard Krupp violence. We have more layers in our music, and a certain kind of humour.

(Andriessen 1996, 45)

Many other improvisers in Andriessen's book suggest that humour is an important characteristic for Dutch improvised music, but they also refer to the connection with contemporary composed music. Andriessen writes that he intentionally mostly interviewed musicians that also identified as composers, because he expected this to be an important element of their music (Andriessen 1996, vii).

I cite these descriptions less to ascertain whether there is such a thing as "Dutch identity" in improvised music, and more to highlight that such considerations continued to be important within this international scene. We saw earlier that Breuker, too, was concerned that jazz had "nothing to do" with Amsterdam or the Netherlands. Mengelberg made references to Dutch folk music from very early on. His "Driekusman Total Loss", from the time of the quartet with Piet Noordijk, can be read as a very early questioning—in a musical form—of the relation between jazz and Dutch music. It uses rhythm changes, but the melody is taken from a Dutch folk song. The song's AABA form corresponds to the basic format of many jazz standards, and even the melodic structure of its A section—aa'ab where a' is an inversion of a and b forms a downward melodic cadence—is structurally very similar to that of "I Got Rhythm" (Misha Mengelberg Quartet 1966; Misha Mengelberg Quartet featuring Gary Peacock 1981).

In an interview for ICP's tenth anniversary, Mengelberg is asked what this "vague" term "improvised music" really means:

Mostly, it means jazz. That's the most developed, urban form of improvisation. In the United States, that is. We renounced jazz for a while [. . .] Dutch and more generally European circumstances are so different, that you end up with different improvised music. In the back of our minds is the music of De Zaaiers, Jack Bulterman, operetta, in short, everything you heard on the radio as a little boy. You have to work that into your music.

('We Zijn Loslopende Honden Samen in Een Kennel' 1977)

On some level, this reference to commercial kitsch is clearly ironic. The use of clichés in their improvisations was something that characterized the ICP's music from the beginning, and was part of what made their performances so funny. A radio broadcast from 1967 that preceded the first ICP record already features "Die Berge Schütze die Heimat" (German for "The mountains guard the homeland", Various Artists 2012). It is an *allemande*, and a very early example of Mengelberg composing classical dance forms for the ICP.[7] The melodic and harmonic simplicity in the context of atonal and a-rhythmic improvisations make for a comical effect. As Bennink told me, the use of such pieces was partly to distinguish themselves from other improvising musicians, suggesting a very early concern with national identity in improvised music.[8]

The duo of Bennink and Mengelberg in fact became particularly renowned for their use of quotations and stylistic allusions (Figure 2.3). However, what was particularly exciting for audiences was their approach to musical interaction. Much of the time in their performances, it seemed they were hardly interacting at all. Bennink would play very loud and fast, using everything around him that could make a sound, while Mengelberg would be slowly figuring out harmonic and contrapuntal structures on his piano. When they do interact, it is mostly antagonistic, and this is where their use of allusions comes in. In line with the aesthetic of "pestering" discussed in the conclusion to the previous chapter, they use such allusions to tease each other, deliberately missing entries the other sets up for them, playing right through what the other is doing, and finally joining in with something when the other has already given up.

An example is "Eine Flasche Für Die Lola", from *Einepartietischtennis* (Mengelberg and Bennink 1974).[9] Mengelberg starts out playing a swing tune with a dissonant melody and accompaniment of chromatically moving chords containing many seconds and clusters, using a stride style. Bennink accompanies him on something wooden—possibly the piano. After the piece ends, Bennink has a short solo, during which Mengelberg starts playing a slow, chromatic ballad, using gestures from Romantic music. Bennink starts playing rolls that have little to do with what Mengelberg is doing, and after a while he starts playing loud crashes to disturb Mengelberg's playing. Mengelberg responds by playing loud clusters and octaves in the bass, but otherwise continues his ballad. Bennink tries again, now also whistling and shouting in German. Mengelberg responds with a chorale-like melody, singing along with his playing in a hoarse, off-key falsetto voice. He continues with his slow chords and Bennink returns to playing fast rolls and loud crashes, and shouting. After that he starts playing a lively tango rhythm. Mengelberg does not respond and plays some chords and clusters out of rhythm. When Bennink stops playing the tango rhythm because he gets no response, Mengelberg finally plays a tango. Bennink responds by screaming. After that, they are finally back together, playing a swing tune similar to the one in the beginning. After a solo by Bennink and one by Mengelberg, the improvisation ends with a minute of music from a music box.

As will be discussed in Part II, this approach was a significant inspiration for the practice of the ICP Orchestra, where Mengelberg's compositions are used to make such interactions possible in a larger ensemble. In the context of the emerging scene of free improvisation in Europe and the United States, it is clear that this approach is far removed from what Derek Bailey would later call "non-idiomatic" free improvisation (Bailey 1993). Rather than playing music beyond existing styles and idioms, the ICP duo actively juxtaposed and deconstructed different idioms in the course of their performances, and from the late 1970s onwards this also again started to include jazz idioms. This iconoclastic approach to different musical idioms corresponds to Mengelberg's views on freedom in musical improvisation, which was such a central aesthetic and political element of free jazz and free improvisation. In the *Jazzwereld* discussion, Mengelberg said:

FIGURE 2.3 The ICP Duo performs in Middelburg, November 1972

Photograph by Pieter Boersma

I just wanted to add that music-technically it's a useless concept, a very dangerous concept. If you look at the concrete facts, the music we just heard, then freedom is the last thing that comes to mind [. . .] Such rebelling for its own sake is trivial, it gives you nothing substantial to deal with. You just end up with new forms of discipline.

(Vuijsje and Witkamp 1966, 225)

In an interview in the 1990s he criticized the 1960s rhetoric of "free music":

They made it into a religion instantly. It had to have power, and whenever it sounded similar to something else it must have been thought of in advance, it had to be spontaneous, etc. I had no use for such slogans. "Free" music was a plague.

(Andriessen 1996, 19)

Free improvisation, because of its attempts to "sound free", was actually experienced as being extremely limited in practice by the ICP musicians.

The use of pieces such as "Die Berge", then, was not only a comment on the impossibility of music without idiom, but also on notions of musical freedom, and in fact the ICP's use of composed material from their very earliest work onwards distinguishes them from many other European improvisers. Lewis notes that part of the second generation of improvising musicians in the United States, specifically the Chicagoans that had been present in Baden-Baden and Frankfurt, also featured much composed material in their performances. Whereas most European improvisers rejected the hierarchical composer–performer relationships that the use of compositions implied (in their eyes), the AACM musicians emphasized:

a hybrid compositional-improvisative discourse that incorporated insights, sounds, techniques, and methods from a variety of areas, including European high musical modernism [. . .] AACM composers were often drawn to postmodern collage and interpenetration strategies that blended, opposed or ironically juxtaposed the two disciplines [. . .] AACM musicians were headed away from, not toward, an exclusive preoccupation with free improvisation, as befits their status as a second generation rather than a first. For these musicians [. . .] this more delicate, nuanced approach was as revolutionary and anti-hegemonic as the previous "free jazz" claimed to be, not just in its challenge to notions of what American free music should sound like, but to notions of the "proper" processes by which working-class black musicians should produce music.

(Lewis 2004)

Much of this also applies to the music of the ICP, and with this we return to the connection between Dutch improvised music and contemporary composition. There are indeed a significant number of Dutch improvisers who have been active as composers or performers of contemporary art music. The claim that European free improvisation builds on principles of western art music is found in various writings by contemporary critics. Sometimes it serves not much more than a rhetorical purpose, valorising a music whose aesthetic credentials were controversial to many. Joachim Ernst-Berendt, for instance, describes the music of the Globe Unity Orchestra as being similar to the music of Schönberg or Webern—in particular, the comparison of 30-minute-long honking improvisations to the carefully composed miniatures of the latter seems quite a stretch (Ernst-Berendt 1977, 225). The claim to contemporary art music seems to secure a cultural capital for European musicians that is not as easily accessible for black musicians. It was perhaps not intended to draw racial boundaries—Ekkehard Jost describes the music of Cecil Taylor in similar terms (Jost 1974, 73)—but this has later been used as a basis for distinguishing different schools or national identities. Such categorizations risk the creation of implicitly racialized conceptual boundaries that do not really hold up to historical reality.

Part of the rhetorical purpose of "instant composition" was to validate improvisation as an art worthy of consideration similar to that of composed music. It did so on the basis of the modernist premise that there is no difference in principle in the kind of musical structural thought that goes into either improvisation of composition—a premise I call modernist because it only concerns the creation of musical structure rather than the social or cultural significance this production process might have. However, as I already showed in relation to the origins of the term in Fluxus performance art, it was not only a rhetorical way of valorising improvisation as a serious art form, but also an acknowledgement of the constraints and limitations inherent to any practice, and a commitment to finding new and creative ways of using them. As Lewis argues, definitions of improvisation play an important role in the implicit distinctions in the historiography of experimental music. Cage, in the 1950s, rejected jazz improvisation because it did not fit his aesthetics of non-intentionality, spontaneity, and a-historicity (Lewis 1996). To Lewis, this ideal of music as completely spontaneous and in the moment is specific to a tradition of western art music with its "binary of notation versus freedom" (Lewis 2004), whereas musics of the African diaspora frequently stress personal expression and historical embeddedness.

The ICP's use of tonal, composed material was a way to discover new forms of musical practice that went beyond traditional definitions of composition or improvisation, and in this sense the group is closer to the musicians of the AACM than to other European musicians. For Mengelberg, part of the challenge of the ICP was to develop a musical practice in which composition could be embedded in a non-authoritarian social practice. Hence, far from claiming the cultural capital of European art music, the practice of instant composition was explicitly a way to find an *alternative* to the hierarchical and conservative practices of traditional composition. In the late 1960s, Mengelberg called this the "Africanization of the twelve-tone row", a phrase that should not be taken literally (although they did experiment with twelve-tone rows at this time), but more as a way of signifying the associations of African music as communal performance and twelve-tone music as the paradigmatic example of abstract, text-focused music that only related to performance in a top-down, hierarchical manner.[10] Whereas for AACM members the use of written material represented "an engagement where composition itself became an act of resistance" (Lewis 2004), for Mengelberg the use of pieces was not necessarily intended to establish a relation to contemporary composition.

This relation was already there: not only had Mengelberg studied composition at the conservatory, but he came from a renowned musical family. His father Karel was a composer and conductor and his mother Rahel Draber played the harp. His most famous family member, however, was his great-uncle and famous conductor Willem Mengelberg, the political opposite of his socialist parents. According to Bennink, "Die Berge" was a reference to Chasa Mengelberg, a chalet in Switzerland that Willem Mengelberg had constructed during World War I, and where he spent much of his time, especially after he had been banned from conducting after World War II because of his friendly ties with the German fascist regime.[11] If anything, his use of compositions in an improvised musical practice was a means to move away from the standard practice of contemporary composition. To understand the context of this desire, however, the next chapter will address the ICP's role in the democratizing movements of contemporary Dutch art music.

Notes

1 Jürgen Arndt argues that neither was it really shared by Jost, and follows this up with a comparison of how Mengelberg and Peter Brötzmann continued to claim influence from American examples (Arndt 2012).
2 Norman Granz had organized nightly jazz concerts there since 1952, which became highly popular and somewhat notorious for their midnight starting time and the liberal drug policy that allowed audience members to smoke marihuana inside the hall (Rusch 2016, 28).
3 The literature on the political meanings of free jazz is extensive; see, for instance, Kofsky (1970); Jones (1975); Wilmer (1987); Hersch (1995); Anderson (2007); Monson (2007); Carles and Comolli (2015).
4 Koopmans' seven-page review of various albums by Albert Ayler might be taken as exemplary; besides the work of Kofsky and Spellman, it draws mostly on French jazz criticism (Koopmans 1969).
5 Evan Parker, conversation with the author, 2 December 2017.
6 See, amongst others, Lacy, Waisvisz, Bennink, and Van Regteren Altena (1978), ICP Orchestra (1982, 1986, 1987), Maslak, Mengelberg, and Bennink (1980), Roswell, Lacy, Carter, Mengelberg, and Bennink (1983), Mengelberg, Lacy, Lewis, Gorter, and Bennink (1985), Lacy, Lewis, Reijseger, Mengelberg, and Bennink (1992), and Various Artists (1997a, 1997b).

7 Different recordings with this same title (in later years) sound different, even though they are all classical dances, suggesting it was originally conceived as a suite.

8 Han Bennink, conversation with author, 27 January 2016.

9 This recording is also discussed in Van den Berg (2009, 148) as an example of the duo's typical interactions.

10 The phrase "Africanizing the twelve-tone row" is on ICP 002 with Mengelberg, Bennink, and John Tchicai (Bennink, Mengelberg, and Tchicai 1968). See also Whitehead (1998, 49).

11 Han Bennink, conversation with author, 27 January 2016. On Willem Mengelberg's political allegiances, see Zwart (2016).

3
POLITICAL ACTIVISM IN CONTEMPORARY MUSIC

In the early 1960s, Mengelberg and his fellow students Schat and Andriessen were looking for alternatives to traditional concert practice, particularly through their participation in the activities of the Mood Engineering Society. Although Andriessen and especially Schat soon left performance art behind them and returned to regular composition, this did not diminish their commitment to reforming the musical infrastructure in the Netherlands. In fact, it was precisely Schat, perhaps the most committed to musical modernism and to the idea that music could not express any ideas (political or otherwise), who was also the most politically vocal, had close connections to the Situationist International and Provo, and would be one of the primary advocates of the various forms of political action of this generation of composers and musicians. Because of their political engagement, Mengelberg and his fellow students—Andriessen, Schat, Reinbert de Leeuw, and Jan van Vlijmen—acquired a reputation as maverick political composers, generally referred to as "The Five" (after the Mighty Handful or Les Six) or the "Notenkrakers" after one of their more notorious political actions. "Notenkraker" literally means "nutcracker", but might also be taken to mean "notesbreaker" or even "note squatter".

As they graduated from the conservatory and tried to get their pieces performed, these composers generally experienced a lack of opportunities for new music: concert programmers and festival directors were not interested in their work, and funding policies heavily favoured pre-twentieth-century classical music. To protest this, they took political action in various ways, and in doing so mobilized musicians across different genres. These practices first came to the fore in 1966, the year in which Provo's actions were at the centre of public attention, and Breuker performed his *Litany* shortly before joining the Noordijk-Mengelberg quartet. It was a year in which there was a general sense of change and revolution: as Niek Pas has written: "There was never a Dutch '1968,' as it were, but there was a 1966" (Pas 2008, 13). Parliament fell in October, and that same month the liberal democratic party D66 was founded, which, although unconnected to Provo or any other countercultural movements, did aim to channel some of the dissatisfaction with traditional political parties into a movement of parliamentary reform, and so "to explode the current political system". Provo itself disbanded in 1967, after which some Provos turned to politics, leading to the "Kabouter" (Gnome) movement advocating green politics, liberal drug policies, and squatters' rights. Although Roel van Duijn had been on the Amsterdam city council since 1966, actual participation in politics was rare for Provo, but the Kabouters were elected to various city councils.

The closing of the decade, then, saw a shift from trying to establish utopia in the here and now through public manifestations, acts of civil disobedience, and artistic events, to actual participation in parliamentary democracy to take more structural forms of action. The 1970s in the Netherlands, for that reason, were in that sense a much more politically conscious decade than the preceding one (Adlington 2013, 309 ff.). Parallel developments were happening in contemporary music, where the Notenkrakers, after a variety of musicopolitical expressions (from ludic to revolutionary), would turn in 1970 to actual political engagement through interest groups, unions, and other institutions. The ICP, which was initially founded more as such a political platform than a musical collective, in that sense precedes some of the actions in the broader musical infrastructure. Mirroring such organizations in the United States as the Association for the Advancement of Creative Musicians, the Jazz Composers Guild, the Black Artists Group, and various others, the ICP was itself an important step in the growing self-awareness of Dutch improvisers and jazz musicians described in the previous chapter. It represented a move beyond representation in the jazz magazines or other media such as newspapers, radio, or television, towards actively trying to reshape the Dutch musical infrastructure so as to improve the possibilities for improvised music.

This chapter thus picks up on various threads presented in the previous two chapters, showing how people in both improvised and composed music were involved in a combined effort of reform, of democratizing musical life in the Netherlands. As I showed in Chapter 1, although there were significant connections between the artistic and the political avant-gardes of the 1960s in the Netherlands, many musicians and artists remained committed to a specialized and modernist form of artistic activity, something which was at odds with the more radical aspirations of some countercultural movements that aimed to abolish professionalized art in favour of an emphasis on collective creativity. Significantly, the political activism of improvisers and composers was similarly mostly intended to secure better opportunities for their art. With this political engagement, the question returned of whether democratization should also include opening up their art to a wider audience, but it was only one question among many, including issues of government funding, the politics within musical practice, and the question of whether music itself could be a means of achieving certain political aims.

It is not my aim to describe all these issues at length—Robert Adlington has done so (at least for the developments in the 1960s) in his book *Composing Dissent*, on which I will frequently draw throughout this chapter (Adlington 2013). Rather, I will focus on the positions of the ICP founders within these debates, and to describe the foundation of the ICP (and subsequent institutions for the support of jazz and improvised music) as part of this movement of democratic reform in contemporary art music. Interestingly, the Notenkrakers generally held on to a belief of aesthetic autonomy of music, arguing that music could not really express political ideas. Bennink has also always denied that his music was political—and indeed has never really shown much interest in politics at all. Breuker, as we saw in Chapter 1, initially also denied that his music was political, while taking some early steps towards audience participation and other ways of democratizing music. In the early 1970s, however, he became simultaneously more overtly political through his music (and musical theatre) while also stepping back from the aim of democratizing musical practice and taking personal control over his own musical collective. Mengelberg, as we already saw in his response to the aesthetics of John Cage, thought that narrative and communication were actually inherent to the way people listen to music. However, he was far from outspoken about the possibility (or desirability) of expressing politics through music. His following comment, from the 1966 discussion with Ted Curson about the politics of free jazz, may be taken as emblematic in its vagueness:

> Schopenhauer once said something like, I forget the exact words, but "Art is an unfolding of truth", it is not beauty that makes for good music, but truth [. . .] and the truth has to do with the totality of circumstances.
> *(Vuijsje and Witkamp 1966, 229)*

In other words, even though music is political through and through, making "political music" does not necessarily contribute anything if it is not true to the social circumstances in which it is made. As we will see, he was quite consistent in this general framework, but would always remain hesitant to say what it meant for music to be "true", or indeed if that ultimately made a difference. Still, the ICP's significant role in these developments had an important impact on the concept and practice of instant composition, particularly in the way it shaped Mengelberg's understanding of the relation between notation and performance.

Politicizing Music

The first public manifestation of the Notenkrakers' political engagement was the so-called "Maderna campaign". In March 1966, the five composers published an

Open Letter to the board of the Concertgebouw Orchestra (De Leeuw et al. 1966). There had been some debate about the inclusion (or rather exclusion) of contemporary music in the Concertgebouw programmes, and orchestra conductor Bernard Haitink had stated that he did not have much knowledge or appreciation of it. The letter suggested that the board consider the appointment of Bruno Maderna (or perhaps Pierre Boulez or Ernest Bour), with whom some of the composers had already worked, besides Haitink as a conductor specialized in modern music. The letter was the start of a campaign consisting of repeated efforts, culminating in a televised debate, to engage the board in a discussion about their programming policy, which scheduled contemporary music in separate concerts and never as part of the more popular regular concerts of classical repertoire. The letter was decidedly modest and polite, but given its timing during a period of increasing social unrest, and because of various comments made by Schat in the subsequent campaign, the efforts of the composers were generally perceived as a parallel in the cultural sphere to the contemporaneous political forms of upheaval that figured so prominently in the public sphere. Various critics reacted to the campaign with warnings of "Provo entering music" (Adlington 2013, 73), establishing a connection that was not really warranted by the contents of the letter or most of the convictions of the campaigners.

As such, the Maderna campaign showcases an ambiguity that I already touched upon in Chapter 1 and that will return repeatedly in this chapter. On the one hand, the Maderna campaign fit in with a general movement of reform, doing away with established structures in the interest of a new generation, and it was certainly perceived as a revolutionary gesture both by some of the campaigners and the public at large. On the other hand, this revolutionary gesture was intended to advocate a concept of music that was purely artistic, and detached from any social concerns. The Maderna campaign ran at the same time as the activities of the Sigma Centre discussed in Chapter 1. There we saw that disagreements emerged between Provo and the musical avant-gardists because the latter ultimately held onto a modernist aesthetic that could not be reconciled with the aims of collective creativity of the former. The Maderna campaign was similarly primarily aimed at the advancement of modernist music rather than a political ideal, and this tension would be a constant throughout these composers' political endeavours. The very argument of the Open Letter was premised on the idea that the work of these composers and their contemporaries represented a continuation of the classical tradition as represented in the Concertgebouw's concert programmes, and should therefore be included in the same concerts. It quoted Maderna saying that "musical evolution is an uninterrupted state of affairs; the public must learn to see this", adding that this perspective could be the only correct one (De Leeuw et al. 1966).

However, the composers' political affiliations would soon become more explicit. In early 1968 Peter Schat and Harry Mulisch, one of the Netherlands' foremost writers who would be an important ally of the group of composers, made a visit to Cuba to see a communist state in action. Later, Mulisch spent some time in Paris, where social and political tensions were on the rise, and Schat and Andriessen both visited him. In May 1968 the five composers organized a "Political-Demonstrative Experimental Concert" in Theatre Carré in Amsterdam. The PDE Concert was intended, in the words of Andriessen, "to clearly underline our political conviction and to declare our solidarity with the world revolution" (Adlington 2013, 85). The venue was decorated with red flags and posters of Fidel Castro, Che Guevara, and Ho Chi Minh. The programme book was filled with excerpts of writings by Lenin, Adorno, Mao, Marcuse, and Trotsky.

Despite these political intentions, even in this concert, the composers generally held onto a view that put music outside of such political considerations. In the concert's programme book, Schat wrote that "music is not able to express anything, let alone transmit political messages. On that every musician will spontaneously and rightly agree" (Schat 1968, 5). In press interviews, Andriessen cited Stravinsky's dictum that music can express nothing other than music, and Mulisch compared it to mathematics, which has meaning only in its application (Adlington 2013, 65). In this, they were once again at odds with the revolutionary youths who made up most of the audience; some (ex-)Provos staged a few interventions during the spoken introductions, to the dismay of Schat who later expressed his anger at people who "think that revolution means undisciplined behaviour" (Adlington 2013, 61).

Mengelberg's position in these matters is an interesting one. Although he would continue to participate in these political actions, he would also increasingly question their aims and premises. Jan van Vlijmen said in 1976: "We were always diametrically opposed to each other. Misha was the most obvious example [. . .] He undermined more than one of our unquestioned assumptions, and I think they needed to be undermined" (Koopmans 1976, 34). In the programme of the PDE Concert, Mengelberg wrote as a postscript that "any connection between my [contribution] and the rest of this political diatribe disguised as a programme book is dismissed" (Mengelberg 1968, 23). This might be interpreted as being in line with (or even a stronger version of) the apolitical musical modernism of the other composers, but in fact Mengelberg diverged from their insistence that music could not be made to express any ideas. After all, in Chapter 1 we already saw that Mengelberg disagreed with Cage that music could even be experienced "for itself" without any expression of narrative or intention. After the PDE Concert, he told a reporter:

> I do not agree with the approach taken here. The pieces have little to do with the political views that are attached to it. It is very topical, and those French students are all fabulous, but the music should fit the ideas.
>
> *("Open Oog" 1968)*

In other words, he did not think that music was incapable in principle of expressing political views, just that the music on the programme that evening failed to do so. Or rather, he thought that there were more effective forms of political action than making music that communicated a political message. As he later put it: "I think you can do much more in music and be much more effective than by sticking a label on it. That's my argument with Peter Schat about this subject. He thinks that music means nothing at all" (Vuijsje 1978, 163). Mengelberg has always expressed his admiration for the Tao Te Ching, not for its spiritual or religious content, but precisely because of the way it relativizes its own message:

> When I was 11 or 12 I got hold of the Tao Te Ching, and I think that has influenced me all my life, on a very low level. I wasn't very fond of the philosophy, just the book. I thought, here we have a kind of world religion based on a little storybook. Everything you can say about Taoism is denied by the book, reduced to nonsense. It's nothing you can ever define.
>
> *(Whitehead 1998, 15)*

In fact, one of the pieces at the PDE Concert was by Mengelberg himself. *Hello, Windyboys!* is a game piece, in which the score specifies rules for a game for the musicians to play. The musicians are divided into two groups, one of which is seated inside a big inflatable dome. The two groups communicate through electronic amplification, and part of the challenge for them is to achieve a common rhythm. Once this is established, there are rules for what they can play as well as instrument-specific penalties for breaking these rules. In the programme, the audience is invited to join in when the musicians are "hopping" (which at the premiere they interpreted as just hooting through the performance when they felt like it). They are also challenged to discover the rules of the game, which is "difficult, but not impossible", and they are given a puzzle in case they get bored (Mengelberg 1968). If Mengelberg demands that "the music should fit the ideas", then this performance came closest to the playful absurdity of Provo. It did so, ironically enough, on the basis of a dismissal of political intentions, which would perhaps have suited the approach of Provo a few years earlier, but as I mentioned above, the group had since turned to participating in professional politics. As I already argued in Chapter 1, it seems again that the primary influence of Fluxus and Provo on Mengelberg's music was how it informed an aesthetic (rather than a politics) of pestering, disagreement, and confusion. Indeed, we can even interpret his piece as a commentary on the composer's actions, as it revolves around a group of musicians who are literally inside a bubble, trying to communicate with people outside (Figure 3.1).

Two years earlier, during the Maderna campaign, he had written *Omtrent een Componistenactie*, "Concerning a Composer's Campaign", which clearly

FIGURE 3.1   Three Provos disturb Mengelberg's announcement of *Hello,
Windyboys!*. The inflatable plastic dome with musicians inside
is visible in the background

Photograph by Pieter Boersma

shows that he was rather ambiguous about the group's political endeavours
from the very start (Figure 3.2). As explained in the programme note, it is
"a kind of lecture in an unknown language accompanied by photographic
slides" (Mengelberg 2012, 23). The music presents "musical equivalents" of
telephone calls and meetings, as well as quotations from pieces by composers involved in the campaign. The programme note reads like a children's
story about the "komprolists" Trunk, Woodie, and Muttermouse and their
friends in the city of Mudbubble. The piece was accompanied by a projec-
tion of slides made by Mengelberg and his wife Amy, illustrating various
scenes of the campaign through humorous collages. The piece is acknowledged to be "incomprehensible" and the audience is told that—provided
they stay awake—they can do no more than watch and listen. Like *Hello,
Windyboys!*, the piece clearly thematizes confusion and miscommunication.

FIGURE 3.2 Two of the twelve slides presented at Mengelberg's *Omtrent een Componistenactie*. To the left: Trunk (probably De Leeuw): "Right, let's write a collective manifesto" and Muttermouse (Mengelberg): "We start by spreading unrest, and then we'll see." To the right: "What a jolly good action. Very jolly. Extraordinarily jolly."

In the next project of the five composers, their most ambitious artistic project, Mengelberg would continue to play this gadfly role. Shortly after Schat and Mulisch returned from Cuba, they began work on the opera *Reconstructie*, jointly written by all composers and with a libretto by Mulisch and Belgian writer Hugo Claus, which would "underline the political conviction" of the group in even stronger terms (Figure 3.3). The opera presented an allegory of Don Giovanni as an American imperialist, who rapes Bolivia and kills her father Che Guevara (who had been killed in reality only a few months earlier). In the course of the performance, an 11-metre-high statue of Guevara as the "stone guest" is built up, who in the end returns to kill Don Giovanni (Adlington 2013, 217–218). A month before the premiere in June 1969, Schat and Andriessen once again expressed the increasingly unlikely sentiment that "music cannot be intrinsically revolutionary or counter-revolutionary" (2013, 220). Mengelberg again made attempts to undermine their serious political rhetoric:

> If I understand anything about Che Guevara, then he would be horrified about this; measuring someone's greatness by the size of his statue . . . ! In a waggish mood I'd suggested, you know what, let's give this Che thalidomide arms. Then at least the people have something to complain about.
>
> *(Koren 2005)*

In response to such remarks, Mulisch and De Leeuw initiated a Bureau for Ideological Purity, a half-serious attempt to make sure that everyone was on the same political page. Mengelberg:

> You were at liberty to laugh heartily whenever the BIP was brought up. But . . . there was a sense of, well, you shouldn't see it as just nonsense what we do here, there are some very serious aspects, something of that order.
>
> *(Ibid.)*

In fact, after the opera had been finished and there was talk of doing a follow-up production (which never took place), Mengelberg was excluded from participation.

Still, despite his relativizing stance on their political ambitions, Mengelberg continued to participate. Indeed, his doubts about the efficacy of their actions should not be taken as an indication that he was any less politically committed.

FIGURE 3.3   Dress rehearsal for *Reconstructie*, with the statue of Che Guevara as the "stone guest"

Photograph by Pieter Boersma

However, he was allergic to the overt political rhetoric of his fellow compos-ers, and also had doubts about the effectiveness of their actions. In a 1988 retrospective interview with the *Reconstructie* composers and Mulisch, he said: "I thought it was a nauseating period [. . .] Overstated expectations, hysteri-cal enthusiasm, gauchisme, without much depth" (De By and De Beer 1988). About his participation in the Maderna campaign he said: "I felt, 'Anything would be better than how it is now,' but I also thought, 'This won't help what we do here.' And it didn't" (Whitehead 1998, 69). Van Vlijmen, of whom Mengelberg said that their ideas on the period are very similar (Koopmans 1976, 28), concurred:

> The methods were borrowed from Provo. Provo also uncovered structures, which was revealing in itself, but that's as far as it went. Provo didn't really set out to change society as such. They had no contact whatsoever with the worker's struggle, with the factories and offices, with strikes. Their actions were something to laugh about—perhaps more negatively than positively. Because they diverted attention from many more fundamental problems and contradictions. And in fact Provo didn't achieve a thing, any more than our Maderna actions or Nutcracker did.
>
> *(Koopmans 1976, 33)*

Despite the Provoisms expressed in his compositions of this period, Mengelberg's continued engagement with the "more fundamental problems and contradic-tions" of musical politics is apparent in a brief exchange with Schat in the 1988 retrospective. Schat had returned to composing for traditional orchestras (including the Concertgebouw) briefly after the group had ceased their political activities, something for which Mengelberg called him out:

M: I would start an action against the Concertgebouw tomorrow, in a manner of speaking, because I don't think that anything has changed. With you I also hear more defeatism than pugnacity.

S: In what sense?

M: You are being performed in the Concertgebouw and you love that, while I think that for your pieces, and Louis' pieces, there still are no properly educated people who can play such music, let alone that such people would ever find their way into the Concertgebouw Orchestra.

S: I have no complaints about these musicians. They are fine musicians.

M: You have no complaints; I remember you used to have certain ideals about what musicians should be able to do.

S: I still do.

M: They do not meet them.
    [. . .]

S: After the Vietnam-era I said: the war is over, let's get back to business.

M: Didn't you think that was rather hyperbolic?

S: To each their own.
M: You needed strings.

(De By and De Beer 1988)

From the Notenkraker demonstration onwards, the focus of these composers increasingly turned from grand themes like their contribution to international socialism to more practical questions of the organization of musical ensembles, the founding of new institutions, and the education of a new generation of musicians. Rather than expressing their political allegiance through musical compositions and performances, they turned back to the theme that originally formed the starting point of their Maderna campaign, namely the political organization of musical practice in the Netherlands. Mengelberg, who had been rather sceptical of their activities so far, would now start to play an active role in trying to reshape the Dutch musical infrastructure, and so did many other ICP musicians. In fact, the foundation of the ICP has to be understood in the context of this broader movement for a democratization of Dutch music.

The Foundation of the ICP

The ICP was founded in late 1967, not so much as a group of performers but as a political movement. A press-release (in English) from 1972 states the aims of the organization as follows:

> The "Instant Composers Pool" (ICP) could be described as a community of interests of a number of musicians working on contemporary developments of instrumental improvisation. The formation of ICP in 1967 was stimulated by the production of a record by Han Bennink and Willem Breuker, at that time performing as the "new acoustic swing duo". Living in discord with the social aspects of their positions, some Dutch musicians, including Bennink and Breuker, decided to put alternatives into effect as regards the production of records, the organization of concerts, in short to improve their living and working conditions. Their common experiences up to that moment can be put in three points:
>
> 1.   An effective distribution of their music was hindered by the arbitrary preferences of managers, youth-leaders and kinds of organizers of concerts;
> 2.   Commercial record-companies were—and they still are—not interested in a consistent research in our field;
> 3.   Apparently society interpreted our activities as some phenomenon in the periphery of musical art.
>
> As a result of this behaviour no infra-structural provisions—neither financially nor didactically—were available.

Since its foundation ICP has worked on these points. As regards the public confrontation: some series of concerts were arranged in cooperation with clubs, cultural institutions and the like. We recall to memory the "Mozart-cyclus" by Willem Breuker's musical theatre and furthermore we refer to concerts in which among others the following foreign musicians took part: John Tchicai, Peter Brötzmann, Derek Bailey, Burton Greene, Frederic Rzewski, Evan Parker, Don Cherry and Paul Rutherford.

As far as our records are concerned: we released 10 records on ICP label. The revenues of each record appeared to be enough to form the financial basis for the production of the next record. Till August 1971 we count 10 ICP records. Not eager to deal with the commercial record-companies and this attitude being reciprocal, we do not have the disposal of the distribution-apparatus of the mass-producers. Apart from some exceptions our records are not for sale in record-shops, but are sold during concerts or by mail. Having no other links between producer and buyer, one of the consequences of this system of selling is that we can offer our records 30 to 50 percent cheaper than comparable productions released by commercial companies. As regards our efforts to come to a further integration in society: ICP supports the plan which was presented to the Dutch ministry of cultural affairs by the foundation "Jazz in Nederland". This plan contains clear proposals to get the improvised music out of its atmosphere of hobbyism by subsidizing of concerts and by taking appropriate social and didactical measures. The members of ICP have a managing influence upon the union of music improvisators: the foundation "Jazz in Nederland".

ICP is alive and kicking; we know that all our goals have not yet been achieved, however in the meantime we keep playing our music.

(Instant Composers Pool 1972)

What is immediately striking about the text is how it describes the ICP primarily as a political organization, with the aim of improving the "living and working conditions" of improvisers. On the one hand, the ICP constituted an independent record label, possibly the first of its kind in Europe. Rudy Koopmans and instrument builder Boudewijn van Grevenbroek had sponsored the release of the first recording, the *New Acoustic Swing Duo* featuring Bennink and Breuker (Bennink and Breuker 1967). The goal was to use the money made with the first record to finance the next one, and so on, representing a conscious decision to find alternatives to the commercial interests of professional record labels (Instant Composers Pool 1968). On the other hand, the ICP was to function as a sort of grassroots organization defending the interests of improvisers and organizing concerts for them to play. The "pool" element of their name meant originally that ICP concerts could feature any number of musicians who were associated with the group; sometimes specific musicians would be billed; other concerts were played by whoever happened to be available (Van den Berg 2009, 130). In a 1971 page-long article for *Oor*, the main Dutch magazine for popular music, Rudy Koopmans quoted Mengelberg:

It's about the people, not the organization. The music will also exist without the pool. The pool is just a means to an end, a community of interests of folks who through music give impromptu shape to time. This fantastic pool was founded to make such musicians filthy rich, fabulously rich, incredibly and extraordinarily wealthy.

(Koopmans 1971)

Indeed, the role of the music remains rather ambiguous in the text of the press-release. We are told not much more than that the group represents "musicians working on contemporary developments of instrumental improvisation". This might seem to indicate that the music was not itself an expression of their politics, but this was not the case. In an interview with the French *Jazz Magazine* in 1974 Mengelberg stated: "ICP is first of all a musico-political organization [. . .] All music is political, our improvised music is political, it is the continuation of our thought, of our political actions" (*Jazz Magazine* 1974, 19–20). Still, these politics were certainly not the collectivism and democratization of Provo, as their aims are clearly geared towards the specialization and professionalization of musicians, in order to get their music out of an "atmosphere of hobbyism". To reach this goal, the ICP worked together closely with some newly founded institutions to be discussed below.

The founding of the ICP, then, was a significant step in the growing sense of autonomy of the Dutch jazz scene described in the previous chapter. There is a strong similarity with the emancipatory aims of the Maderna campaign, which was still being run at the time of the ICP's foundation. Moreover, by taking matters into their own hands and founding their own institutions so as to structurally improve the situation of musicians like themselves, the ICP founders prefigured some of the actions taken by the Notenkrakers, who were similarly concerned with the self-determination of musicians. The Notenkraker demonstration, the group's most famous action, giving them the name that people commonly use to refer to them, took place in November 1969. With it, the composers returned to their concerns with the Dutch musical infrastructure, which had been the initial subject of the earlier Maderna campaign. However, rather than only a discussion about programming policies, they now had more ambitious goals, including the democratization of the Concertgebouw's governance and the self-determination of orchestral musicians. The "notenkrakers", the five composers minus Van Vlijmen but joined by many other musicians and composers, interrupted a Concertgebouw concert conducted by Haitink, playing toy instruments and handing out leaflets, to demand another debate about programming policies and the hierarchical structures of the orchestra's management (Adlington 2013, 237–238). Whereas the earlier Open Letter initiating the Maderna campaign had sought a common interest with the Concertgebouw Orchestra in continuing the orchestra's reputation earlier in the century for playing a contemporary repertoire, these leaflets directly accused it of being elitist, and functioning in the interest of the ruling classes rather than the composers (Adlington 2013, 239).

The demonstration and subsequent actions (including the occupation of the Concertgebouw administration) started a reform movement in 1970 known as the BEVEM, the Beweging voor de Vernieuwing van de Muziekpraktijk, or "movement for the renewal of musical practice" (2013, 242-250). This was a first step from the protests and demonstrations of the 1960s to taking actual political actions towards institutional reform, a development leading towards what is generally referred to as "ensemblecultuur", producing a large number of world-class Dutch music ensembles. This ensemble culture has mostly been understood as a development in contemporary composed music (see especially Schönberger 1996, but it is also implicit in Adlington's book). However, such a description diminishes the role that was played by the upcoming improvisation scene, which included the take-over by ICP musicians of the Foundation for Jazz in the Netherlands (SJN, referred to in the ICP press-release cited above) and the foundation of an improvisers' union, the BIM. In fact, between the worlds of composed and improvised music there was a considerable degree of overlap. Mengelberg himself is an obvious example, but he was certainly not the only one. Theo Loevendie, who also attended the jazz "discussion" mentioned in the previous chapter, had studied composition and clarinet at the Amsterdam Conservatory. Gilius van Bergeijk was an early ICP musician while he was studying with Kees van Baaren and Dick Raaijmakers at the Conservatory of The Hague. Rob du Bois was a classically trained pianist and autodidact composer who played piano with Breuker's ICP groups. Maarten Altena (double bass) was an early ICP member with a classical education on his instrument who would become known mainly as a composer of contemporary music later on. A generation later, with people such as Guus Janssen, Ig Henneman, Peter van Bergen, Paul Termos, Cor Fuhler, and various others, it was almost the norm rather than the exception for improvisers to be involved in contemporary music in some way, usually as composers.

Indeed, the activism of the composers throughout the 1960s had increasingly been a cross-genre affair. The Notenkraker demonstration brought together not only composers and musicians in contemporary music, but also performers in other genres who equally felt that their activities were hindered by the dominating influence of the Concertgebouw Orchestra and its programming policies. Willem Breuker was present, as were other improvising and jazz musicians (Koopmans 1982, 20; Buzelin and Buzelin 1994, 68). *Reconstructie* had featured Breuker as well as Bennink as performers. Perhaps less expected is the participation of Early Music performers, most prominently conductor and recorder player Frans Brüggen, who played a contrabass recorder solo in the opera and was also present at the Notenkraker demonstration. Rather than a lack of interest in contemporary music, Brüggen and his companions criticized the Concertgebouw Orchestra for their lack of interest in "proper" performance of eighteenth-century and earlier music, arguing that "Every note of Mozart and Beethoven that the Concertgebouw Orchestra plays is, musically speaking, a lie" (Rubinoff 2009, 7). The BEVEM was supported by performers from various genres, including Brüggen, Boy Edgar, Loevendie, Van Bergeijk, and Du Bois, and its activities included a "task force" to assess the opportunities in the Netherlands for improvising musicians, consisting of Breuker, Mengelberg, Van Manen, and Loevendie, as well as vocalist Ann Burton and pianist Loek Dikker (Adlington 2013, 247; Rusch 2016, 97–100).

Apart from the diversity in musical backgrounds and outlooks of the musicians involved, there is another important factor of these reform movements that bears pointing out. Although the rise of ensemble culture has often been portrayed as the achievement of a politically engaged young generation against a conservative establishment, this image needs to be qualified somewhat. First, as I also argued in Chapter 1, this younger generation was by no means homogeneous but was characterized by various forms of disagreements and contradictions when it came to its aims and methods of reform in Dutch musical life. Second, the "activists" did not have a carefully thought-out plan for reshaping Dutch music, but rather attempted different kinds of reform on various levels and scales, taking different opportunities as they presented themselves—that is to say, it was a somewhat improvisatory affair. This meant that some of their successes and achievements could be at odds with each other. Third, and perhaps most importantly, not only was this younger generation inherently diverse, but so was the "establishment" against which they opposed themselves, and many of their successes were in fact made possible by the fact that some of those in charge were sympathetic to their aims and wanted to collaborate in their realization.

For instance, the very emergence of the "ensemblecultuur" actually ran against the aims of the BEVEM. The Notenkraker demonstration was met by general condemnation from various orchestral musicians' unions and representatives, who disapproved of the violent methods and argued that the composers had interfered with their work and had not acted in a spirit of "collegial responsibility" (Adlington 2013, 240). In other words, they were concerned that the composers were not actively taking into account their interests as performers, whose employment depended on the performance of the classical repertoire. There was one union, however, the Nederlandse Toonkunstenaars Bond, which supported their action and also helped to found BEVEM. The initial aim of the NTB and the Notenkrakers in founding the movement was to give orchestral musicians a bigger say in the way the orchestra functioned. In a Marxist vein, the musicians were seen to be "alienated" from their product because of the orchestral division of labour (2013, 247–248). As orchestral performers made clear that they felt no need to be liberated, and as the composers were more interested in performers who actually performed their music, their attention turned from the large-scale emancipation of classical musicians to the advocacy of grassroots ensembles dedicated to contemporary music (2013, 255–256).

In fact, founding such ensembles had already been offered as a solution during the Maderna campaign by composer Ton de Leeuw (no relation to Reinbert), who was also one of the initiators of BEVEM. He had suggested that a "mobile ensemble" could be founded that could adjust to the needs of various contemporary compositions. Part of the composers' aims, however, had been to better integrate contemporary music within the programmes of the Concertgebouw, and the idea of specialized ensembles, venues, and programmes was seen as a "ghettoization" of their music. A "mobile ensemble" was precisely the kind of "ghettoization" to which the campaigners were opposed. However, in the course of the 1960s various specialized ensembles started to emerge, and already before the composers turned their full attention to founding their own ensembles, they had employed a "mobile ensemble" in the PDE Concert (Adlington 2013, 85). The foundation of the ICP as a "pool" of musicians suggests an uncertain position between these two poles. On the one hand, their aim was to improve the opportunities for all improvising musicians; on the other, their concept of a "pool" shows great similarities to the idea of a mobile ensemble for contemporary music.

In the press, the ICP was generally discussed simply as an improvising ensemble, and meanwhile the ICP members were pursuing their goals of reform through other institutions. One was the aforementioned "task force" of BEVEM. In a report presenting its findings, it established that very few musicians (only 6%) earned enough to make a living and that there were too few educational opportunities for young musicians. The task force argued that a programme for government funding should be installed to support individual musicians, noting that this had already improved the opportunities of musicians in previous years (including Mengelberg's groups and Boy Edgar's Big Band), and also that steps should be taken to integrate improvised music into conservatory curricula (Stichting Jazz in Nederland and Beroepsvereniging van Improviserende musici 1973, 9). Another was the SJN, which the ICP press-release described above as a partner in their endeavours to professionalize improvised music.

Organizing Improvised Music: SJN and BIM

Stichting Jazz Nederland had been founded in 1963 mainly for awarding the annual Wessel Ilcken prize, but had also put some effort into establishing forms of funding, however temporary and incidental. On 3 November 1970 ICP musicians Breuker, Van Manen, Peter Bennink (Han's brother), and Maarten Altena walked in during a board meeting of the SJN. In line with BEVEM's emphasis on self-determination and democratization, they demanded a stronger say of musicians in their activities, and indeed a larger role of the SJN in discussions about the social and economic situation of Dutch jazz. This "take-over" has often been described as a raid, presenting the event as emblematic of the unfolding revolution, but it is not entirely clear to what extent this really was the case. Rudy Koopmans, a good friend of the ICP musicians, was already on the SJN board, and fellow board member Michiel de Ruyter described the scene in rather colloquial terms:

Willem Breuker, Willem van Manen and a couple of other guys walked in during a meeting and said: "Guys, we'll take over your responsibilities." I thought that was fine. They got things going and I could focus on other matters.

(Van Dixhoorn 1984, 55)[1]

Mengelberg has also described the event in such terms:

I believe they went to a meeting of the Foundation for Jazz in the Netherlands and said: "All you do here is hand out awards to musicians. You'd better leave the board and put us in charge because we know how to do this." To which the others responded: "Well, gentlemen, if you think so, go ahead."

(Buzelin and Buzelin 1994, 62)

The minutes of that meeting tell a more complicated story (Stichting Jazz in Nederland 1970). First of all, Koopmans recalls elsewhere that the musicians had called him the day before to announce their arrival—which seems a dubious tactic for a "raid" (Koopmans 1972b). The musicians came in with no particular purpose, but asked why the SJN appeared to do so little for them. The board members responded that they had formulated a "jazz plan" with the aim of establishing more government support for jazz, and that they had sought collaboration with jazz musicians for putting this plan into effect, but that the musicians had never showed any interest. Van Manen, who had been personally approached by the board previously, responded that he had no interest in collaborating with representatives of the music industry. Interestingly, it was precisely the board members he singled out as representing commercial interests that were willing to offer a greater voice for musicians on the board. Ben Bunders had planned to give up his seat during that meeting anyway, and proposed it be taken by a musician, and Harm Mobach similarly offered to give up his seat if a musician was willing to take it—he had been arguing for a larger say of musicians in the workings of the organization for longer. Koopmans concurred that this was in line with the democratizing aims of their "jazz plan", and proposed that the four musicians immediately become members of the board. The musicians were sceptical, and took the willingness of the board to resign as a sign of their lack of engagement; they refused to collaborate with the foundation as it was organized at that moment. Koopmans acted as a mediator, suggesting that the current board and the musicians work together to reform the SJN and its activities, after which the musicians could take their place on the board, together with former board members Koopmans, Jaap de Rijke, and Hein van Warmerdam (Rusch 2016, 103–104). They agreed, however, that the current board should finalize the awarding of the Wessel Ilcken Prize, lest that raise any trouble between the "raiders" and the prospective winner. The winner of the 1970 prize, ironically, was Willem Breuker.

Far from a revolutionary take-over, then, the growing self-determination of improvising musicians through the SJN was achieved at the suggestion of establishment figures who were sympathetic (to some extent) to their critiques, and despite the initial reluctance of the ICP members to take part. The new SJN board, with the help of an employee of the Ministry of Cultural Affairs (and jazz enthusiast), drafted a new "jazz plan" for structural financial support from the government, consisting of a "Pool plan" and a "Venue plan". The former, obviously influenced by the ICP's way of working, would enable individual musicians to work with flexible ensembles in different settings, while the latter offered support to venues. The plan was initially rejected by the arts council, not because it was opposed to the funding of jazz, but because the process of distributing the money was unclear. To this end, the musicians founded a Union for Improvising Musicians (Beroepsvereniging van Improviserende Musici), the BIM, of which Mengelberg became the chairman—he had initially advocated that SJN become a union after the take-over, so he was a logical candidate (Koopmans 1972b). From 1971 onwards, the SJN and BIM together established a programme for the funding of improvised music, which was increasingly successful: to receive funding, a musician had to be a member of the BIM, and the SJN had a regulatory function, requesting funds and overseeing their distribution. This funding, though very modest compared to other forms of arts government, enabled the improvisation scene to flourish immensely, and the 1970s saw the foundation of countless new collectives. Furthermore, it enabled the establishment of the BIMhuis, a concert venue specialized in jazz and improvised music, in 1974.

Again, however, these achievements were partly due to a sympathetic establishment with which the musicians collaborated. The establishment of a union was to some degree a controversial step. The BEVEM campaign had been fuelled by a general critical stance towards trade unions. The Notenkraker demonstration had grown from (and in turn amplified) a general dissatisfaction with the role of the composers' union Geneco, and part of the NTB's reason to join them also had to do with their unhappiness about the way musicians' unions represented their interests. This reflected a more general perspective among the Dutch left in the 1960s, which saw trade unions ultimately as running against the interests of workers: although in the short term they defended their immediate interests against exploitation from their employers, in doing so they accommodated capitalist labour relations and thus impeded the long-term goal of overturning the capitalist system that was seen to cause this exploitation in the first place. Although the ICP's founding as an independent label and interest group fits into this broader call for self-determination among workers, the "take-over" of the SJN and the foundation of the BIM certainly saw a move towards functioning within—and thus accommodating—existing power structures.

This raises the question of how such power relations were negotiated within this community. The ICP has relied on government funding virtually throughout its existence, and would in all probability struggle to survive should this funding be discontinued. In this, it is not much different than the Willem Breuker Kollektief and various other improvising collectives in the Netherlands, or indeed the other Notenkrakers and their ensembles. Various commentators have recently questioned whether this reliance on government funding was consistent with their revolutionary actions. Richard Taruskin, writing about Andriessen, suggests that "the indulgent treatment Andriessen has received (and accepted) from the state his music ostensibly challenges has cast his musicopolitical agenda in an equivocal light: is it genuine activism, or is it just another show of radical chic?" (Taruskin 2005, 398). Loes Rusch, in her account of the political activities of improvising musicians through SJN and BIM, similarly writes: "Paradoxically, the musicians that ten years earlier had fought on the barricades for freedom, self-control, and against the estab-lished authorities, now began to secure their place within boards, councils, and committees" (Rusch 2016, 106). However, the question of political com-mitment is rather more complex than such either/or questions. The activities of avant-garde musicians could certainly not be reduced to being for or against the state and/or established authorities; their "genuine activism" was often geared precisely towards securing a place within boards, councils, and com-mittees. Their critique of the government had partly been that there was too little funding available for new forms of art, and so accepting government funds, once established, was not really a paradox at all, but consistent with their socialist views of how the state should function.

Still, of course, considering their critical perspective on the power structures inherent to the organization of traditional orchestras, and their aims of democ-ratization in Dutch musical life, it is interesting to note how they themselves negotiated their newly won positions of influence. In order to present jazz as worthy of funding, it had to be presented as having true artistic value, and the associations with popular music that it still very much had in the Netherlands had to be severed. Of course, as we saw in the previous chapter, critics had long aimed to dissociate "true jazz" from its "commercial" excesses. With the diminishing commercial popularity of jazz, in the 1960s this valorisation of jazz increasingly hinged on a presentation of jazz as art music, comparable to contemporary composed music. The ICP's description of their activities as a "contemporary development in instrumental improvisation" thus drew upon and strengthened a discourse that had been building over the course of the previous decade. Indeed, the BIM's concern with "improvising" rather than "jazz" musicians implied a particular position within the "richtingenstrijd" between traditional jazz musicians and avant-garde improvisers mentioned in the previous chapter. Within the BIM there were discussions from the very beginning as to what the nature of the organization should be—a proper union for professional musicians or an interest group for avant-garde improvisation? Mengelberg (as chairman) and treasurer Peter Bennink opted for the latter, while other board members were in favour of a general membership (Vuijsje 1972). After putting this to a vote, the members opted for general membership—Bennink left the BIM board, while Mengelberg stayed on. Still, in 1976 rumours started spreading that Mengelberg, who was in charge of negotiating with SJN (which was of course managed by close companions of his) and the ministry about funding allocation, was pushing forward his own groups and those of his friends (Schulte 1976). In 1980 these problems had still not been solved. Jazz magazine *Jazz Nu*, for the sake of clarity, published some of the correspondence between BIM, SJN, and the ministry, as well as three open letters by various BIM members, all demanding that Mengelberg step down as president, which he did (*Jazz Nu* 1980).

Meanwhile, similar internal pressures had led to a break-up in the ICP. Tensions between the three had been building: Breuker and Bennink felt that Mengelberg was lazy and that they were doing most of the work. Breuker also was increasingly developing as a composer and felt he could not rely on Mengelberg or Bennink to reliably play his compositions. The final reason for Breuker to leave the ICP in December 1973, however, had to do with the way the ICP was structured. Although the group has been initiated as a "pool", Breuker increasingly worked with a standard line-up. Mengelberg and Bennink often performed as a duo, and occasionally played in larger formations of different musicians. Breuker wanted his band members to become official members of the ICP and thus to have a say in its organization, while Bennink and Mengelberg wanted to keep the direction of the pool in their own hands (Koopmans 1974). This also had financial implications, as the funding for the ICP was distributed among the three founders to dole out to the musicians with whom they worked. As mentioned earlier, Mengelberg saw the ICP mainly as a means to improve improvisers' working conditions, not as an end in itself. With the SJN and BIM in place, Breuker probably rightly foresaw that the ICP's role had to change. The development of the ICP's musical practice, especially in the context of broader calls for democratization among the various ensembles emerging in Dutch music, thus deserves a closer look.

Democratizing Musical Practice

The democratization of music had of course been an important theme in the Notenkrakers' actions, and in the burgeoning "ensemblecultuur" this increasingly extended to musical performance practice itself. Such aims were certainly part of the ICP. For Mengelberg, more than for Breuker or Bennink, the ICP was a conscious decision to move away from the official high culture of classical, composed music. In fact, part of the reason that improvised music successfully attracted government funding was a policy of "cultuurspreiding" or spreading of culture, meaning that the cultural policy aimed to spread their funding not just regionally across the Netherlands, but also over different cultural genres, including those outside of formally recognized forms of high art (Adlington 2013, 75–80). The questioning of distinctions between high and low art was also an important aim of BEVEM. Following the example of a "Musicians for Vietnam" event a few weeks earlier, the BEVEM organized an "Inclusive Concert" in May 1970 (Adlington 2013, 248). The purpose of such a concert was explained in their press-release:

> Exclusive is: *one* sort of music; *one* sort of ensemble; the concert ritual, the sort of space, the rigid programs, the entrance fee . . . Therefore this "inclusive concert" will be defined by: collaboration with musicians and ensembles from different sectors of music (classical, pop, jazz, etc.); program assemblage based on the initiative of the participating musicians; informal use of the space; free entry.
>
> *(Quoted in Adlington 2013, 248–249)*

These inclusive concerts were so popular that they started to be emulated on a large scale.[2] They testify to the turn that BEVEM was making from the emancipation of orchestral musicians to the development of alternative forms of musical practice.

Emblematic of this change in orientation among Dutch composers was orchestra De Volharding (Perseverance), founded in 1972 by Andriessen and Breuker. De Volharding was to be a fully democratic collective, consisting of both classically trained musicians and improvisers, where all musicians had an equal voice in discussions about repertoire and performance venues, there would be no conductor, and Andriessen and Breuker would be performers in the group themselves. *De Volharding*, Andriessen's first composition for the group, premiered at an inclusive concert. Drawing on the ideas of Hanns Eisler, they played outside of traditional concert venues, on the streets and at political demonstrations, presenting a combination of socialist workers' songs (including Eisler's *Solidarity Song*) and contemporary compositions, which could be either arrangements of existing work or new music especially composed for the group (Adlington 2004; see also Buzelin and Buzelin 1994, 67–71). The goal was to attract working-class audiences and educate them musically, subverting the associations of contemporary composition with socio-economic elites. The democratization of De Volharding, then, was both internal, in that it applied to the social organization of the ensemble itself, and external, in that it attempted to open up difficult music for non-specialized audiences.

Similar developments were taking place in improvised music. Since the late 1960s, various workshops had been organized, which became increasingly popular during the 1970s.[3] In these workshops, musicians learned various improvisation strategies, as well as to write their own music (Bouman 1978, 21–23). Herman de Wit, perhaps the most prominent advocate of workshops for improvisation, had formerly led a big band of the youth movement of the Dutch communist party (Tra 1978a, 14). He said: "They [these workshops] are also musical cultural politics of the utmost importance, these open clubs, because we don't just talk about music, but also about one's political position, one's musical-political position" (Bouman 1978, 44). The form of collective music-making that was practised at these workshops had political connotations for him:

> We have to fight the soloist concept, the ego trip, which is disastrous. Life-threatening for our music [. . .] It is a totally new mentality, because we all have to work together [. . .] You get rid of the quartet state of mind, the quintet-style playing, like "we can do anything better than you"; that is what we need to avoid.
>
> *(Ibid.)*

Small orchestras such as the Boventoon Orchestra and the Oktopedians were formed at these workshops, and like De Volharding they would play at political events and demonstrations, as well as inclusive concerts (1978, 59-61).[4]

As we saw in Chapter 1 in the case of his *Lunchconcert*, Breuker had attempted to find new ways of reaching the audience before. During this time with the ICP, he organized various street concerts to bring his music into the public sphere. His theatrical work was similarly informed by such an egalitarian concern. Already in 1965 he said:

> It's quite understandable that many people don't like jazz, because nothing happens. Musically something happens, but you have to have listened to the music for some years to experience that. I think eighty percent of the audience is just there to tap their feet and bob their heads [. . .] For that eighty percent there has to be something visual on stage, a kind of musical theatre.
>
> *(Vuijsje 1965, 85)*

Breuker's theatrical works were light-hearted and farcical compared to the absurdist chaos of Mengelberg and Schippers' productions. Most if not all of his theatre pieces were allegories about arts policy, funding distribution, the Dutch jazz scene, and political hypocrisy and corruption (Buzelin and Buzelin 1994, 71–76, 89–92). His music, especially compared to his first ICP recording with Bennink, quickly became much more accessible, using clear rhythms and metres, triadic harmony, and attractive melodies. Although solos could still be quite radical, part of Breuker's soloing style (and that of his other Kollektief musicians) was characterized by its theatrical nature. Drawing on the ideas and music of Eisler, Weill, and Ennio Morricone, he aimed for innovative music that nonetheless had a direct popular appeal (1994, 135-150). A press-release for the Willem Breuker Kollektief (which, incidentally, antedates its foundation to 1971, when Breuker was still a member of the ICP) notes that "the result of their collective efforts is an approach to music which combines great originality with a definition and clearness that guarantees accessibility to a wide audience" (Willem Breuker Kollektief, n.d.).[5]

The irony of the name "Willem Breuker Kollektief", founded in 1974, was not lost on anyone. This "collective" had an undisputable leader, even though it had been Breuker himself to insist that the ICP should have a name that did not contain any of the founders' names.[6] As mentioned above, Breuker was increasingly developing his compositional style and needed musicians who were willing to play his compositions as he intended. Bennink was not: "I don't want to leave one fixed point to arrive at the next fixed point. I like to take the plunge, and the struggle to get to the other end" (Buzelin and Buzelin 1994, 78). Breuker himself acknowledged his change in perspective when it came to the democratization of musical practice. In 1975 he said: "I am authoritarian. I like it when things happen the way I think they should. Others can be bothered by that" (1994, 89). In December 1974, Breuker had also left De Volharding, fed up with the internal political discussions and the need to play at every political demonstration. In fact, both De Volharding and the workshop orchestras were quickly realizing how difficult it was to combine high musical quality with fully democratic and egalitarian politics. For the improvisation workshops this was a particularly pressing concern; as the abilities of the participating musicians increased, discussions arose about whether the workshops should stay as open and noncommittal as they had been or whether they should demand more discipline from the participants to achieve better musical results (Bouman 1978, 65–70). A similar debate was held in De Volharding, which after some internal political conflicts resolved to focus less on political performances and more on concert performances (Koopmans 1982, 58–64). This was not only for party-political reasons, but also because the orchestra members felt that the political performances stood in the way of the "development of an individual musical identity" (1982, 64). As the orchestra improved and composers started writing more complicated music for it, De Volharding decided that they would even employ a conductor.

Breuker's firmer leadership role in his Kollektief was meant not just to advance his own artistic development, but also explicitly to make his music more accessible to a larger group of people, and so to make it more egalitarian. In other words, the clash between Breuker and his two co-founders can be seen not so much as one between democracy and authoritarianism, but rather between opposing views of musical democratization.

Mengelberg's use of tonal, dance-like material such as "Die Berge", discussed in the previous chapter, also includes very accessible musical material. In fact, in the 1970s, Mengelberg's compositional style (also for ensembles and orchestras outside the ICP) was radically changing. _Dressoir_, for instance, written for De Volharding in 1977, is a pastiche of polkas, marches, sarabandes, can-cans, and other traditional dance forms with a very folksy character ("Die Berge" itself also makes an appearance). Compared to his Cageian works of a decade earlier, this really is a radical departure, and this was not just intended to subvert the modernist standards of contemporary free jazz, but similarly of classical composition. As I argued in the previous chapter, it also was an attempt to develop ways of improvising beyond the frameworks of jazz. It was not intended, as Breuker's use of accessible musical material was, to reach audiences. Recall Mengelberg's statement, quoted in Chapter 1, that he was not in principle against elites if these were made up of a small group of specialists. In other words, he saw no need to open up the ICP to a general audience. In a report about a festival for the tenth anniversary of the ICP, he acerbically describes a performance by Keith Rowe and Cornelius Cardew, ridiculing their attempt to make music to support the working class:

> It appears that the improvising ambitions have made way for a concept of "revolutionary music", which does not exclude improvisation, but aims primarily at creating awareness in the people of an anti-capitalist or socialist attitude. A highly laudable concept, made concrete by Cardew by [. . .] performing a revolutionary song composed on the spot, which proffered to the audience that in the battle against the capital, there is nothing to lose and everything to gain [. . .] I hope it does well in the charts, so that the people actually may be reached.
>
> *(Mengelberg 2012, 59)*

Bennink had similar ideas. A newspaper article from 1972 quotes Bennink as saying:

> We formed a pool of musicians with no other intention than to improvise musically in a way of which we personally approve [. . .] We do not see it as our duty to bring the music to the people, that is something that happens automatically if people notice that you enjoy playing.
>
> *(Friesch Dagblad 1972)*

In one of our conversations, he recalled:

> My brother said the other day: "Misha and you were not very social, Willem was social. He thought about social issues." We never did, we just thought in forms. Not even so much about ourselves, but just . . . that's what you have to do, that's art or something, whatever that means.[7]

Certainly, democratization was an important aspect of the ICP's performance practice. In 1977, in an interview with Rudy Koopmans, Mengelberg stated:

> I have been working on a democratization of music itself for years, it is essential [. . .] Delegating decisions to performing musicians is an aspect of it. Such delegation is only a weak form. In the Instant Composers

Pool the distinction between composer, musician and conductor has virtually disappeared.

(Koopmans 1977a, 208)

However, neither Mengelberg nor Bennink was keen on aligning their music with politics as explicitly as De Volharding or the workshop orchestras—moreover, as I discussed in the previous chapter, their performances as a duo were virtually predicated on the competitive clash of egos criticized by De Wit. Although they would later become involved in teaching improvisation, and Mengelberg had a job at the Sweelinck Conservatory in Amsterdam, the ICP never aimed to fulfil such an educative function. Clearly, Bennink and Mengelberg held on to a certain modernist outlook that put the development of their musical art over the expectations and understanding of their audiences, or the broader participation of larger groups of improvisers in the ICP. However, as I stressed earlier, this was not a modernism that saw music as entirely removed from social issues. For one, Mengelberg was not wholly unconcerned with his audience. The following exchange is from an interview with the duo by Bert Vuijsje, published in 1978:

M: I have a number of hypotheses, about which I can elaborate but which are not of much use to anyone. Like the hypothesis that music represents a mode of thought and as such socially is a reflection of something or that it may even have some influence.

V: With such a hypothesis you quickly get to tedious words like engagement.

M: Yes, say it! Let's have it!

V: Well, at the moment the number of artists that claim to be engaged is countless.

M: Innumerable! Immense!

V: How do you see your own position in that crowd?

M: I'm under the impression I'm singing my part with this choir. If [Han and I] play together our approach is so destructive with regard to all sorts of formalities, that we're dealing with a musical expression that immediately informalizes things, one code after the other is blown up, and perhaps replaced by new codes that are subsequently questioned—that should in one way or another, with people who are sensitive to it, lead to the thought: yes, I always do things this way or that, but I could do it very differently. I thought that may have a social purpose, because if everything just stays the way it is now, then that becomes disastrous before too long. Yes, this is extremely general and vague.

V: It's about things that are implicit in your music, not about explicit verbal messages.

M: I called a piece Vietcong once.

B: The name alone got us ten thousand gigs.

M: But the name could have been Aunt Betty.

(Vuijsje 1978, 162)

As is clear from this exchange, however, Mengelberg was not quite sure what the political efficacy of the ICP's music could be. In a 1977 interview with Koopmans he reflected on their influence on the Dutch musical infrastructure in the past decade: "Hopeless. At most you could say: the class struggle needs to be fought, and the result should be a classless society. What happens in the meantime however . . . " (Koopmans 1977c). Koopmans responds that they might make some music in the meantime. "Sure, but as to how that connects to anything, I am more and more confused. I don't have the impression anything I do contributes to this battle" (Ibid.). He repeated that the combination of different musical idioms might stimulate a flexible mind in the listener, which should be a good thing. In 1978, Mengelberg stated:

> ICP's direct social intervention in the improvisation seems to be over, unless there should be developments necessitating fresh action on our part. People are beginning to realize that improvised music can be stimulated by the community in the same way as symphonic music, and we now have the musicians' union we wanted ten years ago. This means that concentrating on the development of music has again become our main objective.
>
> *(Tra 1978b, 8)*

Mengelberg's attitude at this point is similar to that of many other musicians and composers of his generation at the end of the 1970s. Many of them were returning to a concern with music for its own sake rather than as a means to engage in politics (Adlington 2013, 318–319). Partly, this resulted from a disappointment about the efficacy of their political and musical projects. However, as Mengelberg indicates, there was also a sense in which some of the most important short-term goals had been achieved.

The Pragmatics of Composition

The development of "music", however, was by no means wholly distinct from politics. Not only did Mengelberg speculate that the iconoclastic musical interaction between him and Bennink might have a beneficial effect on potential listeners, but he also considered music itself primarily in terms of the interaction between performers. The duo's way of working, where different stylistic allusions are combined and alternated, fits in with the general popularity of neoclassical quotation and allusion in composed music in the Netherlands from the late 1960s onwards. The work of Charles Ives was particularly influential.[8] However, improvising rather than composing such collages sets the ICP apart from the aims of Andriessen and De Leeuw. Contrary to the usual understanding of neoclassicism, and indeed the aims of Ives himself, De Leeuw and Andriessen did not employ such quotation and allusion for their musical connotations, but held on to their notion of musical autonomy. Indeed, as Adlington describes, through the use of an abundance of quotations, they tried to achieve a "stylelessness" in their music (Adlington 2013, 203–217). In what may be understood as an early postmodern gesture, they tried to avoid authorial intent through an endless play of signifiers. Mengelberg clearly had different aims with his style quotations. In the interview with Bert Vuijsje mentioned above, after Mengelberg puts forward the idea that the "informalizing" approach of the duo may encourage flexibility of mind in the listener, Vuijsje questions their use of quotations:

V: When you suddenly play a Schubertian passage, that does evoke a world of meanings.

M: Yes, but the same thing happens in conversations when you refer to something to make a point. You can say that they are quotations, but there is a kind of literature that constantly uses quotations and that is scholarly literature, with continual footnotes. That is frequently the most tedious kind of literature, indeed it's not really literature at all. The quotation itself barely has any literary force. I almost never cite literally. I make style quotations, and usually in such a way that it is clear that *I* am citing, and that I am citing *wrongly*. I feel no need to just play a tidy piece of Schubert. In a quotation I use what I find relevant at that moment [. . .] When I'm playing something and I feel it's a futile enterprise to continue, then I refer to a stereotype from the classical repertoire at my disposal, which has the same futile qualities. That usually clears things up, at least for myself. It helps me to go back to a point that perhaps had more possibilities for development.

(Vuijsje 1978, 163)

The significance of allusions in the ICP Duo is primarily on the level of musical practice, affording possibilities for creative interaction rather than considerations of meaning or authorial intent. The meaning of allusions becomes pragmatic rather than semantic. This ties into matters discussed in the conclusions to Chapters 1 and 2. It brings to mind Mengelberg's idea of improvisation being an everyday activity; it is not a matter of pure, unmediated expression, but rather always happens within a certain context, according to a specific aim. Like the bricolage of Fluxus performances, for Mengelberg improvisation does not consist in letting go of any pre-given forms or structures, but occurs precisely in the development of given musical material. "Free" or "non-idiomatic" improvisations are, in that regard, oxymorons. When discussing his use of stylistic allusions, Mengelberg suggests that certain musical materials can have certain implications for the process of musical interaction, much like materials in Schmit's jar or a specific kind of typewriter might influence the meaning of his poetry.

I briefly bring these matters back into focus in order to make clear how the ICP's performance practice might be understood against the background of the political considerations discussed in this chapter. After Breuker left the

ICP, Mengelberg started to work on organizing a regularly performing group of musicians rather than a loose "pool" of improvisers. It was at this time that Mengelberg was making the first steps towards the ICP Tentet, which was the precursor to the ICP Orchestra (the name used from 1980 onwards) that forms the main subject of the second part of this book—the "tentet" is featured on two recordings from the late 1970s (ICP Tentet 1977, 1979). For this orchestra, Mengelberg started to write an extensive repertoire for them to play. Although he had always written some material for his groups, these compositions now started to play a much larger role in their performances. This shift in performance practice was certainly noticed by reviewers, who generally praised the new direction of the group—since Breuker had left the ICP, most concert reviews had been quite critical, wondering if the group still had a future. Koopmans, always happy to advertise for the ICP, wrote that one of their 1979 concerts would be considered "legendary" in the future, for the way in which the compositions provided some coherence and variety, while still leaving it entirely up to the performers how to play them (Koopmans 1979). This new way of working also required a stronger leadership role from Mengelberg. In an interview from 1997, he describes this process:

> In the beginning we played wild music, without rules. Fun, but there was little commitment. I soon started to work on making this constellation sound "good". With some people, it turned out to be difficult to get any further. Some musicians were good improvisers, but could not really deal with the written material. Let alone that they could engage with the musical ideas. To prevent all pieces from sounding the same, I had to find some new people.
>
> *(Polling 1997)*

Such a way of working might seem to turn against the earlier aim of democratization, to make the distinction between composer, musician, and conductor disappear. For Mengelberg, however, what was essential about his way of working was that musicians could engage with the written material entirely on their own account, without regard for prescribed ways of playing them or his intentions as a composer (paradoxically, thereby fulfilling his intentions as a composer).

> I try to create conditions such that other people can function in the kinds of landscapes that I imagine. My pieces are nothing but starting points for the members of the orchestra to come up with their own ideas. I have no other ambition but to take care that they are in a position to do things that are nice and interesting—things that do then stand on their own.
>
> *(Ibid.)*

As opposed to the more anarchistic approach that characterized the early years of the ICP, Mengelberg now took charge of the group, writing compositions for them and leading regular rehearsals, but with an explicit democratic aim of ensuring equal and autonomous participation by all musicians.

An article from 1979 for the *Neue Zeitschrift für Musik* may be regarded as his most explicit theoretical statement on this problem, and perhaps on improvisation in general. Although it is certainly not without its ambiguities and absurdities—this is the text from which the quote on the "socio-popular simplifications" of the connections between race and class was drawn in the previous chapter—it does attempt to put Mengelberg's views on improvisation in a broader, explicitly political context. He discusses the fixation of musical form in industrial capitalism in order to turn music into an article of consumption—something he sees exemplified in popular music hit songs. He also notes that the impact of colonialism can be to similarly fix and formalize a culture's music as a "musical museum piece", mentioning the fixation of Gamelan music under Dutch colonial rule as a specific example (Mengelberg 1979b, 258). Still, he does not oppose such formalization in principle:

> The question is not: can we detect some kind of formalization, but: what has been formalized and how? [. . .] One could say: the goal is "good" music—it does not matter how it comes to be. But that is just the thing, the quality of music is inseparable from its coming into being—that is, with both method and context.
>
> *(1979b, 259)*

It is at this point that he mentions jazz as an improvised music, and as an anti-racist expression, and his uncertainty about the relation of black power to Marxist thought should thus not only be understood as uncertainty about the relation of European improvisation to American improvisation (as highlighted in the last chapter), but about the way in which musical performance and its division of labour connects to a political context more generally.

Interestingly, Mengelberg approaches the problem of the division of labour in musical performance from the perspective of a *composer* rather than an improviser, whom he notes would not have to deal with this dilemma. He writes:

> Delegating musical ideas to performers can serve a purpose—subordination, however, is in that case a fact [. . .] For many composers this dilemma does not arise at all. It is simply how things are. What else are all these fantastic interpreters, soloists and musicians going to do but perform compositions? Dead and living composers compete for their interest. The division between musical impulse and performance practice is for such composers a given of the creative process. Just like technology has given us washing machines and televisions, of which we do not need to know their inner workings in order to use them. So the composer employs performers without asking them whether or not this fixed role-playing

game of composition meets with their approval. It's all part of the same thing—washing machines and performing musicians—why improvise, when there are such clever solutions at hand [. . .] For me, however, the case is still more complex. Methods and results are by no means congruent. When in his time the composer Karl H.S. let his time pass by way of pseudo-scientific speculations about a pitch-duration continuum, this resulted in a wind quintet that did not essentially distinguish itself from the serialist style of its Darmstadt environment. Nothing wrong with that, but as I said, methods do not guarantee results. Quite the opposite. Misunderstandings on all compositional levels characterize my experiences with music from all times and places.

(1979b, 259)

In his Marxist reading of music history, compositions have become articles of consumption, produced and standardized as finished objects, to be played by interchangeable performers. His compositions are in that sense an attempt at subverting this commodity status of compositions, bringing the moment of creation back from the moment of writing to that of performance. Mengelberg's critique of Stockhausen and his famous essay on "How Time Passes" echoes similar critiques by Fluxus artists, for whom the limited efficacy of such intricate compositional methods in Darmstadt was also a point of contention. Dick Higgins had written: "No matter how diverse the notations look, the performance always comes out the same [. . .] [T]he number of roads they take to get to the same place is perfectly incredible" (D. Higgins 1964, 44). He particularly criticizes the neglect of the musical result in performance:

> In all the copious quotes in Die Reihe, in all the precise analyses of Stockhausen and Pousseur (et al, et al, et al) nobody ever questions the situational or philosophical basis of anything or any piece. All attacks, or the critiques, or the praises, are always on the basis of the means used to reach an ignored end.
>
> *(1964, 45)*

For Mengelberg, this relation between means and ends obviously also had a political significance. During the 1970s, he had been the artistic director of STEIM, the studio for electro-instrumental music, which had been set up by the Notenkrakers plus Dick Raaijmakers and Konrad Boehmer to provide the electronics for the PDE Concert as well as *Reconstructie* (of which Mengelberg had been in charge) (Mengelberg 1978, 17). What distinguished STEIM from other institutions for electronic music in the Netherlands was the emphasis on live music-making. Within a few years this turned into a more radical aim to include technology within a wider vision of musical performance as a democratic social practice. Emblematic of their ideas is the invention of the cracklebox, a small portable synthesizer where the musician completes the electric circuit by putting their fingers on the contacts attached to the top (Waisvisz n.d.). The inventor was Michel Waisvisz, who can be heard playing the instrument on several ICP recordings. Apart from the idea that musician and instrument formed a kind of unity, the cracklebox more simply involved a gesture of decommodification, as its development came about by hacking synthesizers, which were increasingly standardized and made circuit experimentation increasingly difficult (Mengelberg 1978, 19). Mengelberg describes this development with a familiar metaphor:

> The end product of pre-programmed sound synthesis is analogous to that of fully automatic cameras, washing machines, television sets or what have you; nothing can go wrong, expect in the case of a composer attempting to go beyond the bounds of predesignated response. For STEIM, an alternative, however makeshift, had to be developed: the criterion for STEIM equipment was that both "possible" and "impossible" uses of it could be controlled and exploited.
>
> *(Ibid.)*

When Mengelberg stated that misunderstandings on all levels characterize his experience with music, he was not just being facetious, but expressing an ideal of composition that acknowledges the role of the unexpected in performance. To use the terms I introduced in the conclusion to Chapter 1, it is a form of composition that approaches the creative process of performers in terms of bricolage rather than engineering.

Conclusion

As has been shown over the course of the previous three chapters, instant composition was a result of a complex negotiation of different influences, and as such it is many things at once. It is a term that valorised improvisation as a serious form of musical art. It is a Fluxus-inspired reconceptualization of musical performance. It is a Provo-inspired slogan signifying the possibility of alternative forms of social interaction. It is a way to creatively engage with the constraints that make musical expression possible. It is an attempt at formulating an alternative method to jazz improvisation at a time when European improvisers were looking for their own ways of doing things. It is an attempt to rethink and subvert the traditional composer–performer hierarchy inherent in western art music.

In the second part of this book, I will take a step back from the different meanings that have historically emerged around the concept in order to turn to an ethnographic investigation of the ICP Orchestra. In describing the practice of instant composition as crystallized in the orchestra at the end of

Mengelberg's life, we will see that many of the historical considerations above did not play a significant role in the practice of the group in the early 2010s. Still, this closer analysis of their creative processes will show the significance of Mengelberg's thought to theories of creative and social interaction in musical performance today.

Notes

1 Strangely, De Ruyter is not mentioned as a board member in the minutes.
2 Theo Loevendie organized similar concert series under the name STAMP—Stichting Alternative Muziekpraktijk, or foundation for an alternative musical practice (Schönberger 1996, 166–168; Andriessen 1996, 9). Reinbert de Leeuw organized "rondom" ("around" or "roundabout") concerts, combining different musical genres around a central theme (Koopmans 1977b, 43).
3 Theo Loevendie and Nedly Elstak had been organizing such workshops together since 1967, Breuker organized workshops from 1969 to 1970, and in 1972 Herman de Wit began organizing workshops in Amsterdam. Niko Langenhuijsen was an important figure in the organization of workshops in Tilburg in the south of the Netherlands (Rusch 2007, 41).
4 Bouman mentions an anti-apartheid meeting supporting the ANC, manifestations for social housing, an event of the Dutch Communist Party, and demonstrations against the atom bomb.
5 This popular accessibility was praised by composer and critic Konrad Boehmer, who was very critical of most of the political actions described in this chapter, but who wrote an essay on Breuker portraying him as the saviour of modern Dutch music, writing that "his music for the people is music for a potentially intelligent mass audience. It is not written for a stupid common people (which does not exist), nor for a stupid elite (which certainly does exist)" (Boehmer 1971).
6 Han Bennink, interview with the author, 3 January 2012.
7 Han Bennink, interview with the author, 3 January 2012.
8 Reinbert de Leeuw had published a book and several articles about Ives, De Volharding played pieces by Ives, and Andriessen, who had studied with Berio after finishing at the conservatory, repeatedly expressed his admiration for Ives. All three founders of the ICP hold him in high regard, even Bennink, who does not usually listen to composed music. In Whitehead's account of the Amsterdam jazz scene he is possibly the most frequently mentioned non-Dutch composer.

PART II
Beyond Jazz Practice

4

THE ONTOLOGY OF INSTANT COMPOSITION

From its foundation onwards, the ICP has committed to developing a performance practice exploring the interstices between improvisation and composition. Since the emergence of the ICP Orchestra in the mid-1970s, this musical practice has revolved particularly around a repertoire of notated material composed by Mengelberg. These pieces show a broad stylistic diversity and they include various forms of indeterminacy to create different opportunities for improvisatory creativity: there are arrangements of jazz standards, graphic scores, game pieces, and small ideas to use as a basis for further improvisation, as well as more elaborate compositions such as theatrical songs and even a fully composed fugue. Moreover, not only do these pieces construct different situations for musicians to improvise *in* or *on* them, the musicians can also improvise *with* them as they make transitions between pieces, interrupting and combining them in various ways. That is to say, they don't just establish structures within which to improvise, but the establishment of such structures is itself one of the ways in which the ICP improvises. A given ICP performance is usually an improvised collage of the different pieces in their repertoire.

Around 2000, Mengelberg stopped composing—the latest composition I have is dated 1999, although he did not date all of his compositions consistently. In a 2005 documentary about his life and work, he explained this decision as follows:

> The reason was that I was curious to know if we could finally do what we wanted to do in the seventies. That is, to improvise. To not be dependent on songs, pieces, outside inspirations. You'd think we'd be able to do that by now. Those are the ideals behind the Ornette Coleman Double Quartet. They still are. Those are the ones. The difference is that, back then, there were no solutions, and nowadays there are, for some reason.
>
> *(Dekker 2008)*

Some musicians in the group felt that Mengelberg may already have been suffering from dementia when he stopped composing, so his reasoning may not be entirely truthful. Nonetheless, this is a significant statement, because it testifies to Mengelberg's particular understanding of improvisation. After he stopped composing, the ICP did not cease to play his compositions; they started reusing old material they had not played for a while, while other musicians in the group increasingly composed material for the group. When Mengelberg says they are now ready to improvise, this is clearly not intended to mean that they will stop playing his compositions. Rather, it means that they have developed a certain performance practice and a dexterity with the material that allows them to negotiate with it on their own terms, rather than constantly having to learn to play new material.

Ab Baars indicated that he sees this acceptance of the product within the process of improvisation, the integration of compositional elements within improvisatory practices, as a central aspect of Dutch improvised music:

> The first generation of improvisers in the Netherlands contained many trained composers [. . .] And those are people that are concerned with shaping things, how to create length with a restricted set of given ideas, and are very conscious of the importance of form, of creating structure in something given. I think that is a hallmark of improvised music [here] [. . .] and in the ICP you hear this very well.[1]

Thomas Heberer described the two terms in a way that is very similar to Mengelberg's statements about this issue. When I asked what he thought about Mengelberg's idea that composition and improvisation are not categorically different, he answered:

> Well, it's all music. I don't see much difference, because composition is also improvisation, but slower and you can get rid of mistakes. But it is essentially the same, also in improvisation it should *make sense*, you know. And improvisation should not be diminished by the fact that it's done like it is, and you have an additional advantage that . . . creating in the moment has a certain element of excitement that sometimes is very difficult to get from music that is entirely written. Both have advantages and disadvantages, but I don't think there is a significant difference between the two.[2]

Both Baars and Heberer show a pragmatic approach to the distinction between improvisation and composition, and the use of written material in an improvisatory performance practice. In this chapter, we will get a general idea of how this plays out in the practice of the ICP. It forms an ethnographic account of their approach to performance and their ideas on composition and improvisation, and how these challenge our usual understanding of these terms.

The ICP's musical practice developed over the course of the group's history. It changed with a growing repertoire, changing performance contexts, and changing line-ups, and it has developed further again since my fieldwork with the group. As Heberer told me:

> The strategies that the ICP incorporates have not been invented by a composer. They have not been invented by Misha, they have developed. And the development started forty years ago. So the way the ICP operates now is the result of thinking about certain musical problems for decades And both Misha and Han . . . I don't think they had a vision beforehand, I think Misha had certain ideas about blending different aesthetics, from early on, but he didn't know how to get there, and he didn't have the musicians to do this.[3]

We have previously seen the cultural and historical context in which these ideas emerged. The aim of developing a way of working in which notated compositions could be participants in a non-hierarchical performance practice rather than dominating frameworks was a response to a variety of historical developments in music, art, and contemporary politics in the Netherlands and abroad. Developing this practice within the group, as Heberer points out, was not just an implementation of ideas, but similarly a historical process, and the result of social, collaborative experimentation.

As sociologists Robert Faulkner and Howard Becker have argued, with reference to the standards repertoire of jazz, the concept of repertoire is best understood not as a canonical list of pieces, but as "something continuously made and remade as people acquire, exchange, learn, and teach the relevant elements" (Faulkner and Becker 2009, 194). Repertoire is thus not a stable set of objects, but a reciprocal process of negotiation between the musical material and the creative skills of musicians, as well as the social contexts in which these are performed. The ICP repertoire is obviously shared amongst a much smaller group of musicians than the jazz repertoire, but the same reciprocity is key to understanding it and its relation to performance practice. The pieces mediate the creative interaction between the musicians, which in turn reshapes these pieces, as they are rearranged or deconstructed in performance.

Compared to the jazz repertoire, however, the ICP repertoire foregrounds the materiality of their notations. Musicians usually learn the jazz repertoire from playing along with recordings, from fellow musicians, from lead sheets in Fake or Real Books, or even in the course of performance itself when participating in a jam session. In any case, although for larger groups arrangements might be especially written, the physical presence of notated repertoire is usually not very relevant to the musical performance. As we shall see, however, for the ICP's musical practice this presence of the written music is very important to their approach to performance—and not because they are always playing "from" the notation as we might imagine classical musicians do, but because it is essential to their particular form of improvisation.[4] This sheds another light on the reciprocity between skills and repertoire identified by Faulkner and Becker: in the practices they describe, musicians learn harmonic and melodic skills as they learn and remember the chord schemes and melodies of pieces in the repertoire, while in the ICP this reciprocity is mediated by the material presence of notations.

The practice of the ICP therefore demands a reconsideration of the terms "notation" and "improvisation", which form basic categories for describing musical performance, and so for how we understand and appreciate the creativity of musicians. We tend to categorize musical performance either as the creation of music in the course of performance, or as the reproduction of a "work", an ideal piece of music created before the performance. With ICP performances, audiences often wonder which "parts" are improvised and which are written down. Phrased like that, however, the question is not really answerable, as it assumes that the two categories are mutually exclusive. Such matters are ontological, as they concern the type of things music can *be*.

The ICP Repertoire

The ICP repertoire, as a collection of physical objects, consists of big folders carried around by each of the orchestra's ten musicians. These folders contain around 150 to 200 printed compositions each. Most of these were handwritten (in very clear musical handwriting) on staff paper and then copied, although some show signs of having been copied quickly by hand, with sketchy notes and hand-drawn staves. When a new musician joins the group, they learn to play the most frequently performed pieces through a series of rehearsals, copying these pieces in the course of them to start their own folder. Although they form part of the physically distributed memory of the group, these folders constitute a leaky archive. No one folder is "complete", and each folder contains pieces missing in others, or doubles of the same pieces. Moreover, pages or parts may be missing from pieces, and pages may be stained or torn. Before each concert, the group makes copies of missing pages, which is how I came by most of my own folder. As these pages have been copied again and again, their resolution has faded, and because of hasty copying titles and even bars and systems have fallen off the page. This already says much about the way in which these pieces inform the group's approach to improvisation, as missing notes have to be guessed or improvised, outdated or missing instrumentations have to be adapted to the current line-up, and signs of which the meaning has long been forgotten have to be given a new purpose. Usually such adaptations happen briefly before or during a performance. Sometimes forgotten pieces are discovered in the back of these folders, which are then brought back into the set lists, and in fact some of the musicians have a large collection of old pieces at home that they do not carry around in their folders, but that they sometimes bring to rehearsals to see if they are worth playing again.

Hence, these folders are constantly changing, just like the repertoire has changed over time. The nature of the ICP repertoire in their earliest period is somewhat unclear. Both Breuker and Mengelberg had composed work before the ICP, including jazz pieces and experimental compositions, but whereas Breuker kept on composing for his ICP groups, most of Mengelberg's recordings sound freely improvised. Still, there is some evidence that he was aiming to integrate improvised and composed material from the start, and not just with a piece like "Die Berge Schützen die Heimat". I have already mentioned the idea of "Africanizing the twelve-tone row", which Mengelberg described as "Taking a small amount of musical material and subjecting it to all kinds of manipulation: shrinking it, blowing it up, retrograde, inversion, multiplication" (Whitehead 1998, 49). Evan Parker, who played with the ICP around 1970, told me:

> Misha had some pieces about . . . probably twelve-tone rows broken into three boxes of four tones, four boxes of three tones, three or four, I don't know. I can't remember exactly how it worked, but they weren't 2-5-1s, let's put it that way.[5]

Parker's reference to the standard harmonic building blocks of jazz suggests that they were looking for ways to structure improvisation beyond the traditional model of jazz. Breuker speaks of the time when he and Mengelberg had just met, shortly before the founding of the ICP:

> Misha came over to my place one afternoon, brought his music, mostly graphic stuff, and I showed him my notes, and we tried to play. That was the beginning. Very small ideas, maybe just a couple of bars, then you can improvise from that, then we go on to the next phrase, and so on, and maybe combine them. Discover the music.
>
> *(Whitehead 1998, 37)*

The use of such "small ideas"—short pieces, graphic scores, pitch-class sets, tone rows—marks a first attempt at integrating notated and improvised material, while the combination and juxtaposition of such ideas foreshadows some of the later working methods.

An example of such a "small idea" is "Where is the Police?", written in (or just before) 1970 (Figure 4.1).[6] It opens with a kind of hunting call voiced in a simple three-part harmony, which resolves to a marching rhythm on the dominant, played in unison. This rhythm is repeated and serves as a background for a solo. Another hunting call can serve as a transition to a new solo over

FIGURE 4.1 "Where is the Police?"

Used with permission

the same rhythm, before the rhythm is played finally on the tonic (most of the pieces that will be discussed can be heard on one or more of the ICP's recordings). In practice, the dominant and tonic rhythmic ostinati may be alternated behind the same soloist, or the hunting calls may be repeated more often. Such a small piece can be introduced into a free improvisation to go in a new direction, and with such a clearly outlined tonal and rhythmical framework it serves as a clear background to a soloist, which may also be a challenge to break out of the clearly demarcated form. Various other pieces in the repertoire work similarly. "Tuinhek" (Garden Fence) (Figure 4.2), for instance, similarly opens with two loud calls, but then goes into a more complex rhythm than the marching rhythm of "Where is the Police?". As this rhythm is not repeated, a performance of "Tuinhek" will usually feature more open space, with free improvisations that may use musical ideas from the piece, occasionally punctuated by the phrases written on the page.

There are only a few pieces in the repertoire that could be described as "graphic scores", and many of them still contain normal notation or variations thereof. "Portret" (Portrait) is one of twelve such pieces, each starting with the letter "p" (Figure 4.3). The asterisks indicate musicians, dots indicate notes, and anything in a box may be repeated and varied ad lib. Here, four musicians repeat a short staccato high note followed by a lower long note, then a long low note, and then a high and low note again. Meanwhile, two musicians play short low notes, and one musician improvises freely over this texture.

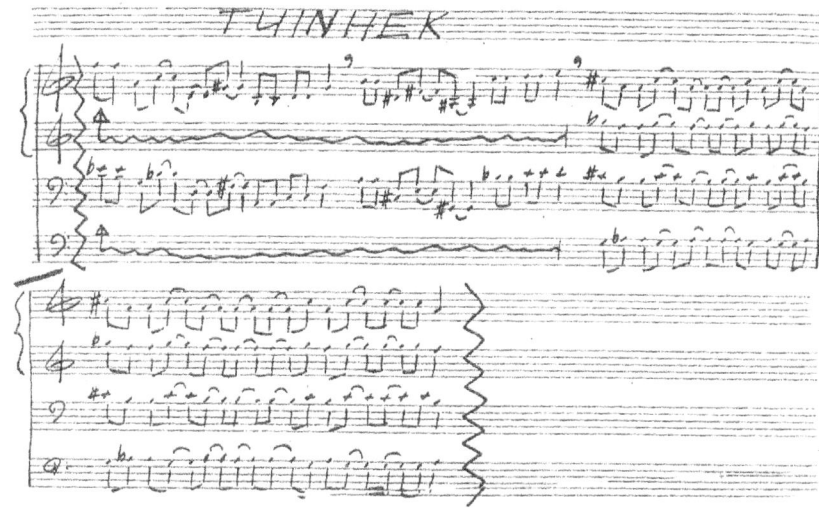

FIGURE 4.2 "Tuinhek"

Used with permission

In "Paling" (Eel), one musician improvises throughout the piece, and groups of one to three musicians take turns joining in (Figure 4.4). Four musicians then repeat upward glissandi, each dropping out until one remains, and then four musicians repeat a high short and long low note, and finally repeat a low note.

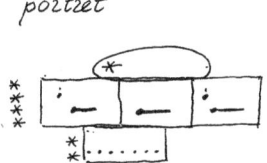

FIGURE 4.3 "Portret"

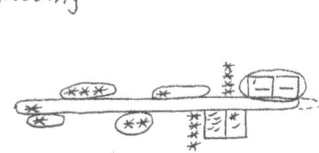

FIGURE 4.4 "Paling"

Such "high" and "low" notes played by several musicians at the same time create dissonant harmonies and clusters in performance. A similar effect is achieved by the use of x-shaped note heads, which indicate general pitch height without specifying a specific pitch. Such notes occur frequently in Mengelberg's compositions for ICP, and they are an effective way to create a common rhythm and texture, without creating a harmonic framework that may limit the options for a soloist. "Kraaloog" ("Kbeady-eye", part of a series of K-pieces that all start with the letter "k" even if their title is a word that does not begin with that letter) consists exclusively of x-shaped rhythmic phrases, played by the whole group, each repeated until another one is cued (Figure 4.5). The boxes again imply repetition ad lib. An early use of them is found in "Rumboon" (Rum Bean, a chocolate sweet with rum—the title might be a play on words connecting the Afro-Caribbean hambone with a Dutch type of confectionery often using exoticist imagery in its packaging) (Figure 4.6). This piece is featured in recordings of the ICP Tentet in the mid-1970s; the version shown here is a later handwritten copy made by Michael Moore. The introduction is a kind of shout figure, while the head is a blues, rendered somewhat harmonically ambiguous because the melody starts on the fourth: this creates subdominant or suspended harmonies rather than emphasizing the tonic, and again generates a harmonic context that is not too rigid. After the head and a repetition of the introduction, a melody follows, notated in x-shaped note heads, creating a series of clusters that suggest a melodic shape rather than a real melody. On the early recordings this melody is sung by the musicians; today it is usually played instrumentally and as a background to solos rather than a section in itself.

"Rumboon" is also an early example of the kind of piece Mengelberg would write more frequently as the ICP Orchestra developed into a more stable line-up in the late 1970s and 1980s. These are somewhat more coherent

FIGURE 4.5 "Kraaloog"
Used with permission

FIGURE 4.6   "Rumboon"; transcription by Michael Moore

Used with permission

and unified pieces like blues, jazz pieces, songs, or dances (waltzes, rhumbas) that feature some indeterminate material that can feature as an introduction, as a background, or as a section by itself, or even as a way to break out of the form of the piece to segue into a free improvisation. "Ktoel" (Kchair, the title has dropped off the page), for instance, consists of a short melody made up of a few basic motifs, with an aa'b structure and a coda leading into harmonically ambiguous territory (Figure 4.7). Some sections of this melody have been boxed in, signifying a brief improvisation of the instruments inside the box, and there is a short game piece put in after the very first motif and again at the end. Such "diamonds" present the option of playing a tone (a note) a noise (an x) or nothing (a blank space), and musicians can follow the lines to successively play these options. "Ktoel" is usually played with the boxes and diamonds the first time, and then with these ignored the second time. Hence, it gives some rules and options for improvisation, ending with a straight melody containing many musical ideas that have been introduced in the improvisation leading up to it. The rhumba "Een beetje zenuwachtig" (a bit nervous) opens with some x-shaped note heads indicating melodic shapes to play as an introduction, before the clarinet cues the head by playing the first repeating notes (Figure 4.8). The piece then contains a chord scheme like a normal jazz standard, and musicians can play solos over these chords. The syncopated x-shaped notes to the right are usually repeated at the end of the

FIGURE 4.7 "Ktoel"
Used with permission

head to lead into the solos, but may also be used as a background or to segue into a free improvisation.

The arrangements of pieces by Herbie Nichols, Thelonious Monk, and Duke Ellington that Mengelberg started to create in the 1980s use such techniques to different degrees. The Nichols arrangements are mostly straight, featuring very

FIGURE 4.8 "Een Beetje Zenuwachtig"

little indeterminate material and focusing on amplifying the complex harmonies of the compositions with lush instrumentation. This underscores Mengelberg's intention, mentioned in Chapter 2, of making clear the harmonic and tonal originality of these pieces. The Monk arrangements variously feature indeterminate techniques as introductions, as well as backgrounds that are either written out or that use x-shaped note heads. "52+", recorded on ICP 026 (ICP Orchestra 1987), is a medley of Monk pieces, starting out with "52nd Street Theme" (with specified pitch), and then featuring a solo with backgrounds of x-note versions of "Evidence" and "Rhythm-a-Ning", first played separately, then simultaneously, building up towards a climax. After a drum solo by Bennink, the medley ends with an arrangement of "Humph" with specified pitches.

The most elaborate arrangements, however, can be found in Mengelberg's arrangements of Ellington. His version of "Mood Indigo" opens with widely spread atonal chords in the clarinets, trombone, and strings. This is an instance of what Mengelberg calls a "zeekip", one of his techniques for creating atonal textures. In a zeekip ("sea-chicken", an archaic Dutch word for a bird flying over a water surface) any intervals between one instrument group are mirrored in the other—so as the clarinets play a minor sixth and a major seventh over the trombone's d flat, the cello and double bass play a minor sixth and major seventh underneath the violin's b flat in the first bar. Various ICP pieces by Mengelberg use this technique, and he has also used it in his compositions for other ensembles and orchestras.[7] These atonal chords loosely follow the contour of the melody of "Mood Indigo" (Figure 4.9), and the second phrase of the introduction contains some contrasting

FIGURE 4.9 Introduction and transition sections of Mengelberg's arrangement of "Mood Indigo"

Used with permission

contrapuntal movement. A transition follows, written as a graphic score, but again following the melodic contours of the head, and then the head is played. The combination of such different compositional techniques, and their integration by drawing on the same formal shape, show Mengelberg's ability to create different improvisatory opportunities while maintaining a compositional unity. It also has a dramatic effect: the emergence of this familiar melody from such an atonal and ambiguous texture creates an effect of surprise, while the transition also appears logical because of its general similarity in shape to the foregoing musical material.

These are just some of the more common ways in which the pieces in the ICP repertoire are embedded in an improvisatory context. Not all of them use such techniques, however, and plenty of pieces are written in a reasonably straightforward way. Many of the theatrical songs are fully written out, as are various pieces by Mengelberg that are modelled on jazz standards. "De Sprong, O Romantiek der Hazen" (The Leap, O Romantics of Hares), for example, might be Mengelberg's most popular composition and features no introductions, backgrounds, or indeterminate material (Figure 4.10). The group even plays a fugue for clarinet, viola, and cello called "A la Russe", although this is sometimes preceded or followed by a free improvisation of these instruments.

Apart from notated material, however, two other important elements that frequently feature in a performance are conducted and free improvisations. Almost every performance will feature a free improvisation by two to four musicians (sometimes more, and sometimes the strings and horns alternate). Once in a while, there will also be a conducted improvisation. This is a widespread but not very well-known practice employed by Sun Ra, Anthony Braxton, Muhal Richard Abrams, and perhaps most famously Butch Morris, but Mengelberg probably came up with it independently (Whitehead 1998, 148–151). An important difference between conducted improvisation as used by the ICP and its use in other groups is that the ICP does not normally use a formalized system of signs and gestures, but reacts to the conductor in a purely intuitive manner. The conductor may be any of the musicians in the group, although some conduct more frequently than others—Tristan Honsinger makes quite a show of it, while Ab Baars uses very modest hand gestures, and Wolter Wierbos likes to use his trombone to conduct the group so he can play along. Conducted improvisation can be seen as a kind of parodic appropriation of the hierarchies of traditional concert practice, but also as a way of turning the conductor's role into one of active participation (or, if you will, emphasizing the participatory aspect of conducting). The signs and gestures are often intentionally ambiguous, and the interaction between conductor and musicians includes much intentional miscommunication and irony.

Finally, a crucial element to understanding the way the repertoire relates to performances is the use of set lists. These were usually made by Mengelberg, shortly before a performance. Baars describes them:

> A few minutes before the concert he'll take a pen and a slip of paper, puts together some groups of people that will improvise, and around that he'll

FIGURE 4.10 "De Sprong, O Romantiek der Hazen"

Used with permission

construct the programme, of the pieces that we play. And I've noticed he'll always take into account the keys the pieces are written in, their atmosphere. Making such a programme is also composing, in a sense. Those set lists are always gratifying, and you can do a lot with them.

(Dekker 2008)

As Mengelberg's mental and physical health deteriorated, the other musicians took over the creation of set lists. Everyone makes a set list every once in a while, although some people do it more than others, and some people like to do it together with one or two others. As a rule, they make the first set list before the concert, usually during dinner, distributing it in the build-up to the concert, and the second set list during the interval. This means that before each set, the musicians will be looking for their pieces, quickly copying any pieces that are lost or comparing different versions of the same piece. This sense of chaos is precisely the point of only making the set lists at the last minute.

Figure 4.11 shows an example, a set list made by Han Bennink and Mary Oliver for a concert at The Vortex in London. The items on the list are "House Party Starting", one of Mengelberg's Nichols arrangements; a free improvisation by Tri(stan Honsinger), Tobi(as Delius), and Ha(n Bennink); then Mengelberg's

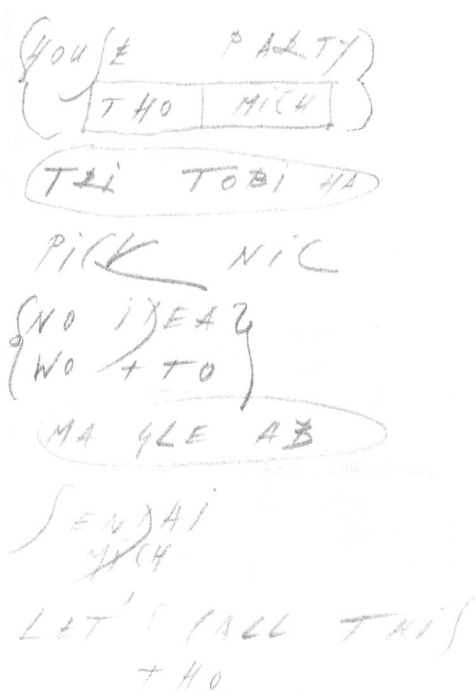

FIGURE 4.11   Set list for a concert at The Vortex, London

"Picnic" and "No Idea"; an improvisation by Ma(ry Oliver), (Ernst) Gle(rum), and Ab (Baars); Michael Moore's "Sendai"; and Mengelberg's arrangement of Monk's "Let's Call This". With each piece, soloists can be suggested, as they are here, in the same abbreviated way as with the improvising groups. There are some tacit rules about what the items on the set list mean, but because they are hardly ever really discussed there is no real agreement on what these rules are, and so they are not very strict. A circle around a name usually means that someone becomes a leader or a conductor. In this case, it indicates improvising groups. Why Thomas Heberer and Michael Moore are in square boxes at the top of the page is unclear, as are the accolades on "House Party Starting" and "No Idea".

The ideal for a set is to play it in one go, improvising transitions between the different elements on the list, and not stopping in between every piece and improvisation. This rarely happens; as in all improvised music, the music may unexpectedly stop when no one decides to contribute anymore, so if nobody continues to play after the ending of a piece, or nobody starts a transition to a piece from a free improvisation, there is a short break in between pieces. Moreover, after a big climactic ending of a piece the audience may of course break into applause. It frequently happens that only 30 minutes into the first set there is a break in which somebody (usually Mary Oliver or Ernst Glerum) can say hello to the audience, mention what they have played—which can have a humorous effect as they try to remember all the pieces so far—and announce the next piece. The set lists indicate a general plan, but they never fully cover everything that happens. People may choose to take a solo when they are not given one, or join in with an improvising group. The orchestra has several strategies of undermining what others are doing, or taking what is happening in a different direction.

From Works to Notations

One of the most important of these is the orchestra's use of so-called *viruses*. Viruses are not so much another class of pieces in the ICP repertoire as they are a specific way of *using* them. "Paardenbloem" (Dandelion) is one of the small graphic pieces mentioned above (Figure 4.12). It has a basic ABA' form. It starts with two repeated rhythmic motifs (indicating only relative pitch height), over which one musician starts playing upward glissandi. Other musicians join in until everyone is playing glissandi, and then drop out until one person remains. The piece ends with a variation on the rhythmic motifs from the A section. "Paardenbloem" can be performed as a piece in itself, but it is mostly used as a virus. That is to say, even if it is not featured on the set list, a musician can start playing it—for instance, in the middle of another piece or improvisation—and hope for others to join in. Like a real virus, the piece can then spread and contaminate the system, or the group can be resistant and the virus is contained. Because it is usually played as a virus, "Paardenbloem" is often performed

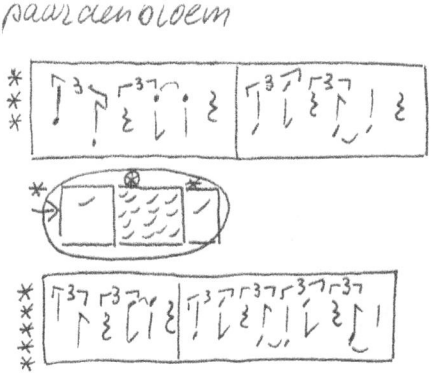

FIGURE 4.12 "Paardenbloem"

differently to the description just given—it can be heard as a virus in a recording of Mengelberg's arrangement of Ellington's "It Don't Mean a Thing" on Bospaadje Konijnehol I (ICP 1992a). The stars indicating the number of musicians are usually ignored, and the two rhythmic motifs in the A section are often played and repeated together as though they were in one box rather than two separate ones. The A' section is usually simply a repetition of this same motif, without the variation indicated in the score. Moreover, a musician can choose to cue the piece by playing the glissandi rather than the rhythmic motif in the A section, which may not provide enough of a contrast in a particularly loud and dense context for it to be noticeable.

Various other small pieces like "Paardenbloem" are played as a virus. "Pilaar" (Pillar) is often used to create an ending, with a long high note followed by a downward glissando (Figure 4.13). This is usually cued with a gesture, moving thumb and index finger up and down in the shape of a pillar. Not all viruses come from this series of "P-pieces", and musicians frequently use other small pieces from the repertoire as viruses.

More generally, however, the idea of the viruses indicates a general way of working amongst the musicians, and this is where the aforementioned reciprocity

FIGURE 4.13 "Pilaar"

between repertoire and practice really comes into perspective. As Tobias Delius put it:

> Some have a name, and then we have decided to keep it and use it more often. But this principle is always there—it's always possible for every-thing to suddenly go in a different direction. Viruses can be composed by Misha, or spontaneously invented on the spot. They can grow from misunderstandings [. . .] It can also be something very banal, pointing at the score and saying "let's play this backwards". Or pointing at a sign for repeating a bar and reading it as a graphic score—beep, booyee bap—or even a title, or a word as a graphic score, or the rhythm of a word or a phrase.[8]

Delius describes the use of viruses as a means to "suddenly go in a different direction". This is indeed a prominent way in which they are used, as an effective way to break out of the form of a piece or create a sudden transition out of a free improvisation. However, the techniques described by Delius are also used to create backgrounds, spurring on soloists, or in transitions between pieces. As a piece ends and the musicians segue into an improvisation, such techniques can be a useful way to introduce musical ideas from the next piece into this improvisation—which might itself continue to use musical ideas from the previous.

This use of viruses in ICP performances is key to understanding their approach to improvisation. Although Delius called these strategies "a little banal", he quickly added that "when you try it in another group you notice it's not as obvious as you think!"[9] The reciprocity between repertoire and practice is so strong in the case of the viruses that they are virtually indistinguishable. In fact, when in the 1970s the ICP grew into the ICP Tentet and later the ICP Orchestra, with a stable line-up of musicians and a steadily growing reper-toire, Mengelberg started to organize weekly rehearsals for the group. In these rehearsals, he actively tried to cultivate a certain way of working. Honsinger was part of this early group (he left in the late 1970s and joined again in the 1990s) and remembers that things did not always go smoothly in these rehearsals:

> Misha is a good leader. He merits being where he is. I couldn't say this when I first started working with him, but now I can. He used to be impossible. He was trying things out, but in such an extreme way, that it was bound not to work somehow. Something changed along the way, when I wasn't there. Something happened where he became an impor-tant leader.[10]

Mengelberg affirmed this, but also explained the necessity he felt to take leadership:

> I thought, I'm not writing this down for nothing, I thought they should play it well [. . .] And I think it was good that I did so, because

at some point they really started to see what I was asking of them, in those arrangements. It was no pettifoggery [. . .] They should be able to do certain important things without mistakes, and we would rehearse that, really concentrate on these matters [. . .] And now all these people, whom you have heard playing, they all have a very good pianissimo, even Han! Haha, I could be nasty to him, but I knew what I wanted.[11]

Obviously, the use of composed material brings into play the figure of the composer, and his authority. Honsinger's comment indicates that this position of authority was something that had to be negotiated between Mengelberg and the other ICP musicians. However, he did point out that this also made possible their specific way of working:

[If there is anything specific to the ICP] it would include the way in which improvisation is exposed. I like these ideas [. . .] but this is the only group where it happens like this, because Misha is a composer. I would say he *is* a composer, as opposed to me; I'm more of an organizer without exactly knowing what I'm doing.[12]

More importantly, the use of viruses, especially the way in which they allow musicians to creatively interpret the written material, alleviates this authoritative role, as it makes clear that the musicians have their own room to play the material in whatever way they wish.

This ties into the issue of ontology. The viruses mean that the ICP musicians are frequently improvising not by filling in the spaces that the score leaves open, but by playing precisely what is written, either because they interrupt the musical situation with a new piece, or because they creatively re-interpret signs and phrases to generate new musical material. Michael Moore argued that the playful approach of the ICP to the pieces in the repertoire consisted in the fact that they treated them as "found objects":

Moore: I think Misha thinks in games a lot.
FS: Do you mean like John Zorn's game pieces?
Moore: Well, no not like John Zorn . . . Zorn studied these board games with all these rules and he thought of rules for people to communicate with each other [. . .] Whereas I see Misha's games as more like . . . okay this is the material, what are we going to do with it? It's that whole found object thing. And a lot of his pieces are like that, they're just little . . . flarden. [Dutch for "snippets"][13]

The approach to notations as "found objects" fits in with the discussion of decommodification in the previous chapter, as well as the interrogation of the functionality of objects in Fluxus. This performance practice also requires a particular approach to composition. Mengelberg told me that the most important thing about the compositions he brought to the rehearsals of the ICP was that they were unfinished.[14] Although we saw earlier that some compositions were completely notated at some point (though they still might have emerged from improvisations), such an incomplete or open quality was mentioned by many of the musicians to be an important aspect of writing for the ICP.

Heberer, for instance, described his experience learning to write for the ICP in some detail:

> Writing for ICP I had some massive failures. Maybe it has to do with my Germanness on the one hand, and writing with computers on the other. For a long time I wrote pieces with their own qualities, but they were closed. So the process of writing them, I thought so much about how things would work out, and from one section to the next, and writing with sequencers and stuff like that, there is always the danger that it sounds beautiful on your machine, but you lose perspective of how the music will develop in the hands of human beings [. . .] So if you write a piece that is a unit in itself, it is too closed, there is no need to improvise anymore [. . .] It has to have loose ends.[15]

As Heberer describes it, the use of these pieces in an improvised context means that they cannot be approached as finished products, or ideal musical objects intended to be accurately reproduced in performance. Rather than taking them as representations of musical structures, the use of viruses emphasizes the status of notations as material objects.

This is a very different understanding of composition than how it is usually described in classical music. The notated repertoire of the classical tradition is often considered as a representation of a musical "work", the expression of the composer's intention, to be accurately followed by musicians in performance. The idea that there are such things as musical works might seem obvious to many—even though we might be hard pressed to specify what kind of things they are exactly—but as Lydia Goehr has argued, they are quite a recent historical development. Only around 1800 did the idea become commonly accepted that a piece of music was an unchangeable, timeless, ideal object represented by notation (Goehr 2007). Music became an *idea* rather than a material and social process, and this idea was thought to have a greater reality than its actual performance. An apocryphal quote by Beethoven, whose career is seen by Goehr as the period in which this work-concept is consolidated, suggests that his music was "in my mind as though cast in a single piece, so that all that is left is the work of writing it down" (Benson 2003, 53). The comment suggests that the existence of the music is independent from its sounding in performance—or even of being written down.

The pieces in the ICP repertoire do not work like this; they do not specify a transcendent musical object to be reproduced in performance, but are themselves subject to change, and as such part of the improvisatory process. The musicians use them as tools to create rapid changes, to make transitions between pieces, or to interrupt what others are doing. They have a role to play within the improvisatory interaction that shapes the music. We can trace at least some of this back to the event scores used in Fluxus. As we saw earlier, the animation of inanimate objects and the mediation of human action through technologies and material objects were an important element of many Fluxus pieces—their performances present "the music of *actions* animating *things*" (Stiles 1993, 65). In a book on the role of written language in art, music, and concrete poetry in the 1960s, Liz Kotz discusses the event scores of George Brecht, La Monte Young, Yoko Ono, and others. She notes how they frequently inhabit a boundary position between prescriptions, descriptions, and autonomous works of word art, and can function alternatively as language, object, or a performance in their own right (Kotz 2007; see also Lushetich 2012). Fluxus' conceptual concern with language, she argues, is not a move towards immateriality, but a reconsideration of the materiality of texts that engages their relationality and multiplicity.

Moreover, Fluxus event scores often generate improvisational processes, which are not improvisational because they leave certain spaces open for the performer to improvise, but precisely because the performer needs to improvise in order to follow the instructions in the score. They emphasize that scores do not need to be considered an obstacle standing in the way of the free expression of the performer, but like the musician's instrument, they can be seen as objects that make possible certain kinds of creative expression in the first place. As such, their role in the creative process has to do less with the space they leave open than with what they give to the performer. The ICP musicians I spoke to about this all mentioned that clarity was an important aspect of the written musical material. Although the openness of the pieces is crucial, this is not the same thing as vagueness. In order to develop a successful way of playing these compositions, it has to be quite clear what is expected. Heberer, when he said that he learned to write pieces with "loose ends", added that "you also have to trigger something that is inspiring and very special, and very specific for that piece, yet it also has to be flexible and open enough that you can see it from different perspectives."[16]

Moore indicated that this was not just a matter of a piece having a specific identity, but also to make sure that the musicians know what is expected from them:

Moore: There are a few ways to improvise that we think are kind of corny. If someone asks us to think in the colour blue, our eyes would glaze over and we would get bored [. . .] I have this kind of ideal, also writing for my own groups, I try to find really simple material that can create really effective music. So that you don't have to tell people much, if anything [. . .]

FS: So what's the problem with improvising over the colour blue? Is it that it's too complicated, or too vague?

Moore: It's too vague, it doesn't mean anything [. . .] It's almost like you could improvise freely, play whatever you want, but you have this nagging idea in the back of your head that maybe you're not doing it right or something.

FS: Like, maybe this is more like purple?

Moore: Yeah or like, what the hell does he mean? What does he want to hear?[17]

Clarity with regard to what a musician is supposed to play, or how a musician can improvise within a piece, thus does not restrict freedom, but means that they are able to play more freely and confidently. As Janssen indicated, if you develop such a dexterity with a piece, it can lead you to discover new musical possibilities:

> In the 1980s I thought the musicians had to submit to the idea of a composition. I would probably say the same today if I were to do something new, but [. . .] I've been playing older material with my piano trio, and it's different every time. That's the funny thing, precisely because you know it so well you can look at it anew. I think the same is true of the ICP. It is very important that Misha stopped composing at some point [. . .] If at some point it just goes without saying, it becomes like breathing and you can take it in any direction. Then it becomes a vehicle for . . . then it's not about playing the piece but a vehicle to take you into some completely unknown territory.[18]

Baars told me something similar:

> We know the paper so well by now, that we can play it in a thousand different ways. It's more a kind of guideline, to achieve certain things that can be very far removed from it. Sometimes very close, very meticulous, but it changes every night, that's what makes the orchestra so special to me.[19]

As Janssen and Baars describe it, the pieces in the ICP repertoire lead a life of their own as they generate different opportunities for improvisation and creative interaction. They do not determine the course of performance, but may precisely be used to go in a new direction. The "virus" metaphor, in this regard, has another advantage, as viruses biologically occupy a position somewhere in between standard classifications of inanimate organic material and living organisms.

Improvising Animals

We have seen how the ICP repertoire requires a reconsideration of how we understand composition; but what about improvisation? The inclusion of notation within improvised music seems to contradict how we normally understand "improvisation". The Grove Online music dictionary defines improvisation as "the creation of a musical work, or the final form of a musical work, as it is being performed" (Nettl et al. 2014). With its emphasis on "works", the definition does not quite capture what happens in an ICP performance. Imagine an

ICP set is played through without any breaks; should an hour of music, combining graphic pieces, arrangements of jazz standards, some free improvisations by different subsets of musicians, a conducted improvisation, and improvised transitions between these elements, be considered a "work"? Moreover, the idea of a "final form of a musical work" does not fit the role of notations in ICP performances; as we saw earlier, these pieces do not have the purpose of "determining" the music in advance, and they do not just leave open space to improvise, but stimulate improvisation precisely by what they *do* specify. The definition seems to assume that the function of notation is essentially to define a work, and to rely on a tacit clause, which might read "as opposed to being determined in the form of a composition or framework in advance". Philosopher Nicholas Wolterstorff, in what reads almost as an aside comment, a statement of something obvious, writes that "a necessary condition of improvisation is that it *not* be the performance of a work" (Wolterstorff 1987, 119), making explicit the logic of opposition by which improvisation has been defined vis-à-vis notation. Indeed, our usual understanding of improvisation as an "oral" as opposed to a "literate" musical practice is deeply governed by the idea that one can "write down" music in the first place (rather than instructions for others to make music).

In this regard, the ICP also distinguished itself from other European improvisers. In his classic account of improvisation in music, Derek Bailey also employs this logic of opposition, suggesting that "true" improvisation can only be impeded by the use of notation:

> Whether reading music is a disadvantage to an improvisor is a question which gets quite a lot of discussion amongst improvising musicians [. . .] There is an unmistakable suspicion that the acquisition of reading skill in some way has a blunting effect in improvising skills, an acceptance that these are very often two things which do not go together. So, of course, in musics where there isn't an "accurate" notation system, that possible problem, or distraction, disappears. But more important than the removal of a possible inhibition or contrary discipline from the performer is the fact that the absence of a music writing/reading tradition gets rid of the composer.
> *(Bailey 1993, 10–11)*

Bailey regularly played with the ICP throughout the 1970s, and has even recorded Mengelberg's "Where is the Police?", so the difference in mind-set should not be seen as establishing irreconcilable boundaries. Still, the development of a performance practice in which compositional and improvisatory elements were completely intertwined signifies an important cultural difference.

Guus Janssen told me how this attitude was important to him as a young musician in the 1970s. He was still studying composition while also making a career as an improviser, and found it difficult because these two worlds were so opposed to each other:

There was an odd sort of tension, because I would be composing at home, knowing I would have a gig that night, and I would drive there with Evan Parker and he would say composition was nonsense. If you really had to compose something, Nam June Paik had composed a piece with durations in terms of light years, so that was good because it was impossible to perform, and you could sit in a chair and read it, or something. Those discussions went really far and they were difficult, especially because Evan Parker is such an intelligent guy. So at the end of the night the conclusion is that composition is forbidden, or at least nonsense. But the following morning I had to get back to work, and my composition teacher Ton de Leeuw would say, well what you guys are doing—improvisation in Indian music is okay, and Dave Brubeck and Oscar Peterson and maybe he liked Messiaen too, but what I did with Evan was just free expression, just nonsense. Like a Rorschach test and at the end you tell each other you had a good time. So I was being butchered from both sides, and if you don't stand your ground you'll be lost. So I looked . . . I thought it has to be possible to connect these two worlds.[20]

Instant composition, as the identification of improvisation as a kind of composition as well as the use of notated pieces within improvised music, offered a certain sense of openness which was experienced as liberating by a number of musicians.

Thomas Heberer equally described how this approach to improvisation really attracted him, and sees it as part of a particularly Dutch approach to improvised music:

In Germany there were basically two streams. I was playing with the legends, the old geezers, you know the Han and Mishas of Germany [. . .] There was a lot of freedom. But German-style freedom, so there were dos and don'ts involved. You had to belong to the club, aesthetically. I assume that in the UK it was even more extreme, people like Derek Bailey and Evan Parker—I mean Evan is a pretty liberal guy, but they developed a certain aesthetic, and if you didn't follow it they didn't want you [. . .] I understand that ICP also by Dutch standards is a very unusual band [. . .] but from my square German perspective I think there is something specifically Dutch there, something I had to get used to [. . .] You know I am a German guy and we like to build cars that work properly, and we have a certain attitude toward things. Great on the one hand, but there's a certain danger that they get too excited about a certain pattern, and they're on a track and they can't get rid of the track. And the ICP taught me to get more open, and not to be too concerned about being brilliant. Misha is an extremely brilliant mind, but he doesn't have to show it all the time, and that's fine with him so there is a sense of understatement. And particularly for me, because I'm probably the squarest, that was very liberating.[21]

Heberer's comment refers to the inclusion of composed and improvised material, but also to the specific ICP strategy of interrupting each other's playing and pestering each other musically, which means that chaos and failure is a frequent and intentional part of ICP performances. Baars also recalled an important moment in learning to play the ICP repertoire, which had more to do with the question of what kind of improvisation is suitable for what kind of piece:

> At one of my first concerts we played "Reflections" by Thelonious Monk, and I had studied and I was playing over the changes and, well, I thought it went okay. But afterwards he came up to me and he said "But Ab . . . you really don't have to play it like that" [. . .] That was a very important remark, because I had always found it difficult to separate those worlds. If you're playing free you're playing free, and if you play changes you play the changes. I had been looking for a way to combine them, to use my free idiom in such a scheme. Apparently he heard that. So the Monk project for me was really a revelation, because I had found a way to play the changes, but not according to the chords, but to make up my own melody that was abstractly related to the original melody. That was very exciting.[22]

Heberer and Baars describe their experiences as liberating, but of course this should not be taken to mean simply that anything goes and anyone can freely play along in the ICP—as I quoted Heberer himself earlier, their repertoire and practice had to be developed over the years. Baars in fact describes his "revelation" not in terms of having an epiphany and suddenly being able to play in a certain way, but rather of seeing a direction in which to develop his playing.

Baars' recollection of this moment does not just tell us something about the ICP's musical style, in which the sounds of free improvisation and of swinging bebop need not be seen as part of mutually exclusive genres. In Baars' solo on "Four in One", recorded on ICP026, for instance, he plays atonal material only abstractly related to the melody of the piece through motivic variation, and experiments with extreme timbres on his clarinet, while the rhythm section plays happy-go-lucky up-tempo accompaniment as though they are accompanying Johnny Hodges (ICP Orchestra 1987). Conversely, a musician might keep to the changes while the music around him transforms into chaos. It also tells us something important about the relation of the notated material to performance. Baars' "revelation" concerned the fact that his playing could engage with the piece in very different ways other than adding melody complementary to given chord changes. However, his development of an alternative approach was not just playing "freely" over the chords either, as he had to find a way to relate the material he played to the musical context. In other words, the freedom of an improviser does not simply consist in what is left unspecified by the score. Rather, it emerges from the relation between musician and the notated material.

When the idea is brought up that all musical performance contains some elements of improvisation, the metaphor of the "continuum" is commonly raised. The idea was perhaps first formulated by Bruno Nettl. Showing the varieties of musical creation in a number of different musical practices, he concluded that improvisation and composition are not categorically different—any performance contains aspects of preparation as well as spontaneity. The continuum between wholly determined performance and wholly free improvisation, neither of which actually exists, is his suggestion to solve this conceptual ambiguity (Nettl 1974, 6). The idea is that even without a compositional framework, a performance will be determined in part by the instruments, a musician's skills, the social context, the acoustics of the room, etcetera. Compositional frameworks of different "degrees" of determination give the musician different degrees of freedom to create their own musical material in the course of performance, hence the idea of a continuum. However, this solution does not deconstruct the basic association of freedom with improvisation and restriction with composition; it does not allow for the idea that the specification of certain aspects in the score might offer new ways of playing an instrument, engaging with other musicians and audiences, or putting certain kinds of musical knowledge into practice.

This was made explicit in a remark by Mary Oliver. Oliver was trained as an interpreter of post-war avant-garde compositions, including graphic scores and the painstakingly notated music of the New Complexity school, performing repertoire from Cage to Xenakis. She has never really learned to "play the changes", and so relied mostly on her ears when playing solos over jazz pieces. In one of our conversations, she talked about her recent experience touring with Bennink and a range of other musicians in the United States, using a small "Real Book" of Mengelberg pieces edited by Michael Moore and published in 2009. She said:

> I'm actually learning a lot more about working with my limitations you know, not being a trained jazz violinist. Recognizing parameters in what a chord or a chart might tell you, listening more to what the bass is doing . . . also it's fun because, playing so much with Han I listen to how he's thinking about rhythmic inflections and things like that [. . .] I used to play very complex music, you know, with different time signatures per measure, Ferneyhough shit like that. So it's kind of calming me down a bit, but it's also giving me new material. So yeah, I like it.[23]

Oliver makes a very important point, as she makes clear that working with particular forms of notation requires particular skills. These jazz pieces, because of the tradition they invoke but also because of the particular texture, harmonies, and rhythms that they set up, require not only a form of playing, but also a way of listening and general conduct that is radically different from the complex scores of Ferneyhough. The crucial point here is that these different forms of conduct are not easily placed on a "scale" or a "continuum" from completely determined performance to completely free improvisation. For Oliver, improvising over chord changes is restricting, because it's something she never really learned, while performing a score by Ferneyhough is less restricting because it is more familiar terrain.[24]

Bennink made a similar remark. Since he does not read, he argued, he is restricted to his instrument and his ears: although he frequently emphasizes his autonomy as a musician who does not have to play what is written, he equally often describes this as "being with his back against the wall", having no other options or footholds than whatever he plays or hears. Far from a position of freedom, then, he experienced not reading as a (self-imposed) restriction. When Mengelberg started writing more material for the group in the late 1970s, this still had an impact on his playing:

> Beautiful pieces, but performing a piece brings a kind of discipline with it. I always had the reputation of playing far too loud—which I think was more about becoming enthusiastic than being really loud—but anyway, I started concentrating on brushes, and the nuances you can have with those and how it feels not to have cymbals in the ensemble . . . that's what I've been working on to this day, it's a work in progress.[25]

Bennink also describes the merits of committing himself to a particular form of playing, having the discipline to learn something new as the musical practice of the ICP was changing. Although Bennink used to be famous for using a wide array of musical instruments—sometimes he still brings one or two to a concert—today he is known to play complete concerts on only a snare drum:

> In the past people were happy with a snare drum that had been stitched up thirty times and then they would still play out of their skin, chasing a whole big band! We're so spoilt, I just want to go back to that mentality [. . .] It's not just the restriction of a snare drum, it's also about what you have and what you do with it. It's rich enough in itself, do you know what I mean? [. . .] *That* is where you can find your freedom, in using those limitations.[26]

Bennink emphasizes how restriction is not just about reducing the sonic possibilities, but about highlighting the creative abilities of the musician when confronted with restrictions—it is about "what you have and what you do with it". Such skills are developed in dialogue with the material at hand, and what goes for instruments also goes for scores. Baars' free playing over changes was not just free playing, but had to adjust to this musical context. Oliver's background as a performer of modern music means she easily and confidently employs phrasing and intonation (not to mention great instrumental technique) but is less adept at improvising a melody over a series of chords.

The continuum metaphor, and the common assumptions of composition and improvisation that it represents, treats freedom individualistically, as the space and ability of the musician to act free from imposed rules or restrictions. The above considerations indicate, however, that this agency is not the capacity of an isolated individual, but is developed in relation to their social and material environment—recall that Mengelberg's fascination for Duke Ellington did not concern the "freedom" on display, but rather the way in which the music could adapt to its environment. The creativity of the musician is developed in a reciprocal relation, in which the piece plays an active role. Art historian Hannah Higgins has argued that Fluxus offers a concept of pedagogy that treats learning and creativity not as the capacity of a disembodied mind, but rather as something that happens in the relation of an embodied subject to their material environment. Fluxus experience, she argues, is neither wholly subjective nor objective, emphasizing a relational and multi-sensory engagement with the world (H. Higgins 2002). She connects the aesthetics of Fluxus to the philosophical aesthetics of John Dewey. Dewey and Fluxus share a basic premise, which is to reconnect art with everyday experience. Dewey opens his *Art as Experience* with the statement that "the existence of the works of art upon which formation of an esthetic theory depends has become an obstruction to theory about them" (Dewey 2005, 1). In other words, because of the museumization of artworks, their isolation from everyday life, and their Romantic association with transcendence, we tend to think of aesthetic experience as categorically different from everyday life, and of artistic freedom as located in this transcendence of everyday burdens. Dewey, conversely, emphasizes the continuity between aesthetic and everyday experience: "Mountain peaks do not float unsupported, they do not even just rest upon the earth. They *are* the earth in one of its manifest operations" (2005, 2).

Moreover, Dewey describes everyday experience not in terms of a material world impacting on a disembodied mind, but as emerging in the interaction of the body with its environment: "Experience is the result, the sign, and the reward of that interaction of organism and environment which, when it is carried to the full, is a transformation of interaction into participation and communication" (2005, 22). Dewey's philosophy of art is also unusual in the attention it gives to the production as well as the experience of art. Here, too, Dewey emphasizes that artistic creation is not a matter of a mind imposing form on raw material, but a process in which subject and object are interrelated: "the expression of the self, in and through a medium, constituting the work of art, is [. . .] a process in which both of them acquire a form and order they did not at first possess" (2005, 67-68). The medium is not just raw material to be shaped to fit the idea of the artist, but itself generates ideas and inspiration. Consequently, both aesthetic experience and production are characterized by a "complete interpenetration of self and the world of objects and events" (2005, 18). In one of the primary expressions of American pragmatist philosophy, Dewey sought to replace the Cartesian dualist account of experience as an encounter between the two fundamentally separate categories of mind and world with an understanding, clearly influenced by Darwinian thought, of the relation between an "organism" and its surroundings. According to Dewey: "Life goes on in an environment; not merely *in* it but because of it, through interaction with it" (2005, 12). Strikingly, Dewey's account describes the aesthetic not as a uniquely human capacity, but in a way that emphasizes the continuities between human and animal behaviour.

The repertoire of the ICP is filled with animals. Apart from the viruses, many of the titles of Mengelberg's pieces feature animals: there are hares, camels, beetles, donkeys, mealworms, pandas, eels, dogs, cats, rabbits, and cows. In the early 1960s, he made a video of his cat Pief and his piano; the cat wakes up lying on the piano, walks back and forth over the keys, and lies down again, stretching himself out, after which another cat comes running along which pulls him down from the instrument. In 1972, the ICP label published a bootleg recording from 1964 with Eric Dolphy. The b-side featured a recording of a duet of Mengelberg and his wife's parrot Eeko. Mengelberg plays a blues accompaniment, while the parrot crows and clicks and whistles a solo. Like Dewey, Mengelberg sought to reconnect music to everyday experience through a consideration of animal behaviour. In a television interview in the early 1980s he took the presenter to a zoo and said, standing in front of a bird cage:

> If at some point you don't know what to do, just go here. They sing a bit, then they fly a bit before they can do something else. It's a unity of music and the rest of their lives, it's not separated.
>
> *(Hülscher 1983)*

Tristan Honsinger told me that "a reason Misha likes animals so much" was that "with animals, it's never overstated. They don't think, or at least not with their heads. Humans think that thinking is something that happens up here".[27] Mengelberg frequently made animal noises: whistling, barking, and bleating. He could be in the middle of a piano solo and stop playing to continue his solo by way of such noises, but he also made them off-stage, a little like other people might hum or whistle to themselves. The first time I went along with the group on the bus, Mengelberg and Honsinger were making animal noises to each other, and describing each other's sounds—a piglet rolling down the mountain was one of them.

Such ideas have also become part of the group's understanding of improvisation, and even if they are rarely made explicit, animals came up in my conversations with ICP musicians with some frequency. In an interview with Ab Baars, I mentioned that it had struck me how his big sound and expressive use of extreme multiphonics make audible the material vibration of his tenor saxophone. He responded by telling me a story about Sidney Bechet:

Yes, it's something I've increasingly started doing, and it has partly to do with playing shakuhachi, because the sound is so important for that. So I'm concerned with that, how to play particular sounds in such a way that you can make a melodic whole out of it. There is a nice story about Sidney Bechet, the soprano saxophone player who lived in Paris. In the same neighbourhood there lived Numar Lubin, a big boss at the Nimbus record company. He used to walk past Bechet's house every day and he would hear him practice. Day after day the routine was the same. He would play scales and arpeggios, and then in the end he would make very strange animal noises. One day he asked Sidney Bechet: "What's all that stuff at the end?" And Bechet said: "You know, I sometimes wonder if what they call music is the real music, where sounds and noise turn into music, and music turns into sound and noise. That's a very interesting place to be." So I thought that was very stimulating, to read this about a guy like that.[28]

Baars' story further underscores the ICP's view of jazz discussed in Chapter 2, acknowledging its history as an experimental and avant-garde genre in its own right. Even if the figure of the animal plays a small role in this story, it serves to explore the limits of what music can be, and what we consider to be "human" expression.

In one of my interviews with bassist Ernst Glerum, he suddenly started talking very matter-of-factly about Mengelberg's arrangement of Duke Ellington's "The Mooche" (the matter-of-factness indicating the extent to which such ideas have become an everyday part of the group's mind-set):

Glerum: Misha put the zoo in "The Mooche", and although I can sometimes get a bit tired of all the zoos and the animals, it does really make it work.
FS: Sorry, what do you mean?
Glerum: There's a zoo in "The Mooche".
FS: What's a zoo?
Glerum: Er, animal sounds, monstrous sounds, scary sounds. That's how it begins, kind of spooky. Mooche-like, whatever a mooche is. And then you get the first theme, with a chorus, and then back into the zoo and then the theme again.[29]

The exchange has several layers of meaning: on the most basic level, the way in which Glerum takes zoos and animals for granted shows the extent to which this has become an inherent part of the mind-set of the group. On a deeper level, the misinterpretation of the slang term "mooche" to signify a fictional animal in a zoo can be seen as a take on Ellington's "jungle style", of which "The Mooche" is a prime example. As Fred Moten and Alexander Weheliye have argued, African-American aesthetics has often turned the dehumanized subject position of black Americans into an in-between position from which to critique traditional humanist accounts of subjectivity (Moten 2003; Weheliye 2005). Moten describes Ellington's band as swinging with "the human animality of its instruments" (Moten 2003, 31). Ellington's adoption of the jungle style was an ironic (and commercially savvy) commentary on the racist associations of black music as expressive of a wild, less-than-human African essence (see Teal 2012 for a discussion of different interpretations of Ellington's jungle style). By turning the jungle into a zoo, Mengelberg creates an arrangement that pays an ironic tribute to Ellington, highlighting his music as one of the models for a form of writing music in which composition and improvisation are intertwined (see also Williams 2012).

Mengelberg's compositions, then, may be considered a "writing for animals". The phrase is borrowed from Gilles Deleuze and Félix Guattari, who ask: "What if one became animal or plant *through* literature, which certainly does not mean literarily?" (Deleuze and Guattari 2013, 3). In an interview with Claire Parnet, Deleuze explains that this "for" should not be understood as "to", but rather as "in their name", and continues to compare it to the signs that animals produce to mark their territory (Boutang and Pamart 1996). There is a long tradition of viewing writing as the expression of the rationality of modern western man. Texts, as representations of rational and scientific knowledge, have been seen as expressing timeless truths rather than as acts of communication, blackboxing social context so as to produce an objective representation of the world.[30] Writing for animals means putting writing back into this context, and seeing it as a means of constructing and negotiating the relation to one's social and material environment, not as exemplary of human rationality and exclusivity.

Notes

1 Ab Baars, interview with the author, 4 January 2012.
2 Thomas Heberer, interview with the author, 20 February 2012.
3 Ibid.
4 As will become apparent throughout the following chapters, I think the idea that playing "from notation" is somehow uncreative (or even necessarily opposed to improvisation) is a fallacy, so my distinction here is mainly rhetorical.
5 Evan Parker, interview with the author, 2 February 2013.
6 It is used in the theatre piece *Hé Hé Hé Waar is de Marechaussee* from 1973, but was recorded before that by Bennink and Mengelberg as well as by Derek Bailey (Bennink and Mengelberg 1971; Bailey 1971).
7 Mengelberg's arrangement of Monk's "Mysterioso" pits the iconic parallel sixths of that piece against a zeekip inversion (ICP Orchestra 1987). His "Kafel" opens with a zeekip canon, as can be heard on Bospaadje Konijnehol II (ICP Orchestra 1992b). Large-scale compositions using this technique include *Zeekip Ahoy* (1984) and *Enige Ervaren Zeekippen Tegen een Achtergrond van Gezanten voor Sour Cream* (1985).
8 Tobias Delius, interview with the author, 21 February 2012.
9 Ibid.
10 Tristan Honsinger, interview with the author, 20 February 2012.
11 Misha Mengelberg, conversation with the author, 25 February 2012.

12 Tristan Honsinger, interview with the author, 20 February 2012.
13 Michael Moore, interview with the author, 23 December 2011. Moore has been living in the Netherlands since the early 1980s, hence using the Dutch word "flarden".
14 Misha Mengelberg, conversation with the author, 15 February 2012.
15 Thomas Heberer, interview with the author, 20 February 2012.
16 Thomas Heberer, interview with the author, 20 February 2012.
17 Michael Moore, interview with the author, 23 December 2011.
18 Guus Janssen, interview with the author, 8 January 2013.
19 Ab Baars, interview with the author, 4 January 2013.
20 Guus Janssen, interview with the author, 8 January 2013.
21 Thomas Heberer, interview with the author, 20 February 2012.
22 Ab Baars, interview with the author, 4 January 2012.
23 Mary Oliver, interview with the author, 2 February 2013.
24 Cook writes at some length about the performance of complex scores (in his case that of a piece by Bryn Harrison by pianist Philip Thomas), arguing that the complexity of the music is precisely what makes it into an object of intense creative interaction between performer(s) and composer, and an opportunity for personal development for the performer, belying any interpretation of New Complexity as the height of composers' authoritative function (Cook 2013, 273–287).
25 Han Bennink, interview with the author, 3 January 2012.
26 Ibid.
27 Tristan Honsinger, conversation with the author, 31 January 2013.
28 Ab Baars, interview with the author, 4 January 2012.
29 Ernst Glerum, interview with the author, 10 January 2013.
30 What David Bleich calls the "sacralisation of texts" in the medieval university indicates how texts have come to be understood as expressing timeless truths rather than as acts of communication (Bleich 2013, 11). In modern scientific writing, moreover, it has become standard practice to use the passive voice to sustain the fantasy that the speaking subject is absent (2013, 385). To paraphrase Cook, this practice suggests that the meaning is "already there in the text", that there can be meaning without an act of communication (Cook 2007, 338). Texts are thus crucial to what Bruno Latour calls the process of "purification" (Latour 1993, 11) in modern accounts of scientific knowledge—the erasure (or "blackboxing", Latour 1999, 183–185) of the various agencies involved in producing knowledge so that it may appear as objective. This association of texts with rational modernity also established a distinction between the western and the non-western world: Gary Tomlinson has argued that music scholarship's concern with notation as the primary way to study music has to be understood against a nineteenth-century mode of writing history that treated the rise of alphabetic writing as the goal of historical development towards increasing sophistication and consequently deemed cultures that used other forms of writing as irrational primitives (Tomlinson 2012).

5
NOTATION AND DISTRIBUTED CREATIVITY

The notated musical repertoire—ranging from fully notated compositions to graphic scores, but also including the use of viruses and set lists—is integral to the way the ICP Orchestra approaches improvisation. As we have seen, this musical practice requires a reconsideration of standard ontological conceptions of both notation and performance. The discussion of viruses and animals in the previous chapter served to shift our focus from works considered as ideal objects to notations considered as material objects, and from improvisation as spontaneous invention to improvisation as an inherent aspect of the way we respond to our environment. But what are the consequences of these shifts in perspective for the way we understand ICP performances as a creative practice? Moreover, can the particular way in which notation is used in their performances shed light on the relation between notation and performance more generally? This chapter tries to answer such questions, drawing on theories of creativity from recent music scholarship as well as cultural anthropology, and illustrating these arguments with specific examples from my fieldwork with the group.

The ontological considerations discussed previously impinge directly on how we understand creativity in musical performance. As Nicholas Cook has argued, the work-based approach of traditional music scholarship, which looks at musical works as such without taking into account the meanings generated in their performance, implies a Platonic ontology: musical works are like Platonic ideas in the sense that they are thought to exist above and beyond everyday musical reality, and as such are only ever inaccurately reflected in performance (Cook 2013, 8–32). Cook calls this state of affairs the "paradigm of reproduction", in which the performing musician's primary task is to reproduce the musical work and/or the composer's intention with this piece as represented by the score (2013, 14–19). At its core, this way of thinking about music is dependent on the idea that there is something "already there in the score, composed into it and just waiting to be released by the performer" (Cook 2007, 338). This Platonist philosophy, he argues, entails a particular understanding of musical communication: the musical work is grasped as an idea in the mind of a composer (we previously saw how such ideas are attributed to Beethoven, as they have been to other classical composers), and this idea is transmitted to the listener who, as musicology's idealized "structural listener", equally grasps the musical work in its entirety (Cook 2013, 13).

The strange thing about this way of thinking is that it not only postulates the existence of music outside of practices of playing and listening, but describes this existence of music as one with a higher degree of reality, from which a performance can only detract. The social and creative interaction between performing musicians is deemed inessential to the existence of music. As Cook writes, it suggests that the performer's "highest ambition should be self-effacement" (2013, 15). As we saw in the previous chapter, however, in improvised music, conversely, the creative autonomy of the improvising musician is often described to the extent that they do not use notation—or use less specific notation. This definition of improvisation leaves intact, and is even dependent on, the idea that music can be contained in the score, "composed into it". With the text as a site of purification, a place where agency is negated, performers are only really seen as creative agents when they do not play from a score.

The ICP does not reject notation, but rather reconsiders what notations actually are. Like Fluxus, their performance practice is obviously iconoclastic, critical as it is of the visual representation of music as defining its essence and value. However, it is an iconoclasm that does not set out to destroy images, but reassesses their function. Anthropologist Bruno Latour maintains that apart from iconoclasm from religious convictions, which wishes to destroy any images deemed heretical, there are also iconoclasts who

> do not believe it possible nor necessary to get rid of images. What they fight is *freeze-framing*, that is, extracting an image out of the flow, and becoming fascinated by it, as if it were sufficient, as if all movement had stopped. What they are after is not a world free of images, purified of all the obstacles, rid of all mediators, but on the contrary, a world *filled* with active images, moving mediators.
>
> *(Latour 2002, 26)*

Seen this way, the ICP's practice might be taken as a case study for rethinking the function of music notation more generally. Notation plays an important role not only in western art music, but also in many other musical practices, not least those normally designated as "improvised". From early jazz to the big bands of Duke Ellington, Charles Mingus, and Sun Ra, and from Fake and Real Books to the more experimental forms of notation in what might be called "post-free" improvisation, notation has also played an important role in the history of jazz, not only as a means of transmitting musical ideas but also by shaping particular forms of musicianship and creative practice. Of course, what actually happens in performance might bear little resemblance to what is written down, but this is precisely what makes these practices interesting: their significance does not rely on an expectation of performers to "comply" with what has been notated, but on the potential of these notations to provide a source of creativity in performance. To quote Cook: "it is only once you think of music as performance that you can start to make sense of scores" (Cook 2013, 1).

Distributed Creativity: Emergence and Indexicality

The philosophy underlying this way of thinking about scores as "works" is by no means unique to music, but underlies ideas about the relation between representation and reality more generally. In the first chapter I mentioned Lévi-Strauss' distinction between engineering and bricolage; the engineer works according to careful planning, with especially purposed materials and techniques, while the bricoleur makes do with whatever is at hand, repurposing available materials and techniques for products that have only a temporary function. Tim Ingold, studying processes of making and design, is clearly on the side of the bricoleurs when he writes that creativity is often wrongly theorized according to a model he calls "hylomorphism", using a term from Aristotelian philosophy (Ingold 2010). This model essentially views creative activity as the imposition of an already existing form on shapeless matter. It rests on the assumption that the human mind gives life and meaning to a stable, meaningless world. However, as it detaches and hypostasizes form from the materials that make it up, this model provides no accurate description of the actual process of making. Ingold conjures the image of a craftsman, for instance a weaver: the weaver does not shape threads into a pre-established form, but lets this form emerge by binding together separate threads. That is to say, even with a pre-established design, the process of making is not so much a matter of "moulding" the material into shape, but of negotiating the motion and the tension of the threads, the various elements of the loom, and the particular characteristics of the fabric—it is a matter of applying force, and working with the forces of materials themselves.

What Ingold calls the "textility" of creative practice is meant to shift attention to the *materials* that are used in creative work, and the "tactile and sensuous knowledge of line and surface" that comes with handling them. Drawing on Deleuze and Guattari, he proposes to replace the conceptual duo of matter and form with that of materials and forces. The hylomorphic model, Ingold argues, reads creativity backwards, working from the formal model that is the outcome of the process rather than attending to the improvisatory process of following materials as they go their way. However, as he and Elizabeth Hallam have argued elsewhere, to understand improvisation as essentially innovative, breaking with tradition or convention, equally reads the creative process backwards, judging the result by a given design rather than attending to the practice itself (Ingold and Hallam 2007).

Music analysis of classical works has traditionally proceeded from hylomorphic principles, focusing on the work as represented by the score and aimed at elucidating part-to-whole relationships in the form of the music. The analysis of jazz, which throughout most of the twentieth century was conducted by music critics and composers rather than musicologists, who have long ignored improvisation as a musical art form, initially followed suit. Solos were treated as little compositions, and through structural analysis it was shown that jazz improvisation was an expression of sophisticated musical knowledge—which of course also had an emancipatory aim, as is the case with Mengelberg's concept of "instant composition", and how it is usually interpreted and used by other musicians. Recent work in improvisation studies has largely moved away from this focus on the creative individual towards an understanding that emphasizes the collective creation of music in the course of performance. In the 1990s, Paul Berliner and Ingrid Monson showed through ethnographic descriptions combined with musical analysis that the forms of musical knowledge and creativity are not attributable only to talented individuals, but are learned and developed through social interaction and enculturation in a broader jazz community (Berliner 1994; Monson 1996).

Monson in particular emphasized that the process of improvisation itself could not properly be understood through an exclusive focus on individual musicians, but is a fundamentally social process. Employing concepts of pragmatics from linguistic anthropology, she described improvisation as a conversation, in which individuals collectively shape the music in the course of performance by responding to and building on each other's ideas. In creativity studies, Keith Sawyer was advocating a similar shift from a product-based conception of creativity to one that focused on the creative process, a reorientation to the *emergence* of creativity through interaction between people rather than the creation of a finished product in the mind of an individual "genius" in a flash of inspiration. Improvised music was central to his argument; one of his early books on the topic featured chapters by both Berliner and Monson, and also pursued the concept of improvisation in theatre, scientific practice, and everyday conversation (Sawyer 1997). The concept of emergence describes a process of causality that is nonetheless characterized by irreducibility. As improvisers react to each other's input, a certain definition of the musical situation will emerge after a few exchanges. In this emergent situation earlier ideas retroactively acquire a particular meaning, and it will also imply a possible course of further interaction, which of course may change again in the light of new ideas being put forward.

Since then, various scholars have built on these ideas to argue that creativity in collective improvisation is *distributed*, and that individual agency is less important than the processes that happen on a group level (Borgo 2005; Hagberg 2016). Thus, in contemporary music scholarship, improvisation is mainly understood as a form of collective action, in which the creative agency of individual musicians cannot be understood without taking into account their interaction with the group. Such ideas have been part of the world of free improvisation for a longer time, as evidenced by the following comment by AACM member Wadada Leo Smith in 1973:

> most of the "musical analysts" who have allegedly transcribed the solo-lines of the great masters, however, have misrepresented them by not transcribing the whole of the line, but by singling out, instead, only one element of the line. in the evaluation of this music, the opinion has been that the solo-line is the creation of a "soloist", and that the other improvisors involved are mere accompaniment. This is an invalid evaluation. The solo-line, in fact, is created by all improvisors contributing to it.
>
> *(W.L. Smith 1999, 321)*

On the one hand, this way of approaching improvisation as emerging in the collective interaction of musicians subverts the hylomorphism identified by Ingold as it describes the creation of form as a process rather than assuming its prior existence. Indeed, it even stresses the importance of interpersonal interaction in a way that seems to be missing in Ingold's examples of solitary craft. However, where Ingold stresses the importance of learning to work with the forces and pressures of one's material, the material aspect of music-making is frequently lacking in these discussions.[1]

In fact, the creativity of improvising musicians is often described as a form of immediate expression, overcoming any material constraints. The story of Charlie Parker playing a cheap, plastic saxophone for one of his most famous concerts is often told to highlight Parker's creative skill to make any instrument sound good. Monson, despite emphasizing the different creative roles for their players implied by different instruments in an ensemble, writes that in jazz, "there are always musical personalities interacting, not merely pitches or instruments or rhythms" (Monson 1996, 26). Such descriptions fit Ingold's hylomorphic model as they describe creativity as developed in opposition to the properties of the material that musicians are working with rather than in correspondence with them.

However, apart from this approach, which emphasizes that improvised music is an emergent result of socio-musical interaction, another theory of distributed creativity has been taking shape mostly outside of jazz and improvisation studies, with a focus on objects and technologies. Georgina Born was one of the first music scholars to explicitly make the argument that the "social and distributed nature of creativity" was evident not only in the social interactions that characterize musical performance or in the divisions of labour in the music industry, but also in the fact that "all cultural production constructs and engages relations not only between persons, but also between persons and things" (Born 2005, 16). She argues that our engagement with objects and technologies is itself deeply social, and thus that the production of music, as "perhaps the paradigmatic multiply-mediated, immaterial and material, fluid quasi-object, in which subjects and objects collide and intermingle", extends and relays such social relations (2005, 7).

Such arguments were quickly picked up in work on digital and electronic music (which is also Born's main area of research), but they also gave rise to a critical turn in organology, the study of musical instruments. In recent years, a wealth of research has appeared on how instruments come to represent or embody national or cultural traditions, how the history of composition might be reconsidered in terms of the innovative use and arrangement of combinations of instruments rather than only in terms of musical structure, or how the history of musical instruments and musical technologies relates to the history of science and technology more generally (Dawe 2001; Doubleday 2008; Bates 2012; Dolan 2013; Tresch and Dolan 2013; Roda 2014). Various scholars have argued that instruments actively participate in the creation of musical history, tradition, culture, and of course sound—that instruments embody musical knowledge, and that musicians, in playing an instrument, are themselves being played by it in return (Rehding 2016; Moseley 2016; Souza 2017).

Born's argument for the role of material objects in distributed creative process in music draws partly on Latour's Actor-Network Theory, which has long argued that the social and technological world are mutually constitutive of each other, and that agency is a result of their interaction, rather than being restricted to individual human actors. As Latour has argued,

> by definition, action is *dislocated*. Action is borrowed, distributed, suggested, influenced, dominated, betrayed, translated. If an actor is said to be an *actor*-network, it is first of all to underline that it represents the major source of uncertainty about the origin of action.
>
> *(2005, 46)*

More directly, however, Born draws on Alfred Gell's anthropological theory of art. In his posthumously published *Art and Agency* Gell outlined a theory that sought the value and purpose of art in its extension and distribution of social relations (Gell 1998). Rather than for its aesthetic properties, Gell argued that an artwork is captivating because of the way it appears as an agent—of the artist's creativity, of the culture from which it came, of the things it represents, of the audience it addresses, or of itself. The distribution of creativity for Gell lies not so much in the forms of collective action that characterize creative work, but in the fact that material objects, especially in artistic practices, can be considered as vehicles for a distributed personhood, or an extension of the (individual or collective) mind. As he writes:

Seen in this light, a person and a person's mind are not confined to particular spatio-temporal coordinates [i.e. their brain or body], but consist of a spread of biographical events and memories of events, and a dispersed category of material objects, traces, and leavings, which can be attributed to a person and which, in aggregate, testify to agency and patienthood [Gell's term for the opposite of agency, i.e. being acted upon] during a biographical career which may, indeed, prolong itself long after biological death. The person is thus understood as the sum total of the indexes which testify, in life and subsequently, to the biographical existence of this or that individual.

(Gell 1998, 222–223)

In other words, an artist's oeuvre or a community's artefacts and other forms of material culture—he discusses Duchamp's many preparatory works for *The Large Glass* as well as Maori meeting houses—are not just a symbol representing their thought, but actually externalize and extend it.[2]

Is it possible to combine these two different accounts of distributed creativity? To describe the role of musical instruments in the processes of emergence would highlight the importance of instruments in opposition to the hylomorphic prioritizing of musicians over their materials. To describe the role of notations, however, would be to subvert not only the common assumptions about "oral" versus "literate" music in discussions of improvisation and performance of composed music, but also the hylomorphism that remains so central to our understanding of music notation (Schuiling 2014; Payne and Schuiling 2017). As I discussed in the previous chapter, this hylomorphism is at work not only in discourses on classical music which see performance as a "reproduction" of the work, but equally in discourses on improvisation which regard any use of notation as an infringement on the musician's creative freedom. Sawyer, for instance, implies that his ideas of collective action, emergence, and distributed creativity do not apply in the case of scripted performance:

A traditional scripted play is composed and prepared by a single creative individual, the playwright. The staging and dramaturgical preparation for a given performance are typically controlled by the director. The actors are thus controlled by two different creative individuals: their words, stage entrances, and emotional expressions by the playwright; their stances, physical positions, and interpretation by the director.

(Sawyer 2003, 36–37)

It is unclear why Sawyer simply lets go of his idea of collective emergence in the case of scripted performance. Sociologists of art would certainly question whether a script is the solitary creation of a playwright (see particularly H.S. Becker 1982), and argue that it, too, is the product of collective action—and we might say the same for the performance. Why does Sawyer not simply include the script, the playwright, and the director in his process of emergence? His description reverts back to the kind of direct, mechanistic, product-focused causality that the concept of emergence so elegantly avoids. Why is the relation between director and actor defined in terms of dominance? Can actors not be quite dominant as well? It is one thing to say that creativity is not a matter of simply following a script. It is quite another to say that following a script is not creative. The process of emergence changes because of the different actors and media involved, but that does not mean the creative process is any less a matter of emergence through collective action.

As Cook has argued, nothing is really "determined" in a score—even if notes are specified to the performers, they still have to work to make them *their* notes, and this involves creative skills and impromptu musical interaction to the extent that performance from a score is still an emergent process to a significant degree. Coming close to Mengelberg's remarks on the difference between composition and improvisation, Cook argues that there is no fundamental difference between improvisation, composition, and performance, except in terms of process: "There are compositional elements in improvisations and improvisational elements in compositions. But in terms of process the difference is categorical: if you improvise off-line then that is composition, if you compose on-line then that is improvisation" (Cook 2007, 334). Rather than seeing the presence of notation as establishing a Great Divide between oral and literate musical practices, then, the concept of distributed creativity, understood both in terms of emergence through musical interaction and of the mediation of musical creativity through objects and technologies, places notation in a broader network of social and technological mediation.

Gell, Monson, and Sawyer all base their theories on the semiotic concept of the *index*. An index, coined by philosopher Charles Sanders Peirce, is a sign that derives its meaning from its practical context of use (Peirce 1991). It may be directly caused by its signified (as smoke is an index of fire) or there may more loosely be a practical connection between sign and signified (as a pointing finger is a sign for whatever it points to). Monson and Sawyer describe the process of emergence in terms of indexical presupposition and indexical entailment, terms drawn from linguistic anthropology. As a statement entails certain ways it might be understood, it sets up a framework of indexical presupposition, which may in due course be adjusted to accommodate the entailments of later statements. To Monson and Sawyer, the process by which musical form emerges from the musical statements and phrases of improvising musicians involves a similar dialectic in which the musical context is creatively adjusted to accommodate new statements. Gell's anthropological theory of art is based on viewing the art object as an index from which the agency of various human and non-human agents may be inferred. The art object, to Gell, may thus be understood to set up its own processes of indexical presupposition and entailment.

In the ICP Orchestra's musical practice, we can recognize how these ideas may be combined. As improvised performances, the musical form is emergent from their interactions, and the musicians creatively negotiate how to collectively shape a musical context to give meaning to each individual's contributions, and how to make an individual contribution that might take the musical context in a new direction. Within this collective give and take, however, a musician's statement may not only be taken as an index of the current musical interaction, but as an index of a piece—for instance, the next piece on the set list, or of a virus. This sets up entailments and expectations for how the musical situation may change, which is then negotiated by the musicians as they transform the musical context, making a transition to the piece (or, conversely, a musician's contribution might entail a move away from the piece that is being played to a free improvisation). Hence, we can see that the pieces in the ICP repertoire become active participants in the creation of musical form in their performances—without having to assume that the music is "already there in the score". In what follows I will make these theoretical arguments more concrete by discussing various examples from performances I attended during my fieldwork with the ICP. First, I will try to make clear what it means to see the score not as a text "containing" the music but rather as one medium in a network of mediating objects and technologies, before going on in the next section to provide some examples of the role of notations in the emergent construction of musical form.

Instruments and Distributed Creativity

Contrary to the idea of jazz improvisation as a form of immediate, spontaneous expression, there are many ways in which jazz performance is mediated and creativity distributed. One of the primary ways that has been addressed by various jazz scholars is the importance of recording media for the history of jazz. They do not just function as artistic products in their own right, but have also been important as a source of creativity for other musicians, as they play along with, imitate, and transcribe the music on recordings by their favourite artists (Monson 1996; Born 2005; Prouty 2006; Tackley 2010). A version of this interplay between performance and recording is also part of the history of the ICP. Mengelberg and Bennink frequently listened to recordings of their duo improvisation—sometimes even between sets, which meant that the interval could last as long as the first set—and Mengelberg often based new pieces on such recordings.[3] Mengelberg's own "De Sprong, O Romantiek der Hazen" appears as "Wie Jeuk Heeft, Als Moet Zich Men Krabben" on the 1978 LP *Pech Onderweg*, which may itself be based on Thelonious Monk's recording of the standard "There's Danger in Your Eyes, Cherie" (Mengelberg 1979; Monk 1959; Whitehead 2015). Ernst Glerum recently continued such practices by making an arrangement of Mengelberg's "Samba Zombie", recorded with the

Misha Mengelberg Quartet in the 1960s (Misha Mengelberg Quartet 1966), which also includes a transcription and arrangement of Mengelberg's solo on that recording as a B section.

However, beyond recordings, the ways in which creativity might be mediated are virtually endless. As Gell argues, any biographical event or memory, or any material object, trace, or leaving, can form part of a distributed personhood. To give but one example, I asked Bennink about the ICP's performance of Mengelberg's ballad "Arm Wiel" (Poor Wheel). The piece was arranged by Moore during my fieldwork. Bennink explained that the title referred to a car accident that Mengelberg's wife Amy had had, which broke the car's suspension or "wielarm". I had noticed that Bennink often used to start whistling during this piece, which he explained was related to a childhood memory:

> Jan Tromp . . . I'm just improvising on the melody. You used to have these butcher's boys who could do it very well, without using their fingers. Tristan can do it too. Jan Tromp, yeah . . . he was a professional whistler, he was very good at imitating birds and had a few hit songs, and he used to know my dad quite well. I do it here because the song is such a "smartlap" so it fits the style of the music.[4]

A smartlap is a Dutch genre, related to the French chanson and German schlager, which consists mostly of lyrical sentimental songs. These performances of "Arm Wiel", then, index many different persons, objects, and events, including not only Mengelberg's agency as a composer and Moore's as an arranger, but more broadly Amy's car accident, Bennink's genre associations, the 1950s Dutch fad for professional whistling, and his own personal biographical history. The performance of the piece assembles a broad aggregate of persons, objects, and events that constitute part of the piece's own biography. In jazz scholarship, such connections have mostly been understood as intertextual references, a way of "signifying" on musical traditions and identities, but I would like to focus here specifically not on how such references are used to create meaning, but rather how they are used as resources for creativity in performance.[5]

Of course, this runs the risk of making the application of the idea of distributed creativity unhelpfully broad. In this section I would like to concentrate specifically on the role of instruments, as well as on how compositions might mediate the relation of musicians to their instruments. A musician's playing style itself "incorporates" a range of social and material influences—Oliver, for instance, told me that she had first been encouraged by her music teachers to learn the cello because she was quite tall. One of the reasons she ended up playing the violin, however, was that her mother and grandmother told her: "I don't think that that's really a proper way for a lady to sit".[6] Such social structures need not entirely determine the relation of the musician to their instrument, of course, as this relation might conversely afford new opportunities for social and musical interaction. In the case of Oliver, she learned to play the viola only later on, and she developed a different playing style on it, partly because of the different relation of the instrument to her body:

> I feel like the viola is closer to my voice than the violin. I still love violin repertoire, and I love the soaring heights and virtuosity that is allowed on the little instrument, and I have a very beautiful violin, it's old and it has a lot of history . . . but the viola, I tend to improvise more with.[7]

On a smaller scale than the gender politics apparent in Oliver's anecdote, the social relations embodied by a musician's playing style may include certain stylistic conventions, particular forms of musical pedagogy, or the instrument's "role" in an ensemble. The concept of distributed creativity implies that there is in principle no contradiction between having one's "own voice" and drawing on a range of inspirations. When I showed Bennink a recording of the group playing an arrangement of Thelonious Monk's "Off Minor", he commented that his way of playing was *"my* way, which has to do with timing, mostly" while simultaneously emphasizing that he learned the placement of the accents and general comping style from listening to recordings: "Yes, you learn that from Art Blakey, of course!"[8] He went on to give a detailed account of how he was playing, as this was one of the performances in which he only used a snare drum:

Bennink: I'm playing one brush and one stick.

FS: Why do you do that?

Bennink: Because that way I can play that upbeat with the wood on the rim, that ticking, and with the brush I can keep going chick-a-chick what I would otherwise do on a cymbal.

FS: So that way you can use the snare drum to . . .

Bennink: Do two very different things, yes. I play the overtones with the brush and the other one is a short tick, you hear that?

FS: Yeah, I've also seen you use the stand of the snare drum as a kind of hi-hat.

Bennink: Yes, that too. Or the legs of a chair, it doesn't matter, they're there anyway.[9]

On the one hand, the development of creative skill is a matter of training and disciplining the body, learning certain motoric skills in correspondence with an instrument. However, this motoric process is itself socially mediated. Bennink's approach to his snare drum is inventive, but this inventiveness stems from a wish to emulate staples of jazz drumming on only a snare drum rather than a whole kit.

This is just to reiterate that in incorporating such social relations, this also creates new opportunities for musical interaction, and new resources for creativity. Janssen compared his own official, educated piano playing style to Mengelberg's more autodidactic style:

> Misha can really . . . I call it rummaging. That is something, once you become an accomplished classical pianist, you lose that. There is a kind of precision in my playing, which is also its quality, I like that, but it's far removed from . . . Misha can goof around, which makes it very jovial [gezellig].[10] I'm more a Bartok pianist, using more martellato, more percussive playing. With Misha it's . . . he has less strength in his fingers of course, especially today, but just the way he sits at the piano . . . I didn't learn it like that! You can't play Beethoven sitting like that! [. . .] So I don't have the means that Misha does. It might sound arrogant if I say I'm too good for that, but just from a technical point of view . . . Misha would be the first to admit that, he told me once that I should play more Art Tatum repertoire, simply because I have the skills. The strange thing is, it makes no difference for the quality of the story you tell. He uses his limited skills incredibly well. The same goes for Monk, quite a limited pianist but he can play exactly what he needs in order to tell his story. But I'm more . . . a classical education gives you something chameleonic, which can be a disadvantage, you can just change colour, from Debussy to Beethoven, which are completely different worlds.[11]

A musician's voice, then, is not a matter of acquiring mastery over one's instrument, making it do your bidding, but is the result of a more interactive, relational process, through which musical knowledge and imagination are constructed.

Instrumentation

Instrumentation might be defined as the way in which notation assumes or intervenes in such embodied relations.[12] The abbreviated nature of lead sheet notations is made possible partly because of their reliance on conventional instrumental roles in performance—although these are of course themselves a re-appropriation of instruments that for the most part were originally associated with very different playing techniques—while modernist scores frequently need highly precise notations to employ musicians' extended techniques. Pieces may group musicians together, implying forms of close coordination during performance, or they might leave open precise instrumentation, which allows musicians room for creative interpretation. Some of the free improvisations on the ICP set lists are characterized only by their instrumentation. Although they usually specify names of musicians (which might imply a certain instrumentation, although many of the musicians play multiple instruments such as saxophones and clarinets, or violin and viola), sometimes they specifically identify instruments. A particularly frequent item on the set list is "strings versus horns", or sometimes "strings versus clarinets", in which the two groups alternate brief improvisations. This practice quite obviously uses the iconicity of these two instrument groups and their associated traditions, as was noted by Honsinger:

> I think I like this piece the most, because of the real . . . I would say, the sound of the different schools [. . .] It's a good way to see the group [. . .] It's a big band, but it's also an orchestra, so an orchestral big band, so it's a good example of what Misha's idea is of the group.[13]

The fact that Honsinger refers to this improvisational set-up as a "piece" indicates the extent to which it is a regular item on the set list. However, it is not just a commentary on the way the orchestra combines these two sound worlds; these sound worlds are also enacted by the musician's playing styles. The three string players all have a classical background, while the horns generally have more of a jazz background. Ernst Glerum started out as a classical double bassist, but has since developed into one the Netherlands' most successful jazz bassists. He frequently switches between plucking and bowing, with an audibly classically influenced vibrato. I commented on his bowing and particularly his use of vibrato:

> Well, yes I like putting that in there. Actually that is just . . . Mary does it too, it's just a classical sound. I'm happy about that [. . .] Tristan has it too, that's really awesome. He has a very special classical tone, I think that's amazing, really cool. For my own playing I also choose to do that, to do it as classically as possible. That's the best way, I think. I think about that a lot, about bowing with the double bass, especially in a jazz context, because what the hell are you going to do with a bow? There are examples: Slam Stewart, Paul Chambers, Christian McBride, John Clayton, there's loads . . . Rufus Reid. They have a particular sound, and that's *their* sound, but I'm looking more in the classical direction. I used to play that a lot, so I can use that.[14]

This closer connection to a classical sound world attracted Glerum to the ICP as opposed to some other groups in the late 1970s that were more in the loud-and-powerful vein of free improvisation, and of course that was also what Mengelberg was looking for with the development of the ICP Orchestra.

Within such pieces that only specify instrumentation, it is clear that the individuality of the musician plays a large role. As I said, the particular relation of a musician to their instrument can be very significant for the way they interact with others. This was apparent in one performance where Guus Janssen was playing a set behind the piano, and a piece on the set list specified an improvisation by "Guus + 3 clarinets". The piece started out with Janssen playing the piano while Delius, Baars, and Moore were switching to their clarinets. His playing was intricate, with up-tempo three-part counterpoint giving way to jazzier harmonic movement. At that point, Moore interrupted with a couple of mocking "duck calls", intentionally playing with bad embouchure.

Janssen: That's funny, tut-tut-tut-tut [. . .] It's an open atmosphere here. I mean, I'm open to their participation. Not in the beginning, I'm just playing something pretty. I start with a solo, really, while here it changes the atmosphere. That's what it's for . . . it needed that, so I find that funny. It can often get hermetic when I play solo. It becomes too much a story in itself. As a musician you have to find a way in, well for instance by playing that, a kind of caricature of a thing I played earlier. You hear me react to that, and then there is this kind of opening.

FS: Was your starting point to play a solo?

Janssen: No, we were to do a group, but I started playing alone because they weren't on their spot yet. I'm the type of pianist who . . . I know this recording of Jazz at the Philharmonic, where Tristano plays with Charlie Parker and this whole big band, and Tristano just doesn't fit in. That's very strange to hear. I'm not trying to be negative about myself, but I tend to fill things up. It kind of works, because those guys also have the tendency to weave this little carpet in the background. It's an interesting phenomenon, how can you be open to other sounds coming in. That's difficult for a composer like me. I'm just thinking, you can hear me think. When I'm playing with a trio, that happens in the extreme.[15]

Apart from another example of individual style resulting from a wide range of influences—Janssen being educated as a composer and a concert pianist, his being deeply influenced by Lennie Tristano, and his usual work as either a solo improviser or with a piano trio—this is a good example of "indexical entailment" as it functions in the work of Sawyer. Moore's intervention clearly serves to create a very different musical structure which is at once a particular social structure, where Janssen is playing solo and the others have no choice but to either not play or accompany him. Moore had a similar experience:

Guus is a . . . soloist. It felt like he was playing a solo piano piece, and he's very good at that, it had a certain shape and a build and . . . crescendo . . . it was almost like a classical form. Where the climax is like two thirds of the way and then it comes down. The clarinets were just creating colours behind him basically. So . . . because of the amplification, that also emphasized the relationship for me, the piano was amplified and the clarinets weren't so . . . the piano was just louder. It's a bit stupid on the part of the sound people, if they see a quartet happening then they can just turn the piano off.[16]

Moore draws attention more to the mediation that is influencing their playing; the balance (or rather the imbalance) of sounds created by the sound engineer behind the deck. There are of course other forms of mediation too, influencing their particular form of interaction. The set list said "Guus + 3 clarinets": the division into a piano and a clarinet trio automatically creates a division of labour, and it becomes difficult to imagine a split into two duos, or a more conversational style between four different players, which would probably have been easier if the instruments had been piano, tenor, clarinet, and alto.

As I already mentioned, the ICP Orchestra is divided into a string section and a horn section in addition to the standard rhythm section in jazz—the usual line-up from left to right during my fieldwork was Mengelberg on piano, then Oliver, Honsinger, and Glerum on violin/viola, cello, and bass, Bennink in the middle on drums, and then Moore, Delius, and Baars on alto and tenor saxophones (or clarinets), Wierbos on trombone, and Heberer on trumpet. The grouping of the musicians in this way effectively creates three groups which have their own internal communication. This is particularly true of the horns, who have a traditional function in big bands to create background riffs. The horns in the ICP do this regularly, but they are also often the ones who introduce the viruses because they are more clearly audible than the strings. Moore explained:

I think the horns have evolved a mechanism to interject riffs, or other kinds of things, into whatever else is going on. I think it's easier for us than it is for the strings, because a lot of the times Ernst Glerum will be playing, or Tristan, they'll be fulfilling other roles. Or at least Ernst will be fulfilling other roles. It's also just a physical thing you know, I mean a lot of those different actions that the horns do are kind of . . . for the purpose of changing the music or, or . . . kind of guerrilla actions.[17]

Because the strings are with fewer musicians, one of whom also has a part in the rhythm section, and are less loud than the horns anyway, they are less suited to creating the kind of backgrounds or interventions that the horns frequently make. However, pieces may create this possibility by giving them certain roles to play.

In Moore's own "Oz", which he had written for the group during my fieldwork, the introduction consisted of downward melodic lines plucked by the string instruments. Notes were suggested, but the musicians could pick their own tempo and were not expected to play their lines together, creating an open, pointillistic texture. Because of this openness, not only in the sound quality but in the way that the musicians are able to pick their own way of playing the suggested notes, this introduction is very suitable for the kind of transitions that the ICP frequently makes. In an improvisation (by the string players or others) the strings can simply start playing these downward lines, which because of the light texture they create does not impose too much on what is happening at that moment but still is recognizable enough so that others can accommodate to making this segue. Later in the piece there is a section of free improvisation, after which the instruments open the next section by quickly repeating an e in irregular rhythms. In both cases, then, "Oz" gave the string players a role they do not often have in the group, namely to initiate new directions within a performance. The piece thus creates new possibilities for the string musicians to influence the socio-musical interaction on stage.

The reliance of pieces on particular roles in a composition may also be a source of disagreement, especially in such a genre where musicians are used to the option of stepping beyond their normally associated instrumental roles. Thomas Heberer had also written a new piece for the group, called "Coming Up for Air", which included a section where the musicians could play a call and response figure at will, but it was his intention that they do this while the rhythm section continued to provide a rhythmic basis. During the first rehearsal of this piece, he interrupted everyone and the following exchange occurred between him and bass player Ernst Glerum:

Heberer: There is a confusion that has to do with the way I wrote it. For the rhythm section in the D part, it's continuous. It's like a no chord situation, but you continue with the walking bass, so . . . those little crosses are just backgrounds if you want.

Glerum: I can't play background (?).

Heberer: Oh y—you could, if you wanted to but eh—it would be . . . for somewhere where the rhythm section has to function . . .

Glerum: No, no, sure, I'll play notes. I just wanted to . . .

[. . .]

Heberer: Let me rephrase that Ernst, if you feel like doing it, that is perfectly fine, but that was not the original idea, so I think from that perspective, it would be slightly . . . it would be a slightly different thing.

Glerum: No worries man, sure.

It is an interesting exchange because it illustrates some of the tensions between the egalitarian impulse of improvisation and the authorship and authority that are inherent to bringing a new piece to rehearsal and explaining how to play it to the group, which explains Heberer's apologetic tone—I will return to this in the next chapter. The confusion stems partly from Heberer's assumption in writing the score that the rhythm section would continue to provide a ground for the rest to improvise with the call and response patterns, and Glerum's expectation that this would be an opportunity for him to stop providing this ground and join in with the improvisation.

Some pieces of course do *not* specify a certain instrumentation. "Paardenbloem" or other graphic pieces do not have any instrumentation, which in its case also suits its function to be played as a virus. Its characteristic riff can be initiated by any musician—although of course the glissandi of its B section cannot be played on some instruments. More importantly, there are many pieces in the ICP repertoire with an outdated instrumentation. Because Mengelberg never wrote out parts, and the scores have been copied over and over again through the decades, the line-ups have changed while the instrumentation has not. Tobias Delius said about this:

> Especially when I joined, there were many arrangements for other line-ups, usually smaller ones, but also for a time there were three altos, two trombones, viola, cello, tuba . . . and we read that score, they were never rearranged, so it's always a search for who plays what and whether nothing is lost, and transposing . . . many things go wrong, but that's the nice thing about Misha's material. You can give it a lot of attention and do everything precisely, but it can also be fun, which happens often enough, when nobody really knows how to play it anymore and you do it half from memory and half from paper and it works really well.[18]

In both cases, then, the missing instrumentation feeds into the improvisatory way of playing of the group, as musicians have to creatively work around the demands of the piece and the affordances of their instruments.

As I mentioned earlier, lead sheets rely on specific instrumental conventions for their abbreviated nature. Considering their importance to jazz performance more broadly, it might be interesting to conclude this section with a brief discussion of a performance involving such lead sheets. During my fieldwork, Bennink, Glerum, Oliver, and Moore gave a short concert at the release of a box set of all the recordings on the ICP label up to that point (which meant fifty recordings at the time). At this concert they played from a kind of "real book" of Mengelberg lead sheets, called *Goedendagjes*, transcribed and edited by Moore in 2009 (Mengelberg 2009). They opened the concert with "Reef & Kneebus" (Figure 5.1), a piece consisting of three parts: a plaintive part consisting of mostly parallel thirds over an f-sharp pedal, then a free transitory improvisation, and finally a more up-tempo jazz piece consisting of an A section with parallel sixths (usually played over an a-flat pedal, not notated in this lead sheet) and a B section consisting of a fairly standard progression of fifths and a turnaround at the end.

Reef und Kneebus (#2 & 4)

FIGURE 5.1 "Reef & Kneebus"

Used with permission

The lead sheet assumes a basic distinction between rhythm section and melody instruments, but other than that it requires the performers to create their own arrangement in the course of performance. The rhythm section will usually include bass and drums, so Glerum and Bennink's roles are quite straightforward, but the sheet does not specify a division of the two melody voices. Moore and Oliver divided the two voices according to the different registers of their instruments, with Oliver playing the top note on her violin and Moore playing the second voice on his clarinet. When they repeated the melody, however, they switched voices. Such an off-the-cuff arrangement to keep some timbral variety, in the course of the performance itself, is typical in using a lead sheet such as this, where only the basic outlines of a piece are given so that it is easily adaptable to different line-ups. When playing "Kneebus", they again proceeded from the build of their instruments to play first and second voice, with Moore improvising a second voice based on the chords that are written in the sheet. When playing "Habañera" (Figure 5.2) later in the concert, a habanera in 3/4 time instead of the usual 2/4, there was more of such impromptu arrangement. The two voices of the melody in the A section were once again divided, but this time with Moore, who had switched to his alto saxophone, playing the top melody. When the B section arrived, Oliver played the main melody, while Moore quickly decided to play the top notes of the chordal accompaniment specified in the sheet. After four bars, Moore switched to playing the melody and Oliver quickly switched to playing the chords in triple stops on her violin.

Such a lead sheet, then, even if it does not really specify particular instruments, does draw on particular instrumental conventions and roles that are commonly used in jazz. In specifying a role, the sheet does not impinge on their creative autonomy, but rather allows the musicians to exercise their creative agency, drawing on their instrumental skills and musical knowledge in making off-the-cuff arrangements and playing the role that is asked of them. "Reef", for instance, clearly allows Glerum and Oliver to showcase their classical tone on their instrument—Glerum used a strong vibrato, adding greatly to the atmosphere of the piece, while Oliver played slight ornamentations typical of classical performance. This chamber music atmosphere was also retained during the ensuing improvisation before going on to "Kneebus". This jazzier piece allowed Glerum to also use his skills in playing walking bass lines, while it might have been more of a challenge for Oliver who is less used to improvising in a jazz idiom, as we saw in the previous chapter. Such details show how a Real Book like this sets its own creative parameters because of the way it distributes agency. This use of lead sheets, however, marks a particular difference from normal ICP performances, in which the scores are used more like "found objects" to be overlapped and juxtaposed in various ways. Having seen how scores may be considered part of a network of distributed creativity, how does this work in normal ICP performances? Specifically, since I have focused specifically on Gell's concept of distributed creativity, how does this work when we shift the

Habañera

FIGURE 5.2 "Habañera"
Used with permission

timescale from Gell's biographical level to that of the performance itself, and focus on the process of emergence as theorized by Sawyer and Monson?

Notations and the Emergence of Form

As with any improvised musical performance, what Monson and Sawyer call indexical presupposition and entailment—the frame of social context and the way it is reshaped by utterances made in that context, which then retroactively acquire a different meaning—are constantly negotiated and used to come up with new ideas. To give one example, at one moment during a concert in The Vortex in London the group was playing "Zombie Zua", shown in Figure 5.3 in an arrangement by Moore, written by Mengelberg in the 1960s for his quartet with Piet Noordijk. The first solo was played by Wierbos, and Moore, Delius, and Baars played some three-part harmonic textures on their saxophones as a background to his solo. When the next solo was played by Oliver, however, Moore sought some different ideas for the horns to play backgrounds. Mengelberg, accompanying Oliver, played some clustered arpeggios that were more the result of a particular wiggling hand movement than of a harmonic idea. This caught Moore's attention, and he imitates the hand gesture to the horn section, who play similarly wobbly sounds.

FIGURE 5.3 "Zombie Zua", arrangement by Michael Moore

Used with permission

But not only was this idea transferred from accompaniment to a background, it was also picked up by Oliver herself, who translated the idea into trills and then into arpeggios. The horns responded with a low trill, while Oliver started to play the arpeggios in stepwise motion, building on the stepwise harmonic movement so characteristic for this piece. As the horn section finally accompanied this with upward stepwise crotchets, this provided a fitting climax to her solo.

Of course, a jazz piece like Zombie Zua still provides a general framework within which such processes can take place. In free improvisations, such interactions shape all of the music. Musicians explore a certain idea for some time, after which the piece may end or transition to a new section because a new idea gets picked up and leads to further exploration in a new direction. It is frequently at such transition moments that ideas quickly acquire a new meaning based on the contributions of others. At one concert at the BIMhuis, for example, Heberer, Wierbos, and Bennink were improvising together. Wierbos and Heberer had started out creating a contrapuntal texture of long intertwining melodic lines— something Heberer told me had to do with the similarity of their instruments. This texture gave way to a section in which both started using flutter-tonguing techniques, which then evolved into a climax as Bennink started playing louder and more dense material on his drums, and Wierbos complemented him by playing long, low, loud notes on his trombone. Bennink and Wierbos clearly wanted to create an ending, but Heberer continues to play, repeating and varying on a quick melodic motif. At this point, Mengelberg, who had been playing for a while but was not audible over the noise, can suddenly be heard playing the piano. As Heberer described this moment:

> When Han stopped and I continued, obviously my impression during that moment was different, but hearing back, I thought, oh, that was a wasted opportunity. But Misha helped me out. At first it sounded like "oh there shouldn't be any more trumpet", but because Misha started it made my misguided statement sound valuable again, because all of a sudden the situation turned and it looked like it was some sort of transition moment.[19]

Mengelberg provided a harmonic accompaniment to Heberer's motivic variations, which turned out to be the start of a new section in the improvisation. Wierbos and Bennink responded by creating sound effects on their instruments. Heberer's motivic variations acquire a new meaning and significance because of Mengelberg's piano playing, generating material for further exploration, which also means that Wierbos and Bennink have to readjust to this new situation, which they had thought to be an ending.

As Monson and Sawyer argue, such processes are typical of much improvised music, where accompanying musicians do not simply provide "background" to a solo, but there is a constant give and take between musicians as they shape the music by responding to each other's contributions. In the case of a free improvisation, this is how all of the musical material is generated, which is where a lot of the excitement of freely improvised music stems from. What role might notation play in such processes? Understandably, notation has frequently been seen to be opposed to such forms of interaction, as the score supposedly determines the music in advance. In the ICP, however, the scores play an integral part of such processes. In the example just described, Oliver and the horn section already make use of the stepwise harmonic and melodic motion of the piece to generate improvised material. The interpretation of parts of the score as graphic material, or playing certain phrases backwards, as described in the previous chapter, is another way in which the notated material can play an active role in the collective emergence of music.

More generally, however, the pieces in the ICP repertoire generate certain forms of improvisatory interaction between the musicians. Heberer made a nice comparison in talking about the way in which many of the scores allow for changes in their formal arrangement in the course of performance:

> I assume the first guy that did this stuff really aggressively was maybe Charles Mingus, who of course comes from Duke Ellington, so there obviously is a connection . . . I've seen that with quite a few, particularly Misha's pieces. They are often very interesting in this regard because on the surface they look very . . . not demanding and simplistic but then there's all sorts of options internally which make them fantastic vehicles for improvisation because they are almost like a modular machine, you can see them from so many angles.[20]

A modular machine is a programming term for software that uses interchangeable parts rather than a single, inflexible, monolithic system. To the extent that it connotes distributed versus centralized control, it also speaks to the way in which these pieces can give the performers a co-creative role rather than dominate their way of working. This was also emphasized by Delius, who said that these pieces often supply a list of ingredients rather than a recipe, and said, speaking particularly about Mengelberg's arrangements of Duke Ellington: "When Misha arranges such a piece . . . or Ab or Michael for that matter, then there are built-in moments from which . . . where it's not about erasing the composition but about improvisationally shaping the material".[21] As Heberer and Delius tell it, then, the pieces in the ICP repertoire anticipate that the music is emergent in performance, and do not specify everything in advance but rather leave room for what I earlier called bricolage in performance, employing elements of the material when they are called for. To use the terminology of Actor-Network Theory, these pieces are not considered "black boxes", presenting the combination of heterogeneous actors and materials as a unified whole, but rather render different concepts and elements compatible while retaining their heterogeneity—something Latour has recently called "composition" (Latour 2010).

"Kneushoorn" (Krhinoceros) is a good example of this (Figure 5.4). It might appear at first as a completely finished piece with no room for improvisation. It has quite a simple form, with twice four bars forming an A section and then twice four bars forming a contrasting B section. Note that the instrumentation of this copy is outdated: the trumpet melody on the second staff, which is the main melody of the piece, is now played by Wierbos on trombone (before Heberer joined in the 1990s, the group had frequent periods without a trumpet player), the tenor saxophones play the baritone and trombone parts, and Oliver joins in with the cello on her viola. However, rather than a monolithic work, the piece is better understood in the "modular" way described by Heberer and Delius. The form is indefinitely repeated, and with each repetition musicians can join in or drop out with their parts as they wish. Every part stands more or less on its own, and with the different combinations of parts the musicians can collectively shape a performance with an interesting build-up and structure. The music of "Kneushoorn" is not "contained" in the score, but emerges through the interaction of performers. Moreover, the different parts also invite creative interpretation; once the rhythm and groove of the piece are established, the musicians frequently experiment with the timing of their parts. They create different accents and syncopations, Glerum often plays fills to alternate the steady oom-pah bass line, Oliver and Honsinger play their line at irregular entries, and Moore and Wierbos lengthen and shorten their melodic phrases.

Again, however, this piece clearly establishes a certain framework within which certain forms of improvisation can take place; to use Sawyer's term, it

FIGURE 5.4 "Kneushoorn"

Used with permission

establishes a framework of indexical presupposition. This is significant in itself, as the notation creates forms of improvisation rather than being opposed to it. However, the notations of the ICP repertoire also play a role in the kinds of creation of musical form and the making of transitions and endings, as we saw in the example of free improvisation discussed above, which are dependent on the creative use of indexical entailment.

To illustrate this, I will describe how the ICP goes through various transitions between pieces over a span of about 15 minutes. As I wrote in the previous chapter, creating such improvised collages is central to the way of working of the group. At a performance in Antwerp, the set list contained the pieces "Toy" (by Heberer), "Een Beetje Zenuwachtig", and "Kehang" (both by Mengelberg) (Figure 5.5).

"Toy" consists of two contrasting textures: slowly moving chords played by the clarinets, contrasted by glissandi played by the brass and strings. Heberer, as the composer of the piece, conducted the piece, counting off and giving some cues to repeat sections. At some point, Heberer cued the clarinets to continue improvising, and their improvisation used ideas from the piece, such as the glissandi and the long melodic arches. The indexicality of their playing was now uncertain; it is not clear if they were still playing the piece and improvising with some of its material, or if they were making a transition to the next piece. At this point Heberer and Wierbos played one of the x-shaped note phrases that clearly indexed a transition to "Een Beetje Zenuwachtig" (see Figure 4.8 in the previous chapter). These staccato notes clearly contrasted with the slow-moving lines of the clarinets, and the clarinets, recognizing the

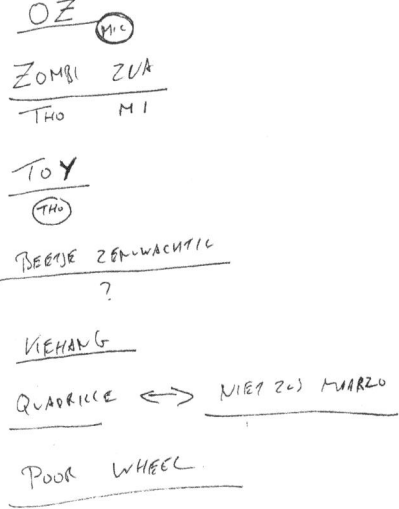

FIGURE 5.5 Set list for a concert at De Roma, Antwerp

Used with permission

material, made an ending by slowing moving up to a long high note. The whole group started playing with these x-shaped figures, before Moore started playing a repeated d which would become the opening melodic figure. After some time, Moore cued the head of the piece.

The pieces in this example clearly participate in the creation of form, without determining the course of the music. They serve as inspiration for the clarinets' improvisation, and they cue a transition to the next piece while also giving material with which to improvise this transition, such as the x-shaped figure and repeated d. Moving on, the musicians had some more extreme ways of improvising with the notated material. Oliver took a solo on "Een Beetje Zenuwachtig", which at some point was interrupted by the horns playing the "Pilaar" virus. This was taken by the rest of the group as an indication to break out of the piece, and the rhythm section stopped playing time and changes. This led to a free improvisation by Mengelberg, Honsinger, and Bennink, who used rhythmic and melodic ideas from "Een Beetje Zenuwachtig". In this improvisation, the horns again played a phrase as an index of a transition to the next piece, namely a phrase that went down and then up, which is another x-shaped figure from "Kehang" (Figure 5.6). The rest of the group responded immediately: Bennink played a short drum fill and everyone was silent for a moment; Mengelberg and Honsinger then continued to use motives from "Een Beetje Zenuwachtig".

However, the horns then looked for different elements in the score for material to use for making this transition. Baars then pointed to the wobbly lines in bar 10 that indicate to tenor and trombone to play the same figure as is notated for alto above. As they interpreted this line graphically and play a wobbly figure, Bennink played a figure on his hi-hat indicating a more regular pulse, to which Mengelberg reacted with a staccato chord. The horns then played the black downward line between the boxed bar 10 and the box in the right-hand bottom corner. Mengelberg kept playing his chromatic block chords, and Baars pointed towards the first three notes of the melody that was scribbled in at the bottom of the page, adding a gesture to play them quietly. This melody is a transcription of the original viola part for trumpet. It seems to contain a mistake, as it turns the third note into a written c sharp, while this was probably originally intended to remain a b flat and not a b natural (which would create a rather unconventional augmented major seventh chord instead of a normal major seventh chord—the b natural also clashes with the b flat in the melody). The horns played this as written, sounding c, b flat, b natural, however, while Wierbos harmonized e, d, c sharp below.

The long notes created a sense of expectation after the clear accents before, which was heightened by Mengelberg playing a trill. The horns then started to repeat the rhythmic motif with which they started, and the strings joined in too. Moore stepped forward to make eye contact with everyone to cue the beginning of the melody by playing the notes in bars 11 and 12. After the head, Baars took a solo, in which he played variations on the x-shaped motif. Moore picked up on this, as the melody reminded him of the first phrase of the jazz standard

FIGURE 5.6 "Kehang"

Used with permission

"As Time Goes By". He communicated with the other horns, and they played this phrase, increasing the energy even more. Bennink greatly increased his basic pulse, and the horns tried out some other riffs before settling on a repetitive rhythm. At the height of textural and energetic density, Moore started playing a high, upward glissando, which was a cue for the rest of the group to immediately open up the musical texture. The glissando was recognized by everyone as the B section of "Paardenbloem", the virus discussed in the previous chapter. The other musicians started playing the rhythm of the A section and everyone slowly took over the glissandi to go into the B section. Rather than returning to A, Oliver played the "Kehang" motif, and the group returned to the head of "Kehang", after which they ended the piece.

I describe this example in detail because this, to me, is what characterizes the performance practice of the ICP Orchestra. In the quick transitions between pieces and free improvisations, the line between what is improvised and what is not becomes completely blurred—at least if we define improvisation in the way in which music scholarship has usually done, in terms of whether something is played from a score or not. In fact, the very use of the term "transition" seems to be inaccurate, as it implies improvised sections between pre-planned stretches of composed music. The example described, which exemplifies the creative practice of the ICP, is better understood as a form of bricolage, in which the musicians shape the music, variously using and repurposing combinations of their creative skills, each other's musical ideas, and the notations on their music stands.

In this example we can recognize various aspects of distributed creativity as I have described it in this chapter. "Kehang", to use Gell's terms, clearly forms an integral part of the "biographical career" of the ICP Orchestra, with its changing line-ups and scribbled-in transcriptions of melody lines for new instruments, which in performance lead to new improvisatory possibilities. The score of "Kehang" is an object that has been shared, copied, reworked, and annotated, and is thus better understood as a distributed material process rather than representing a permanent ideal object. Throughout these transitions as described in this example, the functioning of musical statements and phrases by the musicians as an "index", in Gell's terminology, of an improvised statement or of a part of a piece is essential to the way in which other musicians define the musical situation as a free improvisation, a transition, a performance of a piece, or a breaking out of the piece, and to how they adjust their responses accordingly. That is to say, the agency of the score helps in the process of negotiating forms of indexical presupposition and entailment, and the score thus becomes an integral part of this improvisatory emergence of form. It plays an active role in the social interaction and forms of creative collaboration among the musicians, and does not pre-establish all indexical presupposition and dominate the performance process, but contributes to the heterogeneity of improvisatory possibilities.

Notes

1 This is not to say that instruments have been neglected: Monson's account is predicated on highlighting the role of the rhythm section instead of maintaining an exclusive focus on the soloist, and there have been various studies of particular musicians that explicitly discuss their playing style in terms of instrumental technique (Givan 2003, 2009; Lash 2011). Sawyer's distinction between group creativity and product creativity, between synchronic creativity that is mediated through discourse and product creativity that is mediated through objects, however, seems to make a hard and fast categorical distinction, making the role of material objects in group improvisation theoretically insignificant (Sawyer 2003, 119–120).

2 Ingold has argued the idea of material agency as found (in different forms) in the work of Latour and Gell is actually itself an instance of hylomorphic thinking, as it suggests that there can only be movement when there is an agent behind it (Ingold 2010, 95). However, Latour emphasizes that his account of material agency is intended precisely to dislocate agency rather than seeing it only inherent to minds; Gell's account is subtler, and on the one hand argues that what is important is how art objects are *ascribed* agency (thus avoiding the question of to what extent they "really have" agency), while on the other his account of the extended mind seems to point in a similar direction to Latour's emphasis on the dislocation of agency.

3 Han Bennink, interview with the author, 3 January 2012.

4 Jan Tromp in fact had a hit in the 1950s with "Droomland", a translation of "The Beautiful Isle of Somewhere", which bears some general resemblance to "Arm Wiel", especially in its harmonic progression.

5 The term signifying was introduced to literary studies by Henry Louis Gates, and has been used in jazz criticism by Gary Tomlinson, Robert Walser, Ingrid Monson, and various others (Gates 1988; Tomlinson 1991; Walser 1995; Monson 1996).

6 Mary Oliver, interview with the author, 22 February 2012.

7 Ibid.

8 This form of literacy also brings with it its own notions of literalness. Bennink commented on the ending of the piece that they did not quite play it as Monk had originally recorded it, and that they should probably rehearse it more often.

9 Han Bennink, interview with the author, 4 January 2013.

10 "Gezellig" (from "gezel", companion) is a very common but notoriously untranslatable Dutch word, signifying a convivial, relaxed, and enjoyable atmosphere.

11 Guus Janssen, interview with the author, 8 January 2013.

12 Fabrice Fitch and Neil Heyde, drawing on the ideas of Helmut Lachenmann, have described composition itself as a process of "instrument-making", in the sense that each composition imagines, assumes, or invents particular playing styles. This means that not only does the piece reshape the instrument, but the instrument as such is part of how the composition is constructed (Fitch and Heyde 2007; see also Clarke, Doffman, and Lim 2013).

13 Tristan Honsinger, interview with the author, 30 January 2013.

14 Ernst Glerum, interview with the author, 10 January 2013.

15 Guus Janssen, interview with the author, 8 January 2013.

16 Michael Moore, interview with the author, 9 January 2013.

17 Michael Moore, interview with the author, 23 December 2011.

18 Tobias Delius, interview with the author, 21 February 2012.

19 Thomas Heberer, interview with the author, 15 July 2013.

20 Thomas Heberer, interview with the author, 1 February 2013.

21 Tobias Delius, interview with the author, 31 January 2013.

6
ANTAGONISM, RESISTANCE, AND HUMOUR

In my discussion of the influence of Fluxus and Cage on Mengelberg's aesthetics, I noted his preference for curating situations of disagreement, annoyance, and anger. In my descriptions of the forms of creative interaction in the ICP Orchestra I have not really touched upon this topic yet. We have already seen that the creative practice of the ICP diverges from how improvised music is usually theorized, with its emphasis on orality and its placement of improvisatory creativity in opposition to the use of written music, which is seen as representative of undesirable hierarchies and impeding spontaneous expression. The ICP repertoire, both in terms of the collection of pieces and the creative skills and practical conventions by which these pieces are employed, implies a way of working in which notation is a fundamental part of their improvisatory process and creative interaction.

In the use of viruses and of compositions as "found objects" that can be disassembled and reconstituted in performance, we can already recognize how Mengelberg's taste for mischief and destruction is still apparent in the current orchestra. These practices also show how the competitive way of working of Mengelberg and Bennink in the ICP Duo continues to influence the group's approach to performance. Indeed, the way in which the orchestra continues to interrupt and sabotage each other's playing is very similar to their style, and the ICP repertoire makes it possible for this to happen in a group of ten musicians where the duo was able to do this by means of quotations and stylistic allusions. This was also confirmed by Wierbos:

> The way of working in the ICP is derived from Han and Misha. They've been working together for so long . . . or rather against each other, like in a boxing match [. . .] That has nothing to do with freedom, it's about

egos, competing and showing off. The louder Han would play, the softer Misha would become. And Han wouldn't hear him, and he would become purple and when he stopped you would hear Misha, playing very softly. That was fantastic![1]

This combative way of working stands rather starkly in opposition to the usual emphasis on jazz improvisation as a form of interaction, impromptu collaboration, and as representing a democratic and egalitarian spirit. As Monson argues, "Good jazz improvisation is sociable and interactive just like a conversation; a good player communicates with the other players in the band. If this doesn't happen, it's not good jazz" (Monson 1996, 84).[2] Bennink, however, once remarked that he liked playing with Derek Bailey and especially Mengelberg so much because they did *not* have to interact with each other all the time:

> They are playing whatever they are playing. You can try and work towards them, but it's no use. Sometimes there is some brief contact, but never truly. Misha has that even more than Derek. For me that is a very liberating way of playing, because you don't have to consider the other at all.
>
> *(Andriessen 1996, 39)*

This is not to say that the way of working in the ICP is not interactive or collaborative; the previous chapters have described some examples of musical interaction in detail, and in the historical chapters in Part I we saw that the idea of performance as a social practice was an important concern for the ICP founders. It does imply, however, that there are important differences across musical practices in how social interaction is defined, and how they imagine ideal forms of social practice. Delius spoke about the group's aesthetic ideal as follows:

> Many people say that improvisation can be too chaotic and then there is the "guiding hand" of the composer or a piece to bring some sense of structure, but I think it's the other way around. The purpose of the written material is to disrupt a "nice flow" of improvisation. It can create more anarchy than improvisation sometimes [. . .]. The compositions play their own part.[3]

Apart from underlining the point made in the previous chapter that the pieces in the ICP repertoire actively participate in the construction of social and musical interaction, this comment contains a few other interesting aspects. First, it celebrates the disruption of flow as an important part of their creative practice. Most musicians would probably regard the disruption of flow as a bad thing, and indeed as a form of "optimal experience" (Csikszentmihalyi 2008) flow has generally been described as a positive thing. Second, it suggests that the pieces do not simply dominate the course of the performance but rather provide the musicians with opportunities for creativity in performance—we have already seen examples of this in the previous chapter. Third, it suggests that this way of working neutralizes the authority that composition brings with it; in this approach, rather than the musicians following the will of the composer, the composed material gives them more autonomy.

In his book on the politics of avant-garde music in 1960s Amsterdam, Robert Adlington points out an interesting similarity between the musical practice of the ICP and the anarchism of Provo. He acknowledges the disavowals of the ICP musicians of explicit political ideals; his argument is not to suggest direct influence, but rather "a shared outlook on the relation of self and other, of individual and community" (Adlington 2013, 114–115). Roel van Duijn explicitly rejected the collectivist ideals of earlier Dutch anarchists in favour of a more individualist and antagonist anarchism. Instead of an emphasis on shared responsibility and social cohesion, Van Duijn advocated unlimited individual freedom, in which the "social order [was] subservient to individuality" (2013, 115). In this view, the ideal society was better described in terms of constantly transforming forms of disharmony and inequality than of balance and equilibrium. Adlington's comparison of the early ICP approach to improvisation suggests that not all forms of improvised music might adequately be described in terms of community building, social cohesion, or collaboration, and that there may be very different views on what constitutes desirable forms of socio-musical interaction (Schuiling 2017).

In this chapter we take a closer look at this particular facet of the ICP's musical practice. I will draw on some of my interview material to show how these forms of interaction are understood among ICP musicians and the way they inform their musical aesthetics as well as relations to fellow musicians. In describing examples from moments in ICP performances that I attended that exemplified such antagonism, I argue that moments of resistance, as the complement to moments of flow, can be important sources of musical creativity. Extending the discussion of bricolage and distributed creativity in the previous chapter, I discuss Lydia Goehr's concept of improvisation *impromptu*, which occurs when a preconceived idea encounters resistance. Finally, in describing the playfulness of these moments of tension and disagreement, I want to draw attention to the humour that is such an important aspect of this approach. Humour plays a central role in the ICP's performances, and in every performance of the group I have attended there have been several moments where the audience was laughing out loud. I conclude that the idea of humour, as opposed to that of irony, is not only central to the way of working of the ICP but points to the materiality of creative and improvisatory work more generally.

Antagonism and Counterpoint

The ideal of combining diverse and sometimes even opposing aesthetics and styles can be traced back to the 1960s Misha Mengelberg Quartet. In 1966

Mengelberg wrote of this quartet that one of the primary things he enjoyed about it was its inclusion of different musical perspectives:

> What fascinates me in the collaboration with Han, Robbie, and Piet, besides of course that each plays his instrument really well, is the different musical character of each musician. Piet is very virtuosic, Robbie is outrageous, and Han directs his banging little home altar right through all the oat, potato, and beet fields. The spheres of interest, however, frequently diverge. While Piet and Robbie like rugged swing, alternated with sentimental ballads, Han and I prefer messy swing and mean sounding slow pieces—which does not mean that Robbie and Piet never want to play anything messy or mean, nor Han and I anything rugged or sentimental. The differences in musical outlook do not end there. Piet and Han like to play loud and unequivocally, while Robbie and I play soft and equivocal whimsies, and would like to hear those from the others too. Or not. I don't know how my fellow quartet members feel about this, but my provisional assumption remains that such diversity gives more interesting material for improvisers to work with than regular agreement in a complementary groove.
>
> *(Mengelberg 2012, 22)*

This "provisional assumption" would guide Mengelberg's shaping of his groups for a long time. Moore, speaking specifically about joining the group in the early 1980s, when there were notorious fights and disagreements between musicians in the group, confirmed this:

> I really appreciate Misha, when he does choose people for his band, he doesn't just choose people that have a similar aesthetic [. . .] He liked to create tension in any way possible, and in the beginning a lot of it was . . . putting people together that perhaps shouldn't be together, you know! Seeing what would happen! You know, people that really wouldn't like each other he would put together.[4]

Although the relations within the group are no longer as combative as they may once have been, the aesthetic of competition, pestering, and sabotage still informs the way of working of the group.

Various musicians also commented that when joining the group, this reliance on a multitude of different voices and styles meant that it was difficult for them to decide how to function in the group, as they were not given a particular role to start with. Moore continued that he found it difficult to determine a place for himself alongside the saxophonic violence of Keshavan Maslak and Peter Brötzmann:

Moore: I think I had to find my own niche, I learned to do things that they couldn't do, you know.

FS: What kinds of things?

Moore: I could play clarinet and . . . Peter has his strengths and so does Keshavan, but I think Misha likes different voices, so I sort of had to . . . the whole process of playing and growing is finding your own voice . . . I think at the time I thought I didn't really have much to offer, except maybe on the clarinet, the whole thing was kind of overwhelming![5]

Many of the musicians had a similar experience when they joined the group and had to find out for themselves what they could contribute to the group. Oliver, who joined the ICP in the mid-1990s, describes how she could not rely on any role or place being given to her:

I remember once after a performance I was sitting next to Thomas and I was like . . . I don't know what to do! I don't seem to be able to find a place for myself. And Thomas said, "I've been trying to figure that out since I started!" So that's very different, I wasn't given a role to play. I wasn't given the chick role to play, there were no concessions for me being a girl. I had to find out where to fit, without doing this [strikes a feminine pose] because they wouldn't let me do that either. I tried! You just don't know what you're supposed to do so is it this or this . . . it didn't put me down, but I wasn't coached. There wasn't a lengthy rehearsal process to develop it; I just had to join in.[6]

The inclusion of musicians with different styles and attitudes fits in with the discussion at the end of Chapter 3: that employment of such different styles is not primarily for syntactical or semantic reasons, but primarily pragmatic, offering different forms of making music together. Moreover, by stimulating clashes between different musicians rather than curating a single common ground for his orchestra, the ICP makes it difficult to envision any "division between musical impulse and performance practice", as Mengelberg put it (Mengelberg 1979b, 259), but rather redirects the attention to the music as it is being invented and created by the musicians during performance.

This does, however, provide a challenge to musicians. The juxtaposition of different styles and pieces that demand various musical techniques and stylistic proficiencies constantly requires the musicians to look beyond their usual ways of doing things. As Heberer described it:

I would say that Misha is a master in . . . he's really excited about getting you out of your comfort zone [. . .] Every improviser has his own clichés, and things that they like, maybe things that sounds nice on his instrument, or things that are nice because they have been invented by John Coltrane or Clifford Brown, or something, and everybody copies this because it's beautiful [. . .] So I think from early on Misha, more than Han, was, and still is, looking for something, like an alternative concept of beauty. And there are a lot of things to explore in situations that look like weaknesses, or things that don't go right, and instead of being afraid of those situations, you should seek them and try to deal with a situation that is not entirely smooth. And come up with solutions in a state of disaster, in a state of being fragile.[7]

Delius stated that this also provided their concerts with a sense of excitement and makes for a stylistic and idiomatic variety that is uncommon in much improvised music:

I have heard groups that improvise, you know, sure, but there is a clear consensus on what they are about. To put it crudely, this is a loud energy kind of band, or here it's very subtle and about small sounds, and that can be very interesting, but I find it much more interesting if you do not really know [. . .] So with respect to musical form, some groups have clear models they work with, but I'm more interested in, how are we going to get this ship back to shore, or on the rocks or whatever. It can be great being in a situation where you feel very comfortable, but it is very important not to be comfortable sometimes.[8]

We can relate this to his comment above about the disruption of flow; the suggestion is that there is an important form of creativity in learning to deal with a situation in which the musicians are not quite sure what to do next and where the music is headed.

The musicians sometimes referred to such moments as "stains". Mengelberg had once commented on a piece by Janssen that it was too much like neatly ironed white linen, and that it needed a good coffee stain somewhere. As we have already seen, many of Mengelberg's pieces contain such a "stain" somewhere, a place where things may go wrong, where it isn't entirely clear what to do next. Various pieces discussed in Chapter 4 contain elements that can be used to exit or subvert the form of the piece, but such stains may also be recognized in some of the highly dissonant harmonies amongst the otherwise beautifully flowing chords of "De Sprong, O Romantiek der Hazen". Some pieces, however, are intentionally stain-resistant, as Baars told me:

There was a period when Misha did not like that anymore, because we became too good at these derailments. So he wrote a number of pieces with the idea that we would not know what to do with it. "Moeder aller Oorlogen" [Mother of All Wars] is such a piece; it is hard to open up because the melody is so persistent, and it just keeps going round. And then he thought it would get a sense of freedom, and it only occasionally works, because everyone really has to work at it.[9]

The melody of "Moeder aller Oorlogen" has a very strong motivic coherence and a strong sense of harmonic direction, combined with a tonic pedal that firmly grounds the piece, making it hard to "escape" from it in a way that makes musical sense. Of course, the musicians could simply start to freely improvise, not bothering with the characteristics of the piece, but that goes against their general aesthetic—and this also says something important about these forms of musical disagreement.

When discussing one of my recordings of a free improvisation with Oliver and Wierbos in a previous performance, Bennink was very explicit about how he approaches his performers in a mode of competition rather than collaboration. He commented on his playing in the middle of the improvisation: "I'm working towards an ending, you can hear that clearly. Those dynamics, less less, softer. But because I've been playing so loudly Mary would like to go on for a while, but I keep trying to make an ending".[10] As Bennink stopped playing, Oliver took her chance to play some more now that she was audible. After a few moments, Bennink attempted to sabotage the music by playing a loud crash on his cymbals. He commented:

> Now I don't think it's on the level as where I wanted to end it. You see how selfish this is? It's limping along without the quality that it had when I was still playing, and I was working very hard towards that ending.

When I asked him whether he was just trying to get his way, he replied: "Yes, of course! I'm trying to be in charge". These comments corroborate Adlington's comparison of the ICP to forms of individualist anarchism. However, Bennink's comments simultaneously indicate that his concern is mostly with the form of the piece, seeing the preferences of the musicians as subordinate to this cause.

As Delius already indicated, the question of "how are we going to get this ship back to shore, or on the rocks?" is a question "with respect to form". It is not simply to say that musicians can play whatever they want and the result is a kind of chaos; the clashes and tensions, the musicians generally agreed, are a formal musical consideration, and have to make musical sense, even if this is a matter of great contrasts and divergence. As Delius told me, they are an aesthetic as well as a social matter:

> Misha is a mischievous character of course, he likes spreading doubt and dissatisfaction, but it is also an aesthetic choice. If something goes too well, he loses interest [. . .] You approach it with a certain tension, and with trust, of course [. . .] Everyone is responsible for the material, and everyone in their own ways [. . .] We're all working on making it sound good. Not "pretty", but there is a lot of attention to detail, whether it's dynamics or texture, and everyone is constantly responsible for that.[11]

The musicians generally described this ideal of different musical personalities interacting as a kind of *counterpoint*. This goes back quite a long way, as a version of this idea is already apparent in some of Mengelberg's comments in the *Jazzwereld* discussion described in Chapter 2. Mengelberg, after noting that the free jazz they had listened to as a starting point for their discussion did not signify freedom for him at all, presented his own interpretation:

> In the case of Ayler I see—and don't hold this against me, I've only just heard this for the first time in my life—but I hear a play of densification and dilution, not only as regards the ambitus, so the high and low, but also with regard to multitude. So I see an unconscious, or perhaps conscious, that doesn't really matter, use of contrapuntal possibilities, which did not deserve much attention in bop.
>
> *(Vuijsje and Witkamp 1966, 225)*

Counterpoint is an important part of Mengelberg's compositional style. His dissertation at the conservatory was on the complex contrapuntal style of Gesualdo, and he taught counterpoint at the Conservatory of Amsterdam to multiple generations of Dutch composers, improvisers, and musicians, from the most commercial to the most cerebral. Many of his compositions employ contrapuntal textures—the fugue "A la Russe" is by no means an anomaly in that regard—and his free improvisations frequently contain stretches of improvised tonal counterpoint.

As he continued in the "discussion", he made clear that for him this notion of counterpoint was not just a structural element of the music, but also implied the multiplication of voices and agencies, and thus has a strong connotation of the social aspect of musical practice:

> A few years ago in the Concertgebouw I heard Rollins play a sort of duet with himself. You could say that Rollins was standing on a bridge, commenting musically on Rollins under the bridge. While that was happening Rollins was also coming on the Hudson by boat.
>
> *(Ibid.)*

This specific notion of counterpoint came up a number of times in my interviews with ICP musicians, who often connected it to Mengelberg's preference for tensions and contrasts. Heberer said:

> I think generally speaking the "school of Misha" is a lot about counterpoint and it's about coming up with *different* strategies, to get a richer texture. It's always related to what kind of a personality you are [. . .] People in the ICP differ in this regard. I would describe myself as someone who is usually looking for some kind of common ground, I'm not

> a natural . . . my personality is not such that I am a natural counterpoint player. Like for instance Misha is very much a natural counterpoint player and Ab I would also call a natural, he's always looking for something to like . . . add to the picture, whereas I look more for common ground.[12]

And Moore also described such processes as a form of counterpoint:

> I'm used to—a lot of times, with ICP, there's this thing of counterpoint that is really important to us. It's OK if you're doing one thing and someone else is doing another thing and somebody else is doing another thing.[13]

However, this does not mean that the musicians can simply do anything they want, but precisely creates a sense of responsibility for their musical contributions, and how they shape the music as a whole. As Heberer put it:

> There is a lot of freedom, as long as you're willing to defend your position. If you throw something into the pool, or change the direction, you have to find a way to make it work or when it doesn't find a way to deal with the failure.[14]

Indeed, failure is an ever-present possibility in improvised music, and it is a reality that improvisers have to learn to deal with. The cultivation of moments of failure and disagreement means that they are considered as valuable as the moments of flow, as Heberer told me in a later conversation:

> This band is also about tolerating failure [. . .] I don't want to call it work in progress, that is misleading because the idea of work in progress is really the *programme* of the ICP. I don't think we're like "one day it will be a perfect product", I think it will never be that, that's really not the idea behind it. I think the quality sometimes actually lies in the weaknesses and it going terribly wrong and then figuring out how you deal with them, and that in itself can be a quality that one can enjoy, or say it is terrible rubbish but it's not . . . the rubbish is as important as the really fantastic beautiful Michael Moore solos. That is as valid as the fuck-up of the day. There's no hierarchy in this regard. That is something maybe not specifically ICP, but certainly a specific of the band.[15]

Relational Aesthetics and Material Resistance

In Chapter 1 I referred to Mengelberg's preference for provocation as a "relational aesthetic", one that clearly pursued aesthetic rather than social ideals, yet defined its aesthetics in terms of the kinds of social interaction it generates rather than (only) in terms of abstract structural or formal qualities. We can recognize this again in the particular conception of counterpoint propagated by the ICP musicians. The term "relational aesthetics" was coined by curator and art critic Nicolas Bourriaud, who used it to denote a particular movement in 1990s art, in which "art is the place that produces a specific sociability" (Bourriaud 2002, 16). After a period of postmodernism, Bourriaud writes, in which one either bemoaned the end of historical artistic progress or celebrated the endless play of signifiers, "the role of artworks [became] no longer to form imaginary and utopian realities, but to actually be ways of living and models of action within the existing real, whatever the scale chosen by the artist" (2002, 13). For Bourriaud, it is precisely the aesthetic character of art, its playfulness and relative distance from economic considerations, that forms part of this sociability. Form is central to his argument: "Relational aesthetics does not represent a theory of art, this would imply the statement of an origin and a destination, but a theory of form" (2002, 19). The formal properties of art are both a premise and a result of human relations, and so in a constant state of "formation": "Form only assumes its texture [. . .] when it introduces human interactions [. . .] Through it, the artist embarks upon a dialogue" (2002, 22). Form is not something that is pre-established by the artist, but in line with the discussion of emergence in the previous chapter, arises from the social interactions generated by the artwork.

Although Bourriaud was mainly talking about the work of specific artists in the 1990s, his argument can be considered as a general reconsideration of the relation between aesthetics and social practice. The aesthetic and the social have long been seen as mutually exclusive; since Immanuel Kant, the aesthetic has been defined in terms of its "purposelessness", and its appreciation consequently as "disinterested", distinct from any personal or social interests (Kant 2007), while in sociology, most famously in the work of Pierre Bourdieu, aesthetic considerations have been understood as ideological effects, and functions of social hierarchies and inequalities (Bourdieu 1986). Recently, scholars in both fields have started to reconsider this opposition, and the work of Bourriaud has been an important source of inspiration, as has that of Gell, who equally saw art's aesthetics effects precisely in terms of the way it mediates social relations, and so provides ways of seeing the aesthetic and the social as interwoven rather than opposed (Born 2010b; Born, Lewis, and Straw 2017).

To some extent, discourse on improvised music has long emphasized the interrelatedness of aesthetics and social practice in this genre. With score-based performance as emblematic of a top-down hierarchical way of working, improvisation has often been described in more egalitarian terms, and improvising musicians have frequently shown a conscious awareness of and critical engagement with the socialities of performance—the ICP is no exception in this regard. In the previous chapter, we already saw how there has been a strong emphasis in theories of improvisation on the centrality of collaboration in the process of musical production. Some scholars have translated such ideas into a general critical theory of improvised music, describing improvisation in utopian terms. In recent years, the work of Daniel Fischlin and Ajay Heble has attracted particular attention. In a range of publications including contributions by various other authors since the early 2000s, they argue that improvisational practices have generally shown "concepts of alternative community formation, social activism, rehistoricization of minority cultures, and critical modes of resistance and dialogue" (Fischlin and Heble 2004, 2).

On the one hand, such a utopian perspective is very important, as it alerts us to the ways in which musical practices are not just intended for aesthetic pleasure, but formulate ways of seeing and interacting with the world. Anthropologist Roger Sansi, building on the work of Bourriaud and Gell, argues that all art contains a utopian element, "a reduced model of a possible world, a research process that proposes to imagine the social in different terms; perhaps still imprecise and unstable, subject to revision, but which still contains the promise of a different future" (Sansi 2015, 157; see also Schuiling 2016). However, as he also cautions, precisely because of this, utopian perspectives need to be harnessed by critical attention to their own premises and conditions of possibility. Sansi draws on Claire Bishop's critique of Bourriaud's proposition of relational aesthetics. She confronts his emphasis on sociality, collectivity, and dialogue, arguing that "the social" is not inherently good, but necessitates the question "what *types* of relations are being produced, for whom, and why?" (Bishop 2004, 65). She argues that merely showing artistic practice to be a form of collaboration (and/ or vice versa) is merely ideological if they do not also invite critical forms of resistance: "Without antagonism there is only the imposed consensus of authoritarian order—a total suppression of debate and discussion, which is inimical to democracy" (2004, 66).

Such an argument seems very appropriate to the musical practice of the ICP, although it does not translate directly. As we have seen, ICP musicians were critical of the existing musical infrastructures and the social hierarchies they exemplified, but they did not generally tie their music itself to such forms of societal criticism, or indeed to forms of political critique in general. As I have argued, however, in their musical practice we do see a proposition to see the social in music in different terms, specifically to reconsider scores as objects of social interaction—this in contrast to both a work-centred view of classical composition, which sees scores mainly as representations of musical structures, and the usual discourse on improvisation, which describes its unique form of musical sociality in opposition to the use of scores. Moreover, scores are not just imagined as social objects, but as *resistant* objects, sources of antagonist interaction, as opposed to the imagined conformity and compliance in work-centred views of classical music performance, and to the egalitarian forms of collaboration of free improvisation.

What does it mean to consider notations as resistant objects? In anthropological theories of material culture—the study of the social and cultural relationships between people and things—some have insisted on a categorical distinction between "objects" and "things". The distinction was first drawn by Martin Heidegger, for whom an object, a *"gegenstand"* or standing-against, is a complete and finished product, opposed or indifferent to processes of human interaction, while a thing gathers people, generates collective action, and changes in the process (Heidegger 1971). Ingold, for instance, argues that human creativity can only be developed in correspondence with things, materials in constant formation, rather than objects that establish boundaries and divisions. He cites philosopher Vilém Flusser who writes: "An 'object' is what gets in the way, a problem thrown in your path like a projectile" (Ingold 2012, 436; Flusser 1999, 58). This description of an object, however, although presented as something undesirable and an impediment to creative work and interpersonal contact, is precisely how the pieces in the ICP repertoire are frequently used, and the musicians generally consider this to be an important part of their creative practice. Although I sympathize with Ingold's idea that things should be conceived of as active and adaptive rather than complete and finished entities, I suggest that it is precisely this problematic and resistant aspect of the object that can give it a particularly fruitful role in the creative process.

Lydia Goehr has argued that the concept of resistance indicates an alternative concept of improvisation. When an object is resistant, and thwarts our plans or habits, it calls for improvisation *impromptu*, which she contrasts with improvisation *extempore* or the creation of music in the course of performance. She takes the example of a string breaking in the middle of a performance; no longer able to improvise (extempore), the musician must now improvise (impromptu). Goehr argues that, in opposition to the utopian claims of freedom and authenticity in extemporized music, the concept of improvisation impromptu imagines a form of practice that is more sensitive to the precariousness and contingency of everyday life. Moreover, it is a concept of improvisation that is not merely positive; impromptu improvisation is agonistic, competitive, and divisive (Goehr 2016). Precisely because of this confrontational quality, however, resistant objects highlight the dependence of human action on material environments. In fact, Bill Brown has drawn the thing–object distinction along different lines than Heidegger, arguing that objects are see-through, and only "assert themselves as things" when they stop working, changing our relation to them and thus indicating "how the thing really names less an object than a particular subject–object relation" (Brown 2001, 4).

For Dewey, whose philosophy of creativity I discussed in Chapter 4, resistance forms an essential part of the creative process and of artistic form. In his account of the interaction between organism and environment, he identifies a "rhythm of loss of integration with environment and recovery of union", which forms the basis of aesthetic experience (Dewey 2005, 14). The artist "does not shun moments of resistance and tension. He rather cultivates them, not for their own sake but because of their potentialities" (Ibid.). As Dewey argues, the resistance of the environment generates curiosity and significance:

> Impulsion forever boosted on its forward way would run its course
> thoughtless, and dead to emotion. For it would not have to give an
> account of itself in terms of the things it encounters, and hence they
> would not become significant objects.
>
> *(2005, 62)*

Dewey's ideas form an important inspiration to sociologist Richard Sennett's
work on craftsmanship. Sennett echoes Dewey when he argues that far from
only yielding frustration and anxiety, the resistance of materials can be produc-
tive, as craftsmen need to reconsider the properties of their working materials as
well as their habitual ways of working with them. Resistance thus triggers the
imagination, as it requires a reconsideration of one's work, one's bodily habits,
or one's working materials (Sennett 2008, 214–230).

In the work of these authors, rather than a categorical distinction, as we
find in Heidegger, between natural things that provide an authentic relation to
being and mass-produced objects that corrupt us, in which "objects are against
us, [and] things are with us" (Ingold 2012, 436), the resistance of objects, their
lack of fit to a specific context, may precisely make them significant sources of
social and creative interaction. As Latour has argued, rather than establishing
classifications of objects and things, the central point should be to realize that
the material world is not just a matter of fact, but a matter of concern (Latour
2004). In the ICP, their pieces gain a significance as objects of social interaction
because they are resistant, used antagonistically as ways to interrupt or sabotage
what musicians are playing. Thus, far from the Heideggerian "objects" that
musical works, as standardized and commodifiable entities, might be thought to
constitute, they become things that are part of the social fabric of the orchestra.

Resistance and Play in Rehearsal

For a concrete example of the role that resistance and antagonism can play
in the creative process of the ICP, let's look at the rehearsal process of "Oz",
the piece by Michael Moore mentioned in the previous chapter (Figure 6.1).
The learning of new material is especially interesting in this regard, as it shows
the musicians getting to grips with the particular demands and resistances of a
new piece, while also discovering new forms of resistance as they are getting
to know it better. Moreover, in this process they also have to negotiate the
inevitable hierarchy and authority that composing new material for the group
brings with it. In the dialogue between Glerum and Heberer described in the
previous chapter, we could recognize that Heberer did not want to impress his
intentions of how the piece should be played too hard on Glerum, even though
the latter made clear that he was fine with conforming to Heberer's wish that
the bass would keep playing rhythm rather than join in with the background
riffs played by the rest of the group. This is not just a forced egalitarianism, but

also an awareness that in performance it should be possible for the musicians to suddenly go in a different direction if the situation calls for it, so that Glerum should not feel bound to keep playing rhythm.

Moore is a prolific composer and probably contributes the most compositions to the ICP today, with Baars coming closely behind. As I quoted him in Chapter 4, his ideal is to provide simple ideas that are clear and concise, yet provide a large range of creative possibilities, "so that you don't have to tell people much, if anything". "Oz" fulfils this ideal quite well. It consists of three sections and a coda which each develop a very particular musical idea, with spaces for free improvisation between them to serve as transitions between sections that have no clear sense of structural development on their own. The first section opens with slow downward melodic lines, which segue into tremolos on the strings. The second section establishes a more up-tempo rhythm, with one group of musicians playing long chords in a five-bar cycle, and another playing a rhythmically syncopated and fragmented melody on top. The third section has the strings repeat the note e at a high tempo, with the saxophones playing a series of chords cued by the trombone and the trumpet playing rubato phrases over them. After a final collective improvisation, the coda consists of three notes played repeatedly, slowly expanding into a cluster as the musicians play higher or lower notes, which can be chosen from a specified set.

There is a clear and quite practical rule that whoever composes a new piece is in charge of it both in rehearsal and in performance (for instance, if it requires any cues to be made). Other than that, ICP rehearsals are generally very informal. Although they work effectively and pay attention when they need to, the musicians start doing their own thing when they get bored, and there is a lot of chatter between them when they are not playing. When watching material I had recorded during my fieldwork, I was struck by a brief segment when the group had just quickly gone through the different sections of "Oz" and were about to rehearse it in full for the first time. Moore, however, was not actively leading the group in any way. Wierbos was playing on his trombone, Moore joined in, and Wierbos asked whether they should try playing the whole piece. Moore nodded, but took no action—some people had a brief chat, Baars turned to Moore to ask something about a detail in the piece, while Glerum was practising Monk's "Ask Me Now". He shared some liquorice with Bennink, and they talked about the design of the liquorice box. Meanwhile, Wierbos and Moore were playing again while Baars and Delius talked about something else. At some point, without a cue from Moore, the strings started playing the downward lines that open the piece.

This way of doing things serves to negotiate both of the tensions described above. Moore effectively transfers his authority onto the string players by letting them start the piece, and the free timing of the opening section also means that they can join in when they want to. This is also useful in performances, as Moore anticipates the possibility that they will have to improvise a transition into this piece from a previous item on the set list which may not have finished yet. The notation mediates Moore's status as an author by allowing people to engage with the material on their own terms, distributing leadership over the group. This resolves some of the tension that authority and authorship bring with them, as well as the tension between discipline and spontaneity: the musicians learn to play the notes as they are discovering new possibilities. This is not restricted to the rehearsal, as the musicians keep discovering and experimenting on stage. In fact, the rehearsal for "Oz" only lasted about 20 minutes total, even though the full piece is about 10 minutes long.

FIGURE 6.1   "Oz" by Michael Moore. Reduction of original score by the author
Used with permission

FIGURE 6.1 *(continued)*

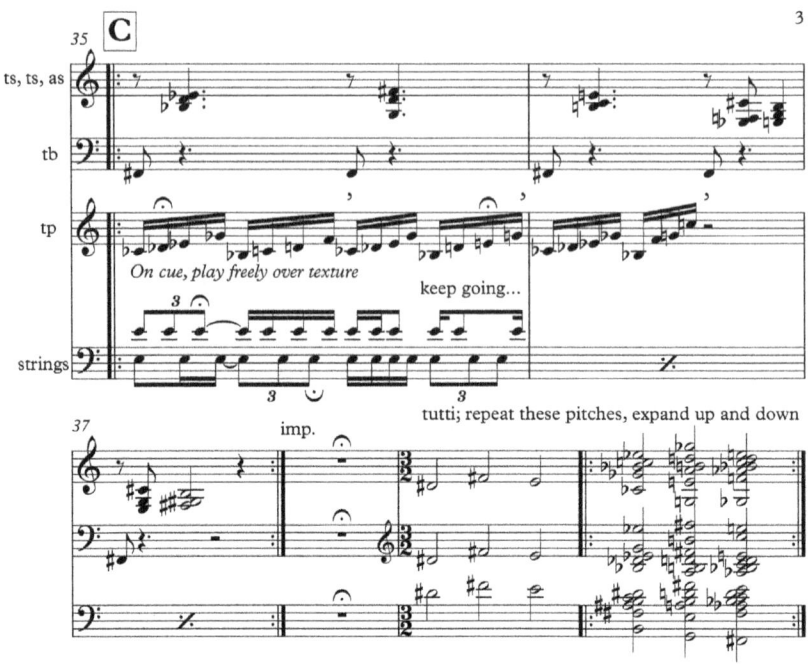

FIGURE 6.1 *(continued)*

In performances, the open texture of the opening section made it suitable to improvise a transition into the piece; the pizzicato downward lines of the strings, though soft, are clearly recognizable as the start of a new piece. The open texture also meant that it allowed for the musicians to add and contribute new ideas, building on the two ideas of downward lines and tremolos in the score. This means that this section could often be quite messy, and rather than a section followed by a free improvisation, it was sometimes more like one long improvisation using ideas from the first section.

In the second section, interruptions and mistakes could be more disruptive. With the first section being so open, the second section appears as a more famil-iar jazz texture, with the rhythm section establishing a firm up-tempo groove, chords being outlined by one group of musicians, and a second group playing a syncopated melody. In an early performance of the piece, Honsinger, who had not been at the rehearsal, started playing his long notes without waiting for a cue. Moore, unlike Mengelberg who always wrote full scores, prints out parts for the different musicians so Honsinger may not have been aware of having to wait for a cue. He also misjudged the basic pulse, playing half-time and making breves out of semi-breves—this actually happened quite frequently; there was one performance where, as if by a miracle, all four musicians simultaneously played these chords at half-time, mistaking the basic pulse for m.m. = 90 rather than 180 at which it was usually played. Perhaps realizing his mistake, Honsinger started improvising with long notes of varying lengths. In principle this created quite a nice contrast between the plaintive rubato cello line and the bass grooving below it, but it created a problem when the other musicians started playing their lines. The other musicians playing these chords, Oliver, Baars, and Wierbos, responded by also simply playing long notes of varying lengths rather than following the written notes exactly. On a cue, the other three musicians started to play the syncopated melody line.

Clearly, mistakes or disruption do not always generate creative and satisfying solutions. Given that the group and especially Honsinger were still very unfamiliar with the piece, in this instance they were not able to come up with an answer to Honsinger's mistake. This is not to say that this section does not tolerate disruptions or mistakes—just like the previous section with its open textures, this section does anticipate some incoherence or disruptions. There is no strong functional harmonic movement in the cycle of five chords, and the syncopated diatonic melody is already written out of sync with these harmonies, meaning that these two elements can be played quite independently and do not need to be closely coordinated. This anticipates the possibility of discrepancies, or of a creative "counterpoint" between the musicians. In fact, some mistakes can lead to new discoveries about this material; when all four musicians playing the held chords played them at half-time, it appeared that the chords were harmonically ambiguous enough to still work with the melody, and even with the bass line even though it was following the proper harmonic rhythm. Honsinger's mistake and the following contrapuntal texture of long notes played by the four musicians also created a nice effect over the bass' b-minor ostinato pattern, which, had the musicians been more familiar with this material, could have been followed by a cue to start playing the chords.

That is to say, a mistake like this one could have led to a new way of performing the piece, a new strategy for making transitions between the different parts. This did happen in section three. While the strings repeat their note e in unison, Wierbos cues chords from the saxophones with his trombone in a free tempo. In the rehearsals, Wierbos actively tried to confuse the saxophones— even during the first time when they played the piece section-by-section to get a feel for the different parts. He played his cues in rapid succession, or at unexpected moments, trying to make the saxophones miss a cue, or even better, to play a chord without a cue being given. At some point, Wierbos made the downward gesture with his trombone as if he plays the note, without actually playing the note—as if he is fooling a dog by swinging his arm but not throwing the ball. The other musicians laughed when they fall for his trick, and this disruption was then used to create a transition to the collective improvisation that follows this section.

As in the first section, there is a certain deflation of the hierarchical relation of Moore as a composer versus the rest of the musicians. The score delegates a leading role to Wierbos, who can also use this role to experiment with the resistances of the material, and to look for strategies that he could later use when performing the piece, which he frequently did. Clearly, the notation here does not dominate what the musicians play, but, at least in the case of the horns in this segment, gives the musicians something to play and experiment with, increasing interaction between them by not only establishing a shared focus but also providing them with an element of contest.

However, this way of working means that Moore had to accept that his piece would not be played quite as he had imagined it—which may mean that the musicians may find creative possibilities he had not foreseen, but also simply that the performances will contain frequent mistakes and failed experiments. When I showed Moore the performance with Honsinger's mistake, which also included some other mistakes, he responded:

> I don't know, it's kind of . . . if you play it right then you don't need to play it anymore. And . . . getting there is half the fun, so . . . Usually, if it was a different band and the people weren't as musical and experienced it might have been really depressing if we didn't get it right, but we can usually come up with something that is quite nice, you know, even if . . . a long time ago I gave up the idea that I wanted it a certain way if I came to bring in a piece to an ensemble. Whatever I had in my mind might be good, but the end result might even be better, that is part of the musical culture.[16]

His comment shows an interesting mix of pragmatic realism and a trust in his fellow musicians, as well as a kind of rationalization of something he is not completely pleased about. He told me in an earlier interview about the ICP's performance practice in general that:

> Personally I would wish that they would leave more space [. . .] My experience with Misha is that, playing in small groups with him, you can work really hard to build up something, creating tensions and . . . And he can just destroy it really easily with just one note, a well-timed, well-placed note. And your whole fantasy just disappears, so there's that element of this group too. It's like . . . "Oh, so you're busy creating something for 30 seconds, okay well it's time to stop that and do something else".[17]

Moore is not the only one who has occasional doubts about this way of working. Glerum, who more than the other ICP musicians often plays in more straight-ahead jazz groups, was quite frank about Mengelberg's taste for stains:

There are certain procedures I question, or at least ask whether they are really for me [. . .] Misha likes destroying things, and I haven't always understood that [. . .] I really support having some kind of friction, because it's often good for a composition to have that, but it's often too soon, and sometimes we haven't even really played the piece, and I think that can be problematic.[18]

Thus the tensions between a sense of antagonism and anarchy and the hierarchies and discipline needed to learn new material (and to keep practising familiar material) continue to be negotiated, and each new composition may bring with it new solutions and new problems.

In the case of "Oz", Moore did not need to do much in order for the group to play his piece well—after the 20-minute rehearsal, he was very reticent to intervene in the way that the musicians were learning the piece, and after a few performances they were able to play it without many mistakes. It is also in this sense that his scores extend his agency as a composer, as what they did specify was clear enough to guide the musicians in this learning process. Moreover, they do not just extend Moore's agency, but attain an independence from his authority and intention, which is significant for the musicians to feel they are engaging with the music on their own terms rather than following Moore's instructions. Moore simply had to accept certain mistakes that were made during this process, as he evidently felt that this would be a more fruitful attitude than to be more authoritative and precise.

In the ICP's process of learning a new piece, then, we can see moments of improvisation impromptu and improvisation extempore in a dialectical relationship, as mistakes and interruptions lead to new creative possibilities for inventing music in the course of performance, and these possibilities in turn provide new opportunities for antagonistic interaction. Such disruptions highlight how the piece constructs relations between musicians, and allows them to negotiate their position in this process. As I argued in the previous chapter, much of the ICP's performance practice revolves around rendering fluid the boundaries between free improvisations, transitions, and pieces. This means that the distribution of musical roles in the ensemble is also constantly in flux. Sennett locates resistance along edges, arguing that there is an important distinction to be made between boundaries and borders. Boundaries are limits that do not allow transgression, while borders are more porous and as such become sites of interest and exchange, interaction and contestation (Sennett 2008, 227). Ambiguity thus encourages improvisation (2008, 235-237).

Sennett illustrates this point by referring to the playgrounds in Amsterdam designed by Aldo van Eyck in the 1950s. These playgrounds contained abstract and minimalist equipment, intentionally ambiguous so that children could use their imagination to construct their own playful narratives around them. Moreover, they contained spatial ambiguities, with uncertain boundaries between sandpits, grassy areas, play equipment, and even surrounding roads. The children, then, had to make up their own rules of play as well as functions for the different elements in the park. The playful provocations that form an important part of the ICP's performances can be traced back to the era of 1960s countercultures discussed in Chapter 1. This playfulness in their antagonism was emphasized by Heberer:

> It is not a test, like let's see how he reacts. It is not a New York kind of survival of the fittest, not this Darwinistic . . . like I have the biggest dick or something like that. It is kind of like a perverted game, but it is play, it is definitely a game.[19]

The pieces in the ICP repertoire can aptly be described as playgrounds for the musicians' games—recall Moore's earlier comment that the games of the ICP are less about following a set of rules and more about a playful approach to their material. Play theorist Miguel Sicart distinguishes play spaces, which afford free play, from game spaces, which are designed in accordance with game rules. He writes: "A play space is a location specifically created to accommodate play but does not impose any particular type of play, set of activities, purpose, or goal or reward structure" (Sicart 2014, 51). The playground triggers the imagination, yet is also resistant to certain narratives; "the relation between space and play is marked by the tension between appropriation and resistance" (2014, 52). In these playgrounds, the ICP musicians negotiate their different roles, and the narratives they construct are emergent in the relation between musicians and scores.

Humour

This brings me to a final point. The performance practice of the ICP, especially in its moments of antagonistic interaction, is often very funny. Both Bennink and Mengelberg have cultivated a stage presence that triggers laughter—and not just in their antagonistic duo performances. In both interviews and his commentary on the music during performances, Mengelberg was renowned for telling stories in wonderfully constructed, slightly archaic sentences (some of the spirit of which I have tried to retain in my translations of his words above), the point of which was not always clear. This prolixity also translated to his musical performance. He would often come on stage late, while the band was already playing, with a cigarette in his mouth, a cup of coffee in one hand and a glass of cognac in the other, wearing a big warm coat. He would make a show of looking for the piano, and having found it, carefully arranged the cup and the glass on top, sat down to smoke a cigarette, and eventually took his coat off and laid it on the piano, half covering the strings.

Bennink's humour is more energetic. He makes a show of playing the drums, accenting a rest by putting his drum sticks behind his head as ears, or getting away from behind his drum kit to play various objects on stage, or sitting down to play the stage floor. He will empty a bag filled with drum sticks over his kit, or throw a stick down on the floor to bounce up and catch it again. Although the duo became well known for the comical visual aspect of their performances, Bennink has always insisted that their behaviour is simply part of the musical performance. He is not merely trying to be funny:

> That's a very delicate point: if it was *only* humor, that would disturb the music. And I *play* what I am and I *do* what I am because I am like that, and it never disturbs the music, it helps the music. Otherwise I couldn't do it that long, you know? [. . .] It's daily life, all differences, and all rules, and you can fight with the rules at the same time.
>
> *(Corbett 1994, 263)*

Indeed, many of the things he does that are perceived as comical are ultimately musical contributions. Emptying the bag of drum sticks creates a particular sonic effect; he also frequently lifts his foot up to push down on his snare drum, influencing the overtones, or puts one of his sticks into his mouth to play it with the other, manipulating the tone by moving his jaws. Such acts always draw a laugh—and intentionally so—but they also have a musical effect.

At one point during my fieldwork, Mengelberg, Bennink, and Moore were playing a free improvisation; Mengelberg and Moore were playing quite softly, with Mengelberg mostly outlining some harmonies and Moore improvising over them, with some exchange of motivic ideas between them, and Bennink was sitting in the middle, clearly bored. He started to play heavy accents on his snare drum, then put a piece of cloth over his drum to dampen the sound, and started "practising" drum rolls. Hitting the drum with a big bang, he checked to see underneath the cloth if he had hit something. Baars and Wierbos, meanwhile, started playing soft notes to accompany the duet between Mengelberg and Moore, ignoring Bennink's interventions. Bennink stood up, and started walking around the stage, while Mengelberg and Moore continued to play. He walked up to Glerum and asked if he had seen the prop he had brought to the concert, a large ratchet of the kind used for sound effects in theatre and early cinema. The fact that he can simply suddenly get up and take the time looking for his prop in the middle of an improvisation is very characteristic of the informal atmosphere of ICP concerts. When Glerum points out the ratchet, Moore and Baars start playing Thelonious Monk's "Hornin' In", meaning that the moment for Bennink to use his ratchet to interfere with their improvisation is gone. Bennink carries the ratchet back to his drums, sets it down, and nonchalantly lets it fall over as he takes his place behind his kit, letting it fall down to create a percussive accent exactly marking the first beat of the repetition of the opening melody.

In that same concert, Cherry Duyns had been invited to read some of Mengelberg's poetry and other writings from *Enkele Regels in de Dierentuin* ("Some

Lines/Rules in the Zoo"—the title refers to a composition by Mengelberg), a book containing a selection of his collected writings, published in 2013. Duyns, a Dutch documentary maker, novelist, and actor, had made a documentary about Mengelberg's last tour abroad briefly before—this was near the end of my fieldwork with the group, shortly before Mengelberg stopped performing altogether. The musicians had made a set list as usual, creating some room for him to read these texts, and played some of Mengelberg's songs where Duyns could read the lyrics. At a rehearsal before the concert, Glerum, Moore, Baars, and Wierbos played "Zing Zang Zaterdag" (Sing Song Saturday) for Duyns. When they were done, Duyns said that he had read the lyrics at home at a much faster tempo, not realizing that it was such a slow waltz. Apologizing, he said: "I'm not trying to put a spoke in your wheels", to which Baars retorted: "Oh but we are in yours!" At a second attempt, while Duyns was reading the lyrics because he felt too embarrassed to sing, Bennink came in singing loudly, throwing Duyns off his guard, and leaving again. Such banter continued during the performance. Before Duyns' first entrance, Bennink said: "Where's Cherry? I thought he was going to be here as well?" At his second entrance, instead of giving him time for a second reading of texts without any accompanying music, the group started playing "Zing Zang Zaterdag", making him have to look up the text in the book on stage while they were already playing.

In the second set, the musicians had just finished playing the march "Rollo IV", after which Mengelberg started to play a bluesy solo, combining thick jazz chords with contrapuntal textures, freely meandering through different tonal areas using his knowledge of counterpoint and voice leading. It was an intimate moment, not only because of the soft and introspective quality of the music, but also because everyone in the audience was aware of Mengelberg's health, and his playing was audibly hampered by his decreased motoric ability. For Duyns, who stepped forward because the set list specifies another reading at this point, this created a moment of great tension, as he did not want to intrude on Mengelberg's solo. As Mengelberg kept playing, it became uncertain whether he was challenging Duyns to interrupt, or perhaps he was simply hoping that he would recite the texts over his piano playing. Mengelberg kept lengthening his solo with new modulations and deceptive cadences, while Duyns stood, with the book in his hand, at the centre of the stage for over 5 minutes, as the atmosphere slowly shaded from intimate to uncomfortable to comical. When Mengelberg, after playing his most elaborate cadence yet, started playing with a more regular pulse, Bennink joined in with his brushes on his snare drum. Duyns decided that he had better simply exit, and he walked off-stage, to the hilarity of the audience, while the horns started playing "Een Beetje Zenuwachtig". When this piece ended, Mengelberg returned straight to his slow solo, marking the moment for Duyns to return to the stage and try again. This time Bennink was on his side, interrupting Mengelberg with his ratchet and a referee's whistle, and yelling "Make way! Make way for the recitation! Of *your* work!" The horns played "Pilaar" to enforce an ending, but Mengelberg kept going, and Duyns finally decided to recite over his playing.

If such actions were merely comical and did not contribute significantly to the music, they would not be as funny. A great deal of the humour in the first example comes from the "counterpoint" between the elegant musical interaction between Mengelberg and Moore, and the virtuosity of the drum fills that Bennink uses to interrupt them, as well as the perfectly timed bang of the ratchet falling on the ground. In the second example, Mengelberg's musicality as well as the musical logic with which his playing led to "Een Beetje Zenuwachtig" rather than a reading by Duyns made this section of the performance so funny. Moore talked about how the humour comes from the forms of musical interaction rather than from "comic acts" as such:

> The humour in ICP is something that comes from the music and the juxtaposition I think. Of styles, and musics. I remember when Thomas first came in the band it would sound like he would try and play things that were funny. Because when he went to hear a concert there would be a lot of humour, and he would try to be humorous, and that didn't work at all. And after a while he realized he didn't really have to do that, it was more the relationships that were funny.[20]

Humour shares with impromptu improvisation a sense of being both contingent and necessary, but whereas the latter is a matter of improvisation becoming necessary because of unforeseen circumstances, humorous moments are extemporized moments that are somehow surprising in their seeming necessity. Philosopher Gary Peters formulates his philosophy of improvisation around the idea that improvisation is a matter of creating the new from the old, reappropriating or repurposing existing ideas rather than a matter of pure innovation. He locates the humour of improvising comedians in their ability to use the same gags and clichés everyone already knows in such a way that they are both obvious because of their necessity and fittingness and surprising because of their richness; they are able to make even the most familiar material *speak* (Peters 2009, 126–129).

The interaction between jazz musicians has often been described in terms of irony. Especially through the African-American cultural practice of "signifying", various jazz theorists have likened jazz improvisation to a creative exchange of wordplay, building on different connotations and homonymic associations in a competitive style. The concept of humour seems to offer a slightly different approach to musical material. Even though it is also clearly based in an antagonistic, competitive style of interaction, it does not revolve around the one-upmanship of outsmarting each other by adding new layers of meaning and nuance. Deleuze distinguishes humour, "the art of the surface", from irony, the "art of depths and heights" (Deleuze 1990, 9; see also Colebrook 2004, 129–149). Rather than playing with meaning, humour points to the richness of the nonsensical and the not yet meaningful; it revolves around the "co-extensiveness of sense with nonsense" (Deleuze 1990, 141).

Although the ICP musicians can certainly be called tricksters, they very seldom use quotations or paraphrase—the "As Time Goes By" quote discussed in Chapter 5 was the only quote that I noticed during my fieldwork. Where irony and signifying are about appearances behind which might lie a truth, humour is about actual reality seeming impossible but no less true. The audience at ICP concerts does not laugh in an "I see what you did there" kind of way; they laugh because they think "I have no idea what is going on, but somehow it still seems to make sense". Irony builds on the existing connotations and meanings of musical ideas, whereas humour is more naïve, looking afresh at familiar material or at the emergent situation for what it is rather than how it might be understood. Humour "descends": "It hurls us into the ground of bodies and the groundlessness of their mixtures" (Deleuze 1990, 135).

In fact, for many people, the humour of the ICP stands out as one of the central characteristics of the group. Many of the examples discussed throughout this book attest to this. Their improvised music theatre was frequently absurd and outrageous. The use of stylized dance pieces in the context of freely improvised music in the late 1960s creates a hilarious effect when heard for the first time. Mengelberg's pestering pieces about Cage and about his fellow activist composers humorously conveyed his disagreements with them. The absurd titles, the animal sounds, and the conducted improvisations continue to amuse audiences, as do the frequent interruptions and on-stage disagreements between musicians. But also the blurred boundaries between improvised and composed material themselves have a humorous effect—as when a composed piece is systematically derailed, or when during a free improvisation two musicians suddenly play a few notes in unison, or even more so when during seeming chaos all the musicians suddenly are back on track in the middle of a swinging jazz piece.

The humour of the ICP highlights the processes of creative interaction between the musicians on stage, and the fact that their approach to improvisation is responding to the emergent situation rather than extemporizing within a set framework. The pieces in their repertoire are not "interpreted", which would be more akin to irony, but are *played*. Instant composition is not just about creating music in the moment; it is about bringing things together, setting them into relation with each other, exploring their oppositions and connections. Rather than establishing the human mind as the primary creative agent, humour decentres the subject and views it as distributed over heterogeneous parts; it acknowledges its position within a world of becoming in which even the most familiar may become a surprise.

Conclusion

I would like to conclude this book with a slightly more personal note, with the most intense and memorable musical experience during my fieldwork. It is 1 February

2013 and I am in The Vortex, a jazz venue in Hackney, London. The ICP Orchestra has been invited by Evan Parker, as part of one of his "Might I suggest . . ." festivals, to play here for a week. After a couple of nights playing freely improvised sets in which ICP musicians teamed up with various UK musicians, this is the first of two closing nights on which the ICP Orchestra plays their own music.

It is nearing the end of the second set, and Mengelberg is still on stage. This is quite a special occurrence; Mengelberg has been suffering from progressive dementia for around ten years now. In fact, this week in London constitutes his last couple of concerts abroad, and Duyns and his film crew have been along all week to shoot a documentary about his situation. As has been clear throughout my fieldwork, the orchestra can function fine without him, and he can choose not to play if he does not want to, or only play a first set. He also frequently decides to stop playing in the middle of a set, gets off-stage, and sits in the audience. For him to play two full sets has become a rare thing.

The band has just finished playing Mengelberg's arrangement of Duke Ellington's "Happy Go Lucky Local" when he gets up from behind the piano, intending to sit down in the audience. However, The Vortex is a very small venue; there is hardly enough room for ten musicians plus music stands on the stage, and the cameraman is on stage as well to shoot material for the documentary. The place is packed with a big audience too, so Mengelberg is stuck.

As we have seen, the ICP knows how to deal with uncomfortable situations—in fact, cultivating them has been a large part of Mengelberg's musical aesthetic— and none of the musicians more so than Honsinger. He gets up to perform a conducted improvisation, guiding the improvising musicians with gestures and body movements, and involving Mengelberg by making some animal noises and vocalizations with him. To add to the confusion, drummer and co-founder of the ICP Han Bennink calls out Honsinger's name to signal the end of his conduction because he thinks he is finished, but Honsinger was not done yet and responds by calling out Bennink's own name. All the musicians start calling out each other's names as well as other things ("bacon!" "sausage!") and Mengelberg, who was initially looking a bit forlorn, is clearly enjoying the absurd scene developing in front of him.

Before Honsinger sits back down to end his conducted improvisation, he turns to Mengelberg, who whistles softly at him, and other musicians start whistling in response. Ab Baars, on clarinet, starts playing "De Sprong, O Romantiek der Hazen", Mengelberg's evergreen lyrical ballad that would no doubt have been a jazz standard had it been written in New York in the 1930s. Mary Oliver, thinking Mengelberg might like to sing the lyrics, tries to turn her microphone his way, and takes his hand to guide him to it. Mengelberg is not interested, and keeps whistling the main melody of "De Sprong", still holding Oliver's hand. The eight other musicians play as softly as possible in order to keep Mengelberg's hesitant and unamplified whistling audible. As the final chords sound, the room is brimming with emotion.

If this moment showed the strength and value of improvisation, it also exemplified the ICP's approach to improvisation as I have described it throughout this book. This was not just a matter of playing a solo or even of collective improvisation; the power of this moment lay in how the musicians responded to the demands of a particular situation, characterized by misunderstandings, competition, absurdity, and adversity. The contingencies of everyday life are not separated from the moment of performance, but permeate what is happening on stage. The pieces and techniques of the ICP form an integral part of the improvisatory response to these contingencies.

I met Mengelberg for the first time in 2010, when he was already suffering from dementia and old age, having had a stroke not too long before. Although he would increasingly play a role in my research, and so in my life, I never knew him other than with dementia. In the beginning of my research he was very welcoming and friendly, offering me a cup of coffee at his house after concerts, and always happy to answer any questions insofar as his memory and aphasia allowed. As my research progressed and his health deteriorated, the painful truth is that I increasingly got to know him as a historical figure rather than as a living person.

In the year he died, the ICP was celebrating its fiftieth anniversary, Bennink turned seventy-five years old, and I had just submitted my proposal for writing this book. Janssen has since replaced him as the group's standard pianist, and the group continues to play dozens of concerts throughout the world each year. The ICP does not merely "keep his memory alive", but through their repertoire, the compositions, and their approach to improvisation, Mengelberg's person continues quite literally to play a role in their music—and the same is true, in different ways, for Piet Noordijk, Willem Breuker, Sean Bergin, and all the others who have shaped the ICP's musical practice over the years. I hope this book may distribute his mind even further.

Notes

1 Wolter Wierbos, interview with the author, 21 December 2011.
2 Benjamin Givan has written an extensive critique of this idea, arguing that the concept of interaction requires further specification (Givan 2016).
3 Tobias Delius, interview with the author, 31 January 2013.
4 Michael Moore, interview with the author, 23 December 2011.
5 Michael Moore, interview with the author, 23 December 2011.
6 Mary Oliver, interview with the author, 22 February 2012.
7 Thomas Heberer, interview with the author, 20 February 2012.
8 Tobias Delius, interview with the author, 21 February 2012.
9 Ab Baars, interview with the author, 4 January 2012.
10 Han Bennink, interview with the author, 4 January 2013.
11 Tobias Delius, interview with the author, 21 February 2012.
12 Thomas Heberer, interview with the author, 15 July 2013.
13 Michael Moore, interview with the author, 9 January 2013.
14 Thomas Heberer, interview with the author, 20 February 2012.

15 Thomas Heberer, interview with the author, 15 July 2013.
16 Michael Moore, interview with the author, 9 January 2013.
17 Michael Moore, interview with the author, 23 December 2011.
18 Ernst Glerum, interview with the author, 25 February 2012.
19 Thomas Heberer, interview with the author, 20 February 2012.
20 Michael Moore, interview with the author, 23 December 2011.

BIBLIOGRAPHY

Adlington, Robert. 2004. 'Louis Andriessen, Hanns Eisler, and the Lehrstück'. *Journal of Musicology* 21 (3): 381–417.
———. 2013. *Composing Dissent: Avant-Garde Music in 1960s Amsterdam*. Oxford: Oxford University Press.
Ake, David. 2002. *Jazz Cultures*. Berkeley, CA: University of California Press.
Ake, David, Charles Hiroshi Garrett, and Daniel Goldmark, eds. 2012. *Jazz/Not Jazz: The Music and Its Boundaries*. Berkeley, CA: University of California Press.
Aldridge, David, ed. 2000. *Music Therapy in Dementia Care: More New Voices*. London: Jessica Kingsley Publishers.
Aldridge, Gudrun. 2000. 'Improvisation as an Assessment of Potential in Early Alzheimer's Disease'. In *Music Therapy in Dementia Care: More New Voices*, edited by David Aldridge, 139–65. London: Jessica Kingsley Publishers.
Allison, Theresa. 2010. 'Transcending the Limitations of Institutionalization Through Music: Ethnomusicology in a Nursing Home'. Champaign, IL: University of Illinois.
Anderson, Iain. 2007. *This Is Our Music: Free Jazz, the Sixties, and American Culture*. The Arts and Intellectual Life in Modern America. Philadelphia, PA: University of Pennsylvania Press.
Andriessen, Bas. 1996. *Tetterettet: Interviews Met Nederlandse Improviserende Musici*. Ubbergen: Tandem Felix.
Arndt, Jürgen. 2002. 'Von Monk Zu Misha Mengelberg'. In *Thelonious Monk Und Der Free Jazz*. Beiträge Zur Jazzforschung/Studies in Jazz Research 11. Graz: Akademische Druck- und Verlagsanstalt.
———. 2012. 'European Jazz Developments in Cross-Cultural Dialogue with the United States and Their Relationship to the Counterculture of the 1960s'. In *Eurojazzland: Jazz and European Sources, Dynamics, and Contexts*, edited by Luca Cerchiari, Laurent Cugny, and Franz Kerschbaumer, 342–65. Boston, MA: Northeastern University Press.
Author Unknown. 1972. 'Concert Announcement: Johnny the Selfkicker, Misja Mengelberg, Michel Waisvisz, Han Bennink, 28 October 1972'. Box: Misja Mengelberg. Nederlands Jazz Archief.

Baaij, Hans. 1965. 'Jazzpianist Misja Mengelberg: "Mooi En Lelijk Zijn Voor Mij Onbruikbare Begrippen"'. *Het Parool*, 27 March 1965.

Bailey, Derek. 1993. *Improvisation: Its Nature and Practice in Music*. New York: Perseus Book Group.

Baraka, Amiri. 1999. 'Jazz and the White Critic'. In *Keeping Time: Readings in Jazz History*, edited by Robert Walser, 255–61. Oxford: Oxford University Press.

Barrett, Frank J. 1998. 'Managing and Improvising: Lessons from Jazz'. *Career Development International* 3 (7): 283–86. https://doi.org/10.1108/13620439810240719.

Barz, Gregory F., and Timothy J. Cooley, eds. 2008. *Shadows in the Field: New Perspectives for Fieldwork in Ethnomusicology*. 2nd Edition. Oxford: Oxford University Press.

Bastien, David T., and Todd J. Hostager. 1992. 'Cooperation as Communicative Accomplishment: A Symbolic Interaction Analysis of an Improvised Jazz Concert'. *Communication Studies* 43 (2): 92–104. https://doi.org/10.1080/10510979209368363.

Bates, Eliot. 2012. 'The Social Life of Musical Instruments'. *Ethnomusicology* 56 (3): 363–95. https://doi.org/10.5406/ethnomusicology.56.3.0363.

Beal, Amy C. 2006. *New Music, New Allies: American Experimental Music in West Germany from the Zero Hour to Reunification*. Berkeley, CA: University of California Press.

Becker, Howard S. 1982. *Art Worlds*. London: University of California Press.

Becker, Jürgen, and Wolf Vostell, eds. 1966. *Happenings, Fluxus, Pop art, Nouveau réalisme: eine Dokumentation*. Reinbek bei Hamburg: Rowohlt.

Beeren, Wim van. 1979. *Actie, Werkelijkheid En Fictie in de Kunst van de Jaren '60 in Nederland*. Rotterdam: Museum Boymans-van Beuningen.

Benson, Bruce Ellis. 2003. *The Improvisation of Musical Dialogue: A Phenomenology of Music*. Cambridge: Cambridge University Press.

Berghaus, Günter, and Tomas Schmit. 1994. 'Tomas Schmit: A Fluxus Farewell to Perfection: An Interview'. *TDR (1988-)* 38 (1): 79–97. https://doi.org/10.2307/1146357.

Berliner, Paul. 1994. *Thinking in Jazz: The Infinite Art of Improvisation*. Chicago, IL: University of Chicago Press.

Bishop, Claire. 2004. 'Antagonism and Relational Aesthetics'. *October*, no. 110: 51–79. https://doi.org/10.1162/0162287042379810.

Bleich, David. 2013. *The Materiality of Language: Gender, Politics, and the University*. Bloomington, IN: Indiana University Press.

Boehmer, Konrad. 1971. 'Willem Is Koning'. *Vrij Nederland*, 27 November 1971. Box: Willem Breuker. Nederlands Jazz Archief.

Bohlman, Philip. 1999. 'Ontologies of Music'. In *Rethinking Music*, edited by Nicholas Cook and Mark Everist, 17–34. Oxford: Oxford University Press.

Borgo, David. 2005. *Sync or Swarm: Improvising Music in a Complex Age*. New York: Continuum.

Born, Georgina. 2005. 'On Musical Mediation: Ontology, Technology and Creativity'. *Twentieth-Century Music* 2 (01): 7–36. https://doi.org/10.1017/S147857220500023X.

—. 2010a. 'For a Relational Musicology: Music and Interdisciplinarity, Beyond the Practice Turn'. *Journal of the Royal Musical Association* 135 (2): 205–43. https://doi.org/10.1080/02690403.2010.506265.

—. 2010b. 'The Social and the Aesthetic: For a Post-Bourdieuian Theory of Cultural Production'. *Cultural Sociology* 4 (2): 171–208. https://doi.org/10.1177/1749975510368471.

—. 2011. 'Music and the Materialization of Identities'. *Journal of Material Culture* 16 (4): 376–88. https://doi.org/10.1177/1359183511424196.

Born, Georgina, Eric Lewis, and Will Straw, eds. 2017. *Improvisation and Social Aesthetics*. Durham, NC: Duke University Press.

Bouman, Eva. 1978. *Workshops: Opkomst En Ontwikkeling*. Zeist: Trezoor.

Bourdieu, Pierre. 1986. *Distinction: A Social Critique of the Judgement of Taste*. London: Routledge & Kegan Paul.

Bourriaud, Nicolas. 2002. *Relational Aesthetics*. Dijon: Les Presses du réel.

Brackett, David. 2016. *Categorizing Sound: Genre and Twentieth-Century Popular Music*. Oakland, CA: University of California Press.

Brill, Dorothée. 2010. *Shock and the Senseless in Dada and Fluxus*. London: University Press of New England.

Brinkman, Els, Sandra Darbé, Laura Stamps, and Hadewych van den Bossche, eds. 2016. *Constant: New Babylon. Aan Ons de Vrijheid*. Lichtervelde: Hannibal.

Brown, Bill. 2001. 'Thing Theory'. *Critical Inquiry* 28 (1): 1–22.

Brummel-Smith, Kenneth. 2008. 'Alzheimer's Disease and the Promise of Music and Culture as a Healing Process'. In *The Oxford Handbook of Medical Ethnomusicology*, edited by Benjamin D. Koen, 185–200. Oxford: Oxford University Press.

Bürger, Peter. 1984. *Theory of the Avant-Garde*. Translated by Michael Shaw. Minneapolis, MN: University of Minnesota Press.

Buzelin, Françoise, and Jean Buzelin. 1994. *Willem Breuker: maker van mensenmuziek*. Translated by Sjaak Hubregtse. Zutphen: Walburg Pers.

Carles, Philippe, and Jean-Louis Comolli. 2015. *Free Jazz/Black Power*. Translated by Grégory Pierrot. Jackson, MS: University Press of Mississippi.

Cerchiari, Luca, Laurent Cugny, and Franz Kerschbaumer, eds. 2012. *Eurojazzland: Jazz and European Sources, Dynamics, and Contexts*. Boston, MA: Northeastern University Press.

Challenge Records. 2012. 'Complete Boxed Catalogue (limited edition): Instant Composers Pool'. Challenge Records International. www.challengerecords.com/products/1326978299.

Clair, Alicia Ann. 2008. 'Music Therapy Evidence-Based Outcomes in Dementia Care: Better Life Quality for Those with Alzheimer's Disease and Their Families'. In *The Oxford Handbook of Medical Ethnomusicology*, edited by Benjamin D. Koen, 201–17. Oxford: Oxford University Press.

Clarke, Eric, Mark Doffman, and Liza Lim. 2013. 'Distributed Creativity and Ecological Dynamics: A Case Study of Liza Lim's "Tongue of the Invisible"'. *Music and Letters* 94 (4): 628–63. https://doi.org/10.1093/ml/gct118.

Colebrook, Claire. 2004. *Irony*. London: Routledge.

Cook, Nicholas. 2001. 'Between Process and Product: Music and/as Performance'. *Music Theory Online* 7 (2). www.mtosmt.org/issues/mto.01.7.2/mto.01.7.2.cook.html.

—. 2007. 'Making Music Together: Or, Improvisation and Its Others'. In *Music, Performance, Meaning: Selected Essays*, 321–41. Aldershot: Ashgate.

—. 2012. 'Anatomy of the Encounter: Intercultural Analysis as Relational Musicology'. In *Musicological Reflections: Essays in Honour of Derek B. Scott*, edited by Stan Hawkins, 193–208. New York: Routledge.

—. 2013. *Beyond the Score: Music as Performance*. Oxford: Oxford University Press.

Corbett, John. 1994. 'Han Bennink: Swing Softly and Play with a Big Stick'. In *Extended Play: Sounding Off from John Cage to Dr. Funkenstein*, 260–9. London: Duke University Press.

Csikszentmihalyi, Mihaly. 2008. *Flow: The Psychology of Optimal Experience*. London: Harper & Row.

Dawe, Kevin. 2001. 'People, Objects, Meaning: Recent Work on the Study and Collection of Musical Instruments'. *The Galpin Society Journal* 54: 219–32. https://doi.org/10.2307/842454.

Debord, Guy. 2011. 'Situationist Manifesto'. In *100 Artists' Manifestos: From the Futurists to the Stuckists*, edited by Alex Danchev. London: Penguin Books.

De By, Henk, and Roland De Beer. 1988. 'Omdat de Instrumenten Er Stuk van Gingen'. *De Volkskrant*, 4 January 1988, sec. Kunst & Cultuur: 5.

De Leeuw, Reinbert, Louis Andriessen, Misha Mengelberg, Peter Schat, and Jan Van Vlijmen. 1966. 'Open Brief Aan Het Bestuur van de Stichting Tot Beheer van Het Concertgebouworkest'. *Algemeen Handelsblad*, 16 March 1966: 9.

Deleuze, Gilles. 1990. *The Logic of Sense*. Translated by Mark Lester. London: Athlone Press.

Deleuze, Gilles, and Félix Guattari. 2013. *A Thousand Plateaus: Capitalism and Schizophrenia*. London: Bloomsbury Publishing.

De Ridder, Willem. 1962. 'De MES'. *Groninger Archieven*. www.archieven.nl/nl/zoeken?mivast=0&mizig=210&miadt=5&miaet=1&micode=2536&minr=6590844&miview=inv2.

De Ridder, Willem, and William Levy. 1983. *De Ridder Retrospective, July–August 1983 Holland Festival/Groninger Museum*. Amsterdam: Groninger Museum/Holland Festival/Van Wulften.

DeVeaux, Scott. 1991. 'Constructing the Jazz Tradition: Jazz Historiography'. *Black American Literature Forum* 25 (3): 525–60. https://doi.org/10.2307/3041812.

—. 2006. 'This Is What I Do'. In *Art from Start to Finish: Jazz, Painting, Writing, and Other Improvisations*, edited by Howard S. Becker, Robert R. Faulkner, and Barbara Kirshenblatt-Gimblett, 118–25. Chicago, IL: University of Chicago Press.

Dewey, John. 2005. *Art as Experience*. London: Penguin Books.

Dezeuze, Anna. 2010. '"Open Work", "Do-It-Yourself" Artwork and Bricolage'. In *The 'Do-It-Yourself' Artwork: Participation from Fluxus to New Media*, edited by Anna Dezeuze, 47–68. Manchester: Manchester University Press.

Dolan, Emily. 2013. *The Orchestral Revolution: Haydn and the Technologies of Timbre*. Cambridge: Cambridge University Press.

Doubleday, Veronica. 2008. 'Sounds of Power: An Overview of Musical Instruments and Gender'. *Ethnomusicology Forum* 17 (1): 3–39.

Drott, Eric. 2004. 'Ligeti in Fluxus'. *The Journal of Musicology* 21 (2): 201–40. https://doi.org/10.1525/jm.2004.21.2.201.

—. 2011. *Music and the Elusive Revolution: Cultural Politics and Political Culture in France, 1968–1981*. Berkeley, CA: University of California Press.

—. 2013. 'The End(s) of Genre'. *Journal of Music Theory* 57 (1): 1–45. https://doi.org/10.1215/00222909-2017097.

Drucker, Johanna. 2013. 'Performative Materiality and Theoretical Approaches to Interface'. *Digital Humanities Quarterly* 7 (1). www.digitalhumanities.org/dhq/vol/7/1/000143/000143.html.

Dumett, Mari. 2008. 'The Great Executive Dream: George Maciunas, Adriano Olivetti, and Fluxus Incorporated'. *RES: Anthropology and Aesthetics*, no. 53/54: 314–20.

Ernst-Berendt, Joachim. 1977. 'Der Deutsche Jazz Und Die Emanzipation'. In *Ein Fenster Aus Jazz: Essays, Portraits, Reflexionen*, 222–46. Frankfurt: Fischer Verlag.

Faulkner, Robert R. 2006. 'Shedding Culture'. In *Art from Start to Finish: Jazz, Painting, Writing, and Other Improvisations*, edited by Howard S. Becker, Robert

R. Faulkner, and Barbara Kirshenblatt-Gimblett, 91–117. Chicago, IL: University of Chicago Press.

Faulkner, Robert R., and Howard S. Becker. 2009. *'Do You Know . . .?'*: *The Jazz Repertoire in Action*. Chicago, IL: University of Chicago Press.

Feld, Steven. 2012. *Jazz Cosmopolitanism in Accra: Five Musical Years in Ghana*. Durham, NC: Duke University Press.

Fischlin, Daniel, and Ajay Heble. 2004. 'The Other Side of Nowhere: Jazz, Improvisation, and Communities in Dialogue'. In *The Other Side of Nowhere: Jazz, Improvisation, and Communities in Dialogue*, edited by Daniel Fischlin and Ajay Heble, 1–41. Middletown, CT: Wesleyan University Press.

Fischlin, Daniel, Ajay Heble, and George Lipsitz. 2013. *The Fierce Urgency of Now: Improvisation, Rights, and the Ethics of Cocreation*. Durham, NC: Duke University Press.

Fitch, Fabrice, and Neil Heyde. 2007. '"Recercar": The Collaborative Process as Invention'. *Twentieth-Century Music* 4 (1): 71–95. https://doi.org/10.1017/S1478572207000539.

Flusser, Vilém. 1999. *Shape of Things: A Philosophy of Design*. London: Reaktion Books.

Foster, Hal. 1996. *The Return of the Real: The Avant-Garde at the End of the Century*. Cambridge, MA: MIT Press.

Foucault, Michel. 1977. 'Nietzsche, Genealogy, History'. In *Language, Counter-Memory, Practice: Selected Essays and Interviews*, edited by D.F. Bouchard, 139–64. Ithaca, NY: Cornell University Press.

Friedman, Ken. 1998. *The Fluxus Reader*. Chichester: Wiley.

Friesch Dagblad. 1972. 'Amsterdams Toneel Op Straten En Pleinen', 22 August 1972. Box: Instant Composers Pool, Folder: Ongedateerde Knipsels. Nederlands Jazz Archief.

Gates, Henry Louis. 1988. *The Signifying Monkey: A Theory of African-American Literary Criticism*. Oxford: Oxford University Press.

Gell, Alfred. 1998. *Art and Agency: An Anthropological Theory*. Oxford: Clarendon Press.

Gennari, John. 2007. *Blowin' Hot and Cool: Jazz and Its Critics*. Chicago, IL: University of Chicago Press.

Gitelman, Lisa. 1999. *Scripts, Grooves, and Writing Machines: Representing Technology in the Edison Era*. Stanford, CA: Stanford University Press.

Givan, Benjamin. 2003. 'Django Reinhardt's Left Hand'. In *Jazz Planet*, edited by E. Taylor Atkins, 19–40. Jackson, MS: University Press of Mississippi.

—. 2009. 'Thelonious Monk's Pianism'. *The Journal of Musicology* 26 (3): 404–42. https://doi.org/10.1525/jm.2009.26.3.404.

—. 2016. 'Rethinking Interaction in Jazz Improvisation'. *Music Theory Online* 22 (3). http://mtosmt.org/issues/mto.16.22.3/mto.16.22.3.givan.html.

Goehr, Lydia. 2007. *The Imaginary Museum of Musical Works: An Essay in the Philosophy of Music*. Oxford: Oxford University Press.

—. 2016. 'Improvising Impromptu, Or, What to Do with a Broken String'. Edited by George E. Lewis and Benjamin Piekut. *The Oxford Handbook of Critical Improvisation Studies, Volume 1*. www.oxfordhandbooks.com/view/10.1093/oxfordhb/9780195370935.001.0001/oxfordhb-9780195370935-e-010.

Hagberg, Garry L. 2016. 'Ensemble Improvisation, Collective Intention, and Group Attention'. Edited by George E. Lewis and Benjamin Piekut. *The Oxford Handbook of Critical Improvisation Studies, Volume 1*. www.oxfordhandbooks.com/view/10.1093/oxfordhb/9780195370935.001.0001/oxfordhb-9780195370935-e-011.

Haraway, Donna. 1988. 'Situated Knowledges: The Science Question in Feminism and the Privilege of Partial Perspective'. *Feminist Studies* 14 (3): 575–99.

Harding, James M. 2013. *The Ghosts of the Avant-Garde(s): Exorcising Experimental Theater and Performance*. Ann Arbor, MI: University of Michigan Press.

Hayles, N. Katherine. 2002. *Writing Machines*. Cambridge, MA: MIT Press.

Hayles, N. Katherine, and J. Pressman, eds. 2013. *Comparative Textual Media: Transforming the Humanities in the Postprint Era*. Minneapolis, MN: University of Minnesota Press. www.upress.umn.edu/book-division/books/comparative-textual-media.

Heffley, Mike. 2005. *Northern Sun, Southern Moon: Europe's Reinvention of Jazz*. New Haven, CT: Yale University Press.

Heidegger, Martin. 1971. 'The Thing'. In *Poetry, Language, Thought*, translated by Albert Hofstadter, 161–80. New York: Harper & Row.

Heller, Michael C. 2017. *Loft Jazz: Improvising New York in the 1970s*. Oakland, CA: University of California Press.

Hendricks, Jon. 1995. *Fluxus Codex*. 2nd print. Detroit, MI: Gilbert and Lila Silverman Fluxus Collection.

Hersch, Charles. 1995. '"Let Freedom Ring!": Free Jazz and African-American Politics'. *Cultural Critique* 32: 97–123. https://doi.org/10.2307/1354532.

Higgins, Dick. 1964. *Postface*. New York: Something Else Press.

—. 1998. 'Fluxus Theory and Reception'. In *The Fluxus Reader*, 217–36. Chichester: Wiley.

Higgins, Hannah. 2002. *Fluxus Experience*. London: University of California Press.

Holbraad, Martin, and Morten Axel Pedersen. 2017. *The Ontological Turn: An Anthropological Exposition*. Cambridge: Cambridge University Press.

Huyssen, Andreas. 1993. 'Back to the Future: Fluxus in Context'. In *In the Spirit of Fluxus*, edited by Janet Jenkins, 140–52. Minneapolis, MN: Walker Art Center.

Iddon, Martin. 2013. *New Music at Darmstadt: Nono, Stockhausen, Cage, and Boulez*. Music since 1900. New York: Cambridge University Press.

Ingold, Tim. 2007. *Lines: A Brief History*. London: Routledge.

—. 2010. 'The Textility of Making'. *Cambridge Journal of Economics* 34 (1): 91–102. https://doi.org/10.1093/cje/bep042.

—. 2012. 'Toward an Ecology of Materials'. *Annual Review of Anthropology* 41: 427–42.

Ingold, Tim, and Elizabeth Hallam. 2007. 'Creativity and Cultural Improvisation: An Introduction'. In *Creativity and Cultural Improvisation*, edited by Elizabeth Hallam and Tim Ingold. Oxford: Berg.

Instant Composers Pool. 1968. 'ICP 001'. Box: Instant Composers Pool, Folder: t/m 1971. Nederlands Jazz Archief.

—. 1972. 'Instant Composers Pool'. Box: Instant Composers Pool, Folder: 1972. Nederlands Jazz Archief.

Jazz Magazine. 1974. 'Allemagne Pays-Bas: Peter Brotzmann Han Bennink Misha Mengelberg' no. 220, 1974: 19–21.

Jazz Nu. 1980. 'Het Subsidiedossier' 3 (1), 1980: 15–38.

Jazzwereld. 1971. 'Prijswinnaar Willem Breuker' no. 33, 1971: 17.

Jazzwereld Editors. 1967. 'Jazzwereld Poll'. *Jazzwereld* no. 12, 1967: 18–23.

Jenkins, Janet, ed. 1993. *In the Spirit of Fluxus*. Minneapolis, MN: Walker Art Center.

Jones, LeRoi. 1975. *Blues People: Negro Music in White America*. Repr. New York: Morrow Quill Paperbacks.

Jost, Ekkehard. 1974. *Free Jazz*. Beiträge Zur Jazzforschung/Studies in Jazz Research 4. Graz: Universal Edition.

—. 1979. 'Europäische Jazz-Avantgarde: Emanzipation Wohin?' *Jazzforschung* 11: 165–95.

—. 1987. *Europas Jazz 1960–1980*. Frankfurt: Fischer Taschenbuch Verlag.

Kamoche, Ken, and Miguel Pina e Cunha. 2001. 'Minimal Structures: From Jazz Improvisation to Product Innovation'. *Organization Studies* 22 (5): 733–64. https://doi.org/10.1177/0170840601225001.

Kant, Immanuel. 2007. *Critique of Judgement*. Edited by Nicholas Walker. Translated by James Creed Meredith. Oxford: Oxford University Press.

Keil, Charles M.H. 1966. 'Motion and Feeling Through Music'. *The Journal of Aesthetics and Art Criticism* 24 (3): 337–49. https://doi.org/10.2307/427969.

Kennedy, James. 1995. 'Building New Babylon: Cultural Change in the Netherlands During the 1960s'. University of Iowa.

Kirschenbaum, Matthew G. 2008. *Mechanisms: New Media and the Forensic Imagination.* Cambridge, MA: MIT Press.

Kofsky, Frank. 1970. *Black Nationalism and the Revolution in Music.* New York: Pathfinder Press.

Koopmans, Rudy. 1969. 'Albert Ayler: New Grass: Een Uit de Hand Gelopen Platenbespreking Door Rudy Koopmans'. *Jazzwereld* no. 24, 1969: 12–18.

—. 1971. 'De Instant Composers Pool Is Een Pool van Instant Composers'. *OOR*, April 1971: 11.

—. 1972a. 'De Jezus van de Jazz'. *Jazzwereld* no. 39, 1972: 12–14.

—. 1972b. 'Beroepsvereniging van Improviserende Musici'. *OOR*, March 1972: 11.

—. 1974. 'Op de Breuklijn van ICP En BV Haast: Presenting the Corona's'. *OOR*, April 1974. Box: Instant Composers Pool, Folder: 1973–1976. Nederlands Jazz Archief.

—. 1976. 'On Music and Politics: Activism of Five Dutch Composers'. *Key Notes*, no. 4: 19–38.

—. 1977a. *Jazz: improvisatie en organisatie van een groeiende minderheid.* Amsterdam: SUA.

—. 1977b. *Over Muziek En Politiek: Een Esssay.* IJmuiden: Vermande Zonen.

—. 1977c. 'Instant Composers Pool Tien Jaar: Dat Wordt Feesten in Uithoorn'. *De Volkskrant*, 8 June 1977. Box: Instant Composers Pool, Folder: 1977–1979. Nederlands Jazz Archief.

—. 1979. 'Oktober Jazzmaand Begonnen: Optreden ICP-Orkest Wordt Legendarisch'. *De Volkskrant*, 10 January 1979. Box: Instant Composers Pool, Folder: 1977–1979. Nederlands Jazz Archief.

—. 1982. *10 Jaar Volharding.* Amsterdam: Van Gennep.

—. 1983. 'Herbie Hancock Quartet'. *Jazz Nu* 5 (55), 1983: 29–30.

Koopmans, Rudy, and Bert Vuijsje. 1970. 'Han Bennink: "Shepp, Sanders, Ayler, Murray, Het Is Om Te Huilen"'. *Jazzwereld* no. 30, 1970: 18–19.

Kop, Anton. 1960. 'De V.A.R.A.-Jazzweek 1960'. *Rhythme* 11 (128), 1960: 7–9.

Kop, Anton, and Skip Voogd. 1960. 'Bij Onze Nieuwe Jaargang'. *Rhythme* 12 (133), 1960: 3.

Kotz, Liz. 2001. 'Post-Cagean Aesthetics and the "Event" Score'. *October* 95: 55–89.

—. 2007. *Words to Be Looked At: Language in 1960s Art.* Cambridge, MA: MIT Press.

Lagerwerff, Frits. 1980. 'Mengelbergs ICP-Orkest: Satire En Muziek Luchtig Vermengd'. *De Volkskrant*, 5 October 1980: 35.

Lash, Dominic. 2011. 'Derek Bailey's Practice/Practise'. *Perspectives of New Music* 49 (1): 143–71. https://doi.org/10.7757/persnewmusi.49.1.0143.

Latour, Bruno. 1993. *We Have Never Been Modern.* Translated by Catherine Porter. Cambridge, MA: Harvard University Press.

—. 1999. *Pandora's Hope: Essays on the Reality of Science Studies.* Cambridge, MA: Harvard University Press.

—. 2002. 'What Is Iconoclash? Or: Is There a World Beyond the Image Wars?' In *Iconoclash: Beyond the Image Wars in Science, Religion, and Art*, edited by Bruno Latour and Peter Weibel, 14–37. Cambridge, MA: MIT Press.

—. 2004. 'Why Has Critique Run Out of Steam? From Matters of Fact to Matters of Concern'. *Critical Inquiry* 30 (2): 225–48. https://doi.org/10.1086/421123.

—. 2005. *Reassembling the Social: An Introduction to Actor-Network-Theory*. Oxford: Oxford University Press.

—. 2010. 'An Attempt at a "Compositionist Manifesto"'. *New Literary History* 41 (3): 471–90.

Leeuw-Marcar, Ank, and Giorgio Anselmo, eds. 1969. *Op losse schroeven: situaties en cryptostructuren*. Catalogus / Stedelijk Museum Amsterdam, nr. 457. Amsterdam: Stedelijk Museum.

Lévi-Strauss, Claude. 1966. *The Savage Mind*. Chicago, IL: University of Chicago Press.

Lewis, George E. 1996. 'Improvised Music After 1950: Afrological and Eurological Perspectives'. *Black Music Research Journal* 16 (1): 91–122. https://doi.org/10.2307/779379.

—. 2004. 'Gittin' to Know Y'all : Improvised Music, Interculturalism and the Racial Imagination'. *Critical Studies in Improvisation / Études Critiques En Improvisation* 1 (1). https://doi.org/http://dx.doi.org/10.21083/csieci.v1i1.6.

—. 2008. *A Power Stronger than Itself: The AACM and American Experimental Music*. Chicago, IL: University of Chicago Press.

Lushetich, Natash. 2012. 'The Event Score as a Perpetuum Mobile'. *Text & Performance Quarterly* 32 (1): 1–19.

MacDougall, Susan. 2016. 'Ethnography: Deviation'. Correspondences, Cultural Anthropology Website. 19 May 2016. https://culanth.org/fieldsights/877-ethnography-deviation.

Maciunas, George. 1965. 'Manifesto II'. George Maciunas Foundation Inc. 1965. http://georgemaciunas.com/about/cv/manifesto-ii.

Mann, Paul. 1991. *The Theory-Death of the Avant-Garde*. Bloomington, IN: Indiana University Press.

Martin, Peter J. 2006. *Music and the Sociological Gaze: Art Worlds and Cultural Production*. Music and Society. Manchester [etc.]: Manchester University Press.

McKenzie, D.F. 1999. *Bibliography and the Sociology of Texts*. Cambridge: Cambridge University Press.

Mengelberg, Misha. 1965. 'Criss Cross Met En Zonder'. *Jazzwereld* no. 1, 1965: 20–1.

—. 1968. 'Hello Windyboys'. In *Muzikale En Politieke Commentaren En Analyses Bij Een Programma van Een Politiek-Demonstratief Experimenteel Concert Met Nieuwe Nederlandse Muziek in Negentienhonderdachtenzestig*, 21–3. Amsterdam: Polak & Van Gennep.

—. 1970. 'ICP'. *Jazzwereld* no. 29, 1970: 21.

—. 1978. 'S.age T.hymes E.at I.nkfish M.mmm'. *Key Notes*, no. 8: 17–19.

—. 1979. 'Werdegang Der Improvisation'. *Neue Zeitschrift Für Musik* 140 (3): 258–9.

—. 1994. 'Misha Mengelberg Spricht über Seine Musik: Von Fahrrädern, Hasen Und Provokationen . . .'. In *Jazz in Europa*, edited by Wolfram Knauer, 169–81. Darmstädter Beiträge Zur Jazzforschung. Hofheim: Wolke Verlag.

—. 2009. *Goedendagjes: Misha's Moments Musicaux*. Edited by Michael Moore. Amsterdam: Muziek Centrum Nederland.

—. 2012. *Enkele Regels in de Dierentuin*. Edited by Erik Van den Berg. Rimburg: Huis Clos.

Monson, Ingrid. 1996. *Saying Something: Jazz Improvisation and Interaction*. Chicago, IL: University of Chicago Press.

—. 2007. *Freedom Sounds: Civil Rights Call Out to Jazz and Africa*. Oxford: Oxford University Press.

Moseley, Roger. 2016. *Keys to Play: Music as a Ludic Medium from Apollo to Nintendo*. Berkeley, CA: University of California Press.

Moten, Fred. 2003. *In the Break: The Aesthetics of the Black Radical Tradition*. Minneapolis, MN: University of Minnesota Press.

Nettl, Bruno. 1974. 'Thoughts on Improvisation: A Comparative Approach'. *The Musical Quarterly* 60 (1): 1–19.

Nettl, Bruno, Michael Collins, Stewart A. Carter, Greer Garden, Robert E. Seletsky, Robert D. Levin, Will Crutchfield, et al. 2014. 'Improvisation'. *Grove Music Online. Oxford Music Online*. www.oxfordmusiconline.com/subscriber/article/grove/music/13738.

Nicholson, Stuart. 2005. *Is Jazz Dead?: Or Has It Moved to a New Address*. New York: Routledge.

Niemans, Rud. 1960. 'Jazz-Parade in Concertgebouw: Artistiek Bankroet Van Nederlands Jazz-in-de-Konsertzaal'. *Rhythme* 11 (124), 1960: 28–9.

Nooshin, Laudan. 2003. 'Improvisation as "Other": Creativity, Knowledge and Power: The Case of Iranian Classical Music'. *Journal of the Royal Musical Association* 128 (2): 242–96.

Orlikowski, Wanda J., and J. Debra Hofman. 1997. 'An Improvisational Model for Change Management: The Case of Groupware Technologies'. *Sloan Management Review*, Winter: 11–21.

Pas, Niek. 2003. *Imaazje! De Verbeelding van Provo 1965–1967*. Amsterdam: Wereldbibliotheek.

—. 2008. 'Subcultural Movements: The Provos'. In *1968 in Europe: A History of Protest and Activism 1956–1977*, edited by Martin Klimke and Joachim Scharloth, 13–21. London: Palgrave Macmillan.

—. 2011. 'In Pursuit of the Invisible Revolution: Sigma in the Netherlands, 1966–1968'. In *Between the Avant-Garde and the Everyday: Subversive Politics in Europe from 1957 to the Present*, edited by Timothy Brown and Lorena Anton, 31–43. New York: Berghahn Books.

Payne, Emily, and Floris Schuiling. 2017. 'The Textility of Marking: Performers' Annotations as Indicators of the Creative Process in Performance'. *Music & Letters* 98 (3): 438–64. https://doi.org/https://doi.org/10.1093/ml/gcx055.

Peirce, Charles Sanders. 1991. 'On a New List of Categories'. In *Peirce on Signs: Writings on Semiotic by Charles Sanders Peirce*, edited by James Hoopes, 23–33. London: University of North Carolina Press.

Peters, Gary. 2009. *The Philosophy of Improvisation*. Chicago, IL: University of Chicago Press.

Piekut, Benjamin. 2009. '"Demolish Serious Culture!": Henry Flynt and Workers World Party'. In *Sound Commitments: Avant-Garde Music and the Sixties*, edited by Robert Adlington, 37–55. Oxford: Oxford University Press.

—. 2011. *Experimentalism Otherwise: The New York Avant-Garde and Its Limits*. Berkeley, CA: University of California Press.

—. 2014. 'Actor-Networks in Music History: Clarifications and Critiques'. *Twentieth-Century Music* 11 (02): 191–215. https://doi.org/10.1017/S147857221400005X.

—. 2017. 'The Afterlives of Indeterminacy'. University of Leeds.

Polling, Kees. 1997. 'Misha Mengelberg: Jazzmuziek Is in 1960 Gestorven'. *Trouw*, 30 October 1997, sec. Kunst. Box: Instant Composers Pool, Folder: Ongedateerde Knipsels. Nederlands Jazz Archief.

Pritchard, Matthew. 2011. 'Who Killed the Concert? Heinrich Besseler and the Inter-War Politics of *Gebrauchsmusik*'. *Twentieth-Century Music* 8 (1): 29–48. https://doi.org/10.1017/S1478572211000272.

Prouty, Ken. 2006. 'Orality, Literacy, and Mediating Musical Experience: Rethinking Oral Tradition in the Learning of Jazz Improvisation'. *Popular Music and Society* 29 (3): 317–34. https://doi.org/10.1080/03007760600670372.

Rehding, Alexander. 2016. 'Instruments of Music Theory'. *Music Theory Online* 22 (4). http://mtosmt.org/issues/mto.16.22.4/mto.16.22.4.rehding.html.

Rhythme. 1958. 'Jazz Club Corner', 9 (103), 1958: 23.

Rhythme Editors. 1953. 'Zonder Commentaar: Meningen van Mensen over Muziek'. *Rhythme* 5 (49), 1953: 22.

—. 1956. 'Hampton Notities'. *Rhythme* 7 (79), 1956: 7.

—. 1957. 'Over de Grenzen'. *Rhythme* 8 (92), 1957: 10.

Righart, Hans. 1998. 'Moderate Versions of the "Global Sixties": A Comparison of Great Britain and the Netherlands'. *Journal of Contemporary European Studies* 6 (13): 82–96.

Roda, P. Allen. 2014. 'Tabla Tuning on the Workshop Stage: Toward a Materialist Musical Ethnography'. *Ethnomusicology Forum* 23 (3): 360–82. https://doi.org/10.10 80/17411912.2014.919871.

Rubinoff, Kailan R. 2009. 'Cracking the Dutch Early Music Movement: The Repercussions of the 1969 Notenkrakersactie'. *Twentieth-Century Music* 6 (1): 3–22.

Ruhé, Harry. 1979. *Fluxus: The Most Radical and Experimental Art Movement of the Sixties*. Amsterdam: A.

Rusch, Loes. 2007. 'Jazzpracticum: Over de Institutionalisering van Jazzonderwijs in Nederland'. PhD Thesis, Amsterdam: Universiteit van Amsterdam.

—. 2016. '"Our Subcultural Shit-Music": Dutch Jazz, Representation, and Cultural Politics'. Amsterdam: Universiteit van Amsterdam.

Sansi, Roger. 2015. *Art, Anthropology and the Gift*. London: Bloomsbury Publishing.

Sawyer, Keith. 1992. 'Improvisational Creativity: An Analysis of Jazz Performance'. *Creativity Research Journal* 5 (3): 253–63. https://doi.org/10.1080/10400419209534439.

—. 1997. *Creativity in Performance*. London: Ablex.

—. 2003. *Group Creativity: Music, Theater, Collaboration*. London: Lawrence Erlbaum Associates.

Schat, Peter. 1968. 'Inleiding'. In *Muzikale En Politieke Commentaren En Analyses Bij Een Programma van Een Politiek-Demonstratief Experimenteel Concert Met Nieuwe Nederlandse Muziek in Negentienhonderdachtenzestig*, 5–6. Amsterdam: Polak & Van Gennep.

Schönberger, Elmer. 1996. *Ssst! Nieuwe Ensembles Voor Nieuwe Muziek*. Amsterdam: International Theatre and Film Books.

Schouten, Martin. 1973. 'Hoe de Zestigers de Nederlandse Muziek Uit de Droom Hielpen'. *Haagse Post*, 3 November 1973: 56–66.

Schuiling, Floris. 2014. 'Compositions in Improvisation: The Instant Composers Pool Orchestra'. *ACT: Zeitschrift Für Musik & Performance*, no. 5. www.act.uni-bayreuth. de/resources/Heft2014-05/ACT2014_05_Schuiling.pdf.

—. 2016. 'The Instant Composers Pool: Music Notation and the Mediation of Improvising Agency'. *Cadernos de Arte E Antropologia*, vol. 5, no. 1 (April): 39–58. https://doi.org/10.4000/cadernosaa.1028.

—. 2017. 'Review: Composing Dissent, Avant-Garde Music in 1960s Amsterdam by Robert Adlington'. *Critical Studies in Improvisation / Études Critiques En Improvisation* 12 (1). www.criticalimprov.com/article/view/4163/4150.

—. forthcoming a. 'Jazz and the Material Turn'. In *The Routledge Companion to Jazz Studies*, edited by Tony Whyton, Nicholas Gebhardt, and Nichole Rustin. London: Routledge.

—. forthcoming b. 'Notation Cultures: Toward an Ethnomusicology of Notation'. *Journal of the Royal Musical Association.*

Schulte, Han. 1976. 'BIMhuis: BIM Moet Kiezen'. *Jazz Press* no. 16, 1976: 2.

Schumacher, Rogier Wernardus Gijsbert. 2010. *Neo-avant-garde in Nederland: Museumjournaal als forum van een nieuw kunstbegrip 1961–1973*. Amsterdam: Amsterdam University Press.

Schütz, Alfred. 1951. 'Making Music Together: A Study in Social Relationship'. *Social Research* 18 (1): 76–97.

Seddon, Frederick, and Michele Biasutti. 2009. 'A Comparison of Modes of Communication Between Members of a String Quartet and a Jazz Sextet'. *Psychology of Music* 37 (4): 395–415. https://doi.org/10.1177/0305735608100375.

Sell, Mike. 2008. *Avant-Garde Performance and the Limits of Criticism: Approaching the Living Theatre, Happenings/Fluxus, and the Black Arts Movement*. Ann Arbor, MI: University of Michigan Press.

Sennett, Richard. 2008. *The Craftsman*. London: Penguin Books.

Sicart, Miguel. 2014. *Play Matters*. Cambridge, MA: MIT Press.

Small, Christopher. 1987. *Music of the Common Tongue: Survival and Celebration in African American Music*. Middletown, CT: Wesleyan University Press.

—. 1998. *Musicking: The Meanings of Performing and Listening*. Middletown, CT: Wesleyan University Press.

Smith, Wadada Leo. 1999. 'Creative Music and the AACM'. In *Keeping Time: Readings in Jazz History*, edited by Robert Walser, 315–23. Oxford: Oxford University Press.

Smith, Owen. 1993. 'Fluxus: A Brief History and Other Fictions'. In *In the Spirit of Fluxus*, edited by Janet Jenkins, 24–37. Minneapolis, MN: Walker Art Center.

Souza, Jonathan De. 2017. *Music at Hand: Instruments, Bodies, and Cognition*. Oxford: Oxford University Press.

Steinbeck, Paul. 2017. *Message to Our Folks: The Art Ensemble of Chicago*. Chicago, IL: University of Chicago Press.

Stichting Jazz in Nederland. 1970. 'NOTULEN van de Vergadering van Het Bestuur van de Stichting Jazz in Nederland, Gehouden Op Dinsdag 3 November 1970 Ten Huize van Piet Koster, Ten Harmsenstraat 17 Te Alphen Aan de Rijn'. Box: SJIN, Folder: Diverse documentatie. Nederlands Jazz Archief.

Stichting Jazz in Nederland, and Beroepsvereniging van Improviserende musici. 1973. 'Herdruk Jazzplan 1970, Herzien 1973'. Box: SJIN, Folder: Beleidsplannen. Nederlands Jazz Archief.

Stiles, Kristine. 1993. 'Between Water and Stone: Fluxus Performance: A Metaphysics of Acts'. In *In the Spirit of Fluxus*, edited by Janet Jenkins, 64–99. Minneapolis, MN: Walker Art Center.

Suurmond, Henk. 1989. 'Pianist En Componist Misha Mengelberg: "Dingen Moeten Ook Kunnen Mislukken"'. *Jazz Nu* 12 (131), 1989: 4–6.

Tackley, Catherine. 2010. 'Jazz Recordings as Social Texts'. In *Recorded Music: Performance, Culture and Technology*, edited by Amanda Bayley, 167–86. Cambridge: Cambridge University Press.

Taruskin, Richard. 2005. *The Oxford History of Western Music*. Vol. 5: The Late Twentieth Century. 5 vols. Oxford: Oxford University Press.

Teal, Kimberley Hannon. 2012. 'Beyond the Cotton Club: The Persistence of Duke Ellington's Jungle Style'. *Jazz Perspectives* 6 (1-2): 123–49. https://doi.org/10.1080/17494060.2012.721292.

Tomlinson, Gary. 1991. 'Cultural Dialogics and Jazz: A White Historian Signifies'. *Black Music Research Journal* 11 (2): 229–64. https://doi.org/10.2307/779268.

—. 2012. 'Musicology, Anthropology, History'. In *The Cultural Study of Music: A Critical Introduction*, edited by Martin Clayton, Trevor Herbert, and Richard Middleton, 2nd Edition, 59–72. New York: Routledge.

Toynbee, Jason. 1999. *Making Popular Music: Musicians, Creativity, and Institutions*. London: Arnold.

Tra, Gijs. 1978a. 'Herman de Wit's Workshops'. *Key Notes*, no. 7: 13–14.

—. 1978b. 'Instant Composers Pool: A Decade of Musical and Political Innovation'. *Key Notes*, no. 7: 7–9.

Tresch, John, and Emily Dolan. 2013. 'Toward a New Organology: Instruments of Music and Science'. *Osiris* 28 (1): 278–98. https://doi.org/10.1086/671381.

Van de Leur, Walter. 2012. '"Pure Jazz" and "Charlatanry": A History of De Jazzwereld Magazine, 1931–1940'. *Current Research in Jazz* 4. www.crj-online.org.

Van den Berg, Erik. 1987. 'Misha Mengelberg: "Ik Hoop Dat Je Bij Ons Niet Terug Verlangt Naar Monk Zelf"' In *Jazzjaarboek 5*, edited by Erik Van den Berg and Frank Van Dixhoorn, 71–9. Amsterdam: Van Gennep.

—. 2009. *Han Bennink: De Wereld Als Trommel*. Amsterdam: Thomas Rap.

—, ed. 2015. *Worp En Wederworp: 26 Interviews Met Misha Mengelberg*. Rimburg: Huis Clos.

Van Dixhoorn, Frank. 1984. *Michiel de Ruyter: Een Leven Met Jazz*. Amsterdam: Van Gennep.

Van Duijn, Roel. 1985. *Provo: de geschiedenis van de provotarische beweging, 1965–1967*. Amsterdam: Meulenhoff.

Visser, Frank. 1967. 'Goed & Gek'. *Jazzwereld*, no. 13, 1967: 20.

Vuijsje, Bert. 1965. 'Willem Breuker'. *Jazzwereld* no. 3, 1965: 84–5.

—. 1972. 'De Onenigheid'. *Jazzwereld* no. 37, 1972: 25.

—. 1973. 'Afscheid: De Laatste Jazzwereld'. *Jazzwereld* no. 43, 1973: 3.

—. 1978. *De Nieuwe Jazz: Twintig Interviewen*. Baarn: Bosch en Keuning.

—. 1983. *Jazzportretten*. Amsterdam: Van Gennep.

Vuijsje, Bert, and Anton Witkamp. 1966. 'Een Jazzwereld Diskussie'. *Jazzwereld* no. 7, 1966: 224–9.

Vuijsje, Bert, and Martin Schouten. 1971. 'Misha En Han over ICP 010: "Een Ontzaggelijk Troebele Vijver"'. *Jazzwereld* no. 35, 1971: 18–20.

Waisvisz, Michel. n.d. 'The Cracklebox'. Crackle. Accessed 27 March 2018. www.crackle.org/CrackleBox.htm.

Wall, Michelle, and Anita Duffy. 2010. 'The Effects of Music Therapy for Older People with Dementia'. *British Journal of Nursing* 19 (2): 108–13.

Walser, Robert. 1995. 'Out of Notes: Signification, Interpretation, and the Problem of Miles Davis'. In *Jazz Among the Discourses*, edited by Krin Gabbard, 165–88. Durham, NC: Duke University Press.

Weheliye, Alexander G. 2005. *Phonographies: Grooves in Sonic Afro-Modernity*. Durham, NC: Duke University Press.

Weick, Karl E. 1998. 'Introductory Essay: Improvisation as a Mindset for Organizational Analysis'. *Organization Science* 9 (5): 543–55. https://doi.org/10.1287/orsc.9.5.543.

'We Zijn Loslopende Honden Samen in Een Kennel'. 1977. Box: Instant Composers Pool, Folder: 1977–1979. Nederlands Jazz Archief.

Whitehead, Kevin. 1998. *New Dutch Swing: An In-Depth Examination of Amsterdam's Vital and Distinctive Jazz Scene*. New York: Billboard Books.

—. 2015. 'Digested Lessons from the Master'. Presented at the Holland Festival: Misha's Middag, Bimhuis, Amsterdam, 6 June.

Wien, Barbara, Wilma Lukatsch, and Kai-Morten Vollmer. n.d. '1963'. Tomas Schmit Archiv.

Willem Breuker Kollektief. n.d. 'Willem Breuker Kollektief'. Box: Willem Breuker. Nederlands Jazz Archief.

Williams, Katherine. 2012. 'Improvisation as Composition: Fixity of Form and Collaborative Composition in Duke Ellington's Diminuendo and Crescendo in Blue'. *Jazz Perspectives* 6 (1-2): 223–46. https://doi.org/10.1080/17494060.2012.729712.

Wilmer, Valerie. 1987. *As Serious as Your Life*. London: Pluto Press.

Wipplinger, Jonathan O. 2017. *The Jazz Republic: Music, Race, and American Culture in Weimar Germany*. Ann Arbor, MI: University of Michigan Press.

Wolters, Gezinus. 1970. 'AACM: Destruction for Creativity'. *Jazzwereld* no. 31, 1970: 8–9.

Wolterstorff, Nicholas. 1987. 'The Work of Making a Work of Music'. In *What Is Music? An Introduction to the Philosophy of Music*, edited by Philip Alperson. University Park, PA: Penn State University Press.

Wouters, Kees C.A.T.M. 1999. *Ongewenschte Muziek: De Bestrijding van Jazz En Moderne Amusementsmuziek in Duitsland En Nederland, 1920–1945*. Den Haag: SDU.

Zack, Michael H. 2000. 'Jazz Improvisation and Organizing: Once More from the Top'. *Organization Science* 11 (2): 227–34. https://doi.org/10.1287/orsc.11.2.227.12507.

Zwart, Frits. 2016. *Willem Mengelberg: Een Biografie 1920–1951*. Vol. 2. 2 vols. Amsterdam: Prometheus.

Filmography

Ad van t veer. n.d. *John Cage in Gesprek Met Misha Mengelberg*. Accessed 13 November 2017. www.youtube.com/watch?v=qXzLcx-qBpw.

Boutang, Pierre-André, and Michel Pamart. 1996. *L'abécédaire de Gilles Deleuze*. Documentary.

By, Henk de. 1963. 'Signalement'. Hilversum: VARA.

Dekker, Jellie. 2008. *Afijn: Misha Mengelberg*. NPS.

De Ridder, Willem. 2008. 'FLUXUS SPECIAL: Slideshow'. Willem de Ridder. 2008. www.willemderidder.com/kunstjes/fluxus/audio/nederlands.m3u.

Flothuis, Trino. 1968. *De Bezetene*. VPRO.

Hülscher, Hans. 1983. 'Muzikale Amalgamen'. NOS.

Hylkema, Hans. 1993. *Last Date*. NPS.

Koren, Yaèl. 2005. 'Reconstructie'. *Andere Tijden*. NTR/VPRO. https://anderetijden. nl/aflevering/423/Reconstructie.

"Open Oog". 1968. Hilversum: NTS.

Van den Bos, Paul. 2015. *Biography Willem Breuker*. www.willembreuker.com/project/ biography.

Van Gasteren, Louis. 1964. *Jazz and Poetry*.

—. 1983. Hans: Het Leven Voor de Dood. Documentary.

Discography

Bailey, Derek. 1971. *Solo Guitar*. LP. Incus: INCUS 2.

Bennink, Han, and Willem Breuker. 1967. *New Acoustic Swing Duo*. LP. Instant Composers Pool: ICP 001.

Bennink, Han, and Misha Mengelberg. 1971. *Instant Composers Pool*. LP. Amsterdam: Instant Composers Pool: ICP 010.

Bennink, Han, Misha Mengelberg, and John Tchicai. 1968. *Instant Composers Pool*. LP. Instant Composers Pool: ICP 002.

Breuker, Willem. 1966. *Contemporary Jazz from Holland/Litany for the 14th of June 1966*. LP. Relax: 33004.

Dolphy, Eric. 1964. *Last Date*. LP. Fontana: 681 008 ZL.

ICP Orchestra. 1982. *Japan Japon*. LP. Instant Composers Pool: ICP 024.

—. 1986. *Extension Red, White & Blue*. Cassette. Instant Composers Pool: ICP 025.

—. 1987. *Two Programs: The ICP Orchestra Performs Nichols-Monk*. CD. Instant Composers Pool: ICP 026.

—. 1992a. *Bospaadje Konijnehol I*. CD. Instant Composers Pool: ICP 028.

—. 1992b. *Bospaadje Konijnehol II*. CD. Instant Composers Pool: ICP 029.

ICP Tentet. 1977. *Tetterettet*. LP. Instant Composers Pool: ICP 020.

—. 1979. *ICP Tentet in Berlin*. LP. FMP: SAJ-23.

Lacy, Steve, George E. Lewis, Ernst Reijseger, Misha Mengelberg, and Han Bennink. 1992. *Dutch Masters*. CD. Soul Note: 121 154–2.

Lacy, Steve, Michel Waisvisz, Han Bennink, and Maarten Van Regteren Altena. 1978. *Lumps*. LP. Instant Composers Pool: ICP 016.

Maslak, Keshavan, Misha Mengelberg, and Han Bennink. 1980. *Humanplexity*. LP. Leo Records: LR 101.

Mengelberg, Misha. 1979. *Pech Onderweg*. LP. BV Haast.

—. 1992. MISHA MENGELBERG 25 juni 1992 interview Bas Andriessen Interview by Bas Andriessen.

Mengelberg, Misha, and Han Bennink. 1974. *Einepartietischtennis*. LP. Instant Composers Pool: ICP 014.

Mengelberg, Misha, Steve Lacy, George E. Lewis, Arjen Gorter, and Han Bennink. 1985. *Change of Season: Music of Herbie Nichols*. CD. Soul Note: SN 1104.

Misha Mengelberg Quartet. 1966. *The Misja Mengelberg Quartet: As Featured at the Newport Festival 1966*. LP. Artone: MGOS 9467.

—. 2011. *Journey (Live in Amsterdam 1966)*. CD. MCN: 1101.

Misha Mengelberg Quartet featuring Gary Peacock. 1981. *Driekusman Total Loss*. LP. VARAJAZZ: 210.

Monk, Thelonious. 1959. *Thelonious Alone in San Francisco*. LP. Riverside Records: RLP 1158.

Rudd, Roswell, Steve Lacy, Kent Carter, Misha Mengelberg, and Han Bennink. 1983. *Regeneration*. LP. Soul Note: SN 1054.

Schlippenbach, Alexander von, and Globe Unity Orchestra. 2001. *Globe Unity 67 & 70*. CD. Atavistic.

Various Artists. 1955a. *Jazz Behind the Dikes*. LP. Philips: P 10078 R.

—. 1955b. *Jazz Behind the Dikes No. 2*. LP. Philips: B 08000 L.

—. 1957. *Jazz Behind the Dikes 3*. LP. Philips: B 08004 L.

—. 1970. *Gittin' To Know Y'All*. LP. MPS Records: MPS 15269.

—. 1997a. *October Meeting 1991: 3 Quartets*. CD. Bimhuis Records: BIMHUIS 003.

—. 1997b. *October Meeting 1991: Anatomy of a Meeting*. CD. Bimhuis Records: BIMHUIS 004.

—. 2012. *Instant Composers Pool*. CD Box Set. Instant Composers Pool: ICP1275-1.

INDEX

Note: Page numbers in *italics* refer to figures.